MASOCHISM and the SELF

MASOCHISM and the *SELF*

Roy F. Baumeister
Case Western Reserve University

Psychology Press
Taylor & Francis Group
NEW YORK AND LONDON

First Published 1989 by
Lawrence Erlbaum Associates, Inc.

Published 2014 by Psychology Press
711 Third Avenue, New York, NY 10017

and by Psychology Press
27 Church Road, Hove, East Sussex, BN3 2FA

First issued in paperback 2014

*Psychology Press is an imprint of the Taylor & Francis Group,
an informa business*

Copyright © 1989 by Lawrence Erlbaum Associates, Inc.

All rights reserved. No part of this book may be reprinted or reproduced or utilised in any form or by any electronic, mechanical, or other means, now known or hereafter invented, including photocopying and recording, or in any information storage or retrieval system, without permission in writing from the publishers.

Trademark notice: Product or corporate names may be trademarks or registered trademarks, and are used only for identification and explanation without intent to infringe.

Production, interior, and
cover design by Robin Marks Weisberg

Library of Congress Cataloging-in-Publication Data

Baumeister, Roy F.
    Masochism and the self / Roy F. Baumeister.
      p. cm.
    Bibliography: p.
    Includes index.
    1. Masochism. 2. Self psychology. I. Title.
RC553.M36B38   1989
616.85'835—dc19   88-26797
                                                  CIP

ISBN 13: 978-1-138-87606-4 (pbk)
ISBN 13: 978-0-8058-0486-7 (hbk)

Publisher's Note
The publisher has gone to great lengths to ensure the quality of this reprint but points out that some imperfections in the original may be apparent.

Contents

Preface   ix

Chapter One
Why Is Masochism Interesting?   1
Definition   2
Prevalence   4
Self   5
Gender   7
Pathology and Morality   8
Things Are Not What They Seem   12
Methods and Evidence   14

Chapter Two
Overview of Main Ideas   20
Primacy of Masochism   20
Escape From Self   26
Relationship and Justification   32
Conclusion   36

Chapter Three
Masochism, Culture, and History   38
Self in History   39
Justification and Fulfillment   42
History of Masochism   45

Cross-Cultural Perspectives   53
Implications   57

Chapter Four
Essentials of Masochism — 60

Pain   60
Loss of Control   76
Humiliation   81
Conclusion   86

Chapter Five
Satisfactions of Masochism — 88

Burden of Selfhood   88
Guilt   93
Escape and Ecstasy   100
Therapeutic Effects   101
Opponent Process Effects   104
Masochism as Life-Scheme   107
Conclusion   114

Chapter Six
Masochism and Sexual Pleasure — 117

Sexual Activities   117
Masochism as Sexually Therapeutic   122
Self-Awareness   128
Relief of Sex Guilt   133
Excitation Transfer   138
Masochism as Foreplay   140
Conclusion   141

Chapter Seven
Femininity, Masculinity, and Masochism — 143

The Great Debate   144
Masculine and Feminine Masochism   152
Summary and Interpretation   166

Chapter Eight
Sadism — 177

What Is Sadism?   177
Sadism and the Self   179
Masochist and Sadist: An Ideal Couple?   180

On Graduating From Masochism to Sadism 182
Intimacy and Sadism   183
Sadism and Sex   184
Conclusion   186

Chapter Nine
Clinical Implications 187

Masochism, Pathology, and Assessment   187
Masochists in Therapy   189
Narcissism Theory of Masochism   195

Chapter Ten
Conclusion 200

Summary of Main Ideas   201
Unanswered Questions   202
Masochism as Self-Destruction   204
Nonsexual Masochism   206
Masochism and Love   208
Conclusion   209

Appendix **211**
References **222**
Author Index **230**
Subject Index **234**

Preface

Several years ago, while gathering material for another project, I decided to check the literature on masochism to see whether that paradoxical behavior might be illuminated by the theory I was working on. It wasn't, but the literature on masochism confronted me with several challenges that kept my interest. It was obvious that psychology's theories of masochism had been made obsolete by recent data that contradicted many basic assumptions—such as the ideas that most masochists were mentally ill or that masochism derives from sadism. Indeed, it seemed that empirical researchers had realized the inadequacy of the old theories but had been slow to find better ones, so that collection of data had proceeded (slowly) in an atheoretical vacuum. In short, a new theory was overdue.

What intrigued me the most was that the evidence about masochism seemed to contradict many of the most common and fundamental assumptions in the psychology of self, an area in which I had done much of my past work. In particular, masochists apparently seek to relinquish control and esteem, whereas most research shows that people generally seek to increase their control and esteem.

I began to wonder how this seeming contradiction between masochism and the psychology of self could be resolved. Soon I suspected that it could not be resolved at all, for it was not a "seeming" contradiction but rather the key to the essential nature of masochism—the denial of self. This suspicion was greatly enhanced when I began to examine the historical and cultural evidence about masochism and found that its distribution corresponded closely to some patterns I had found in a previous work on the problematic construction of individual identity.

Masochism thus emerged as an escapist response to the problematic nature of selfhood.

It was also obvious that many very different things were lumped together under the heterogeneous and controversial rubric of masochism. To make any progress, I felt it necessary to narrow the focus to the original and prototypical form of masochism: sexual masochism. The term *masochism* was originally coined to refer to a pattern of sexual behavior, but it later began to be used to refer to a variety of nonsexual behaviors. The description of nonsexual behaviors as masochistic is based on argument by analogy, and yet analogies cannot be made effectively if the core phenomenon is misunderstood. Accordingly, this book focuses on understanding sexual masochism, and nonsexual analogs are postponed to the final chapters.

Although the notion of escape from self has dominated my thinking about masochism, I gradually came to recognize a second element. Masochism does not only take the self apart but also, to some extent, puts together a new set of meanings in place of the deconstructed one. The construction of new meanings may hold the major appeal for some masochists, whereas for others the removal of meaning is the primary attraction.

This book explains my work on masochism. The escape from self hypothesis is emphasized, and the construction of meaning hypothesis is also covered. Given my background in empirical research, I felt it necessary not only to propose theories but to examine all possible sources of evidence about them. This book integrates past research evidence, current findings, cross-cultural and historical comparisons, and some original data on the masochistic imagination as evidenced in anonymous scripts of fantasies and favorite experiences written by a large sample of masochists (and some of their partners).

The book's style and presentation are a product of the attempt to reach several different audiences. I am a research psychologist myself, and one primary audience is my professional colleagues, especially those interested in self and identity, in paradoxical behavior patterns, and in the construction of meaning. I hoped to have something to offer to researchers and counselors concerned with human sexuality, for masochism has been one of the biggest puzzles in that area. Clinical psychologists have struggled for decades with various aspects of masochism (defined in various ways), and I hoped that my elucidation of the core phenomena of masochism would be useful to them. Students in each of these areas should also find the book accessible.

Finally, this book may offer some reassurance and self-insight to actual masochists. Past psychological works have generally taken a dismal or alarmist view of the masochist, probably unfairly, and this work represents an effort to understand masochism on the basis of common principles in the behavior of normal people.

I was initially attracted to the study of masochism because it seemed to be the ultimate in paradoxical, incomprehensible, and bizarre behavior. It was utterly foreign to me, resembling nothing in the results of laboratory research studies I read nor anything in my personal experience (indeed, I had never met a masochist). I could form neither an intellectual nor an intuitive hypothesis of its appeal, and I recall how astonished I was at the research results of the 1970s and 1980s indicating that most masochists were apparently normal, healthy, capable, and successful individuals. Gradually, over several years, I came to see that masochism has very systematic resemblances to many other behavior patterns that have been found among normal people, and as a result I was able to furnish this account of the psychology of masochism. I suspect it will be many years before we know why people come to choose masochism rather than other activities that might produce similar results, but the similarity itself places masochism in an intelligible context.

Psychology has debated for decades whether it is preferable to work as a detached, uninvolved observer, with pretensions of scientific objectivity, or rather as a highly involved participant who can benefit from firsthand knowledge, experience, and intuition. Probably both sides have some merit. In masochism, the difference is quite apparent. Explanations of masochism written by masochists run the risk of being superficial, self-serving rationalizations for one's own deviant behavior, prone to place undue emphasis on intuition and personal experience at the expense of rigorous examination of data. And explanations written by nonmasochists run the risk of being completely out of touch with reality, especially given the difficulty of obtaining reliable, objective data about masochism.

For better or worse, my own stance is that of the uninvolved observer. If good psychological work requires firsthand knowledge and intuitive understanding of the phenomena, then this book is highly suspect, for it has neither. Indeed, there were times when I was acutely aware of groping in the dark to construct a theory about a mysterious, elusive, and paradoxical phenomenon. On the other hand, my lack of involvement has the benefit of being able to approach the available evidence in a relatively fresh, unbiased fashion, armed with recent conceptual and empirical advances in social and personality psychology.

So I can assert with some confidence that this work offers an integration of the available evidence about masochism with psychology's current, broad knowledge about human behavior. The force of this book's conclusions solely depends on the fit of theory to data (although the data include many firsthand reports and accounts of masochistic experiences written by masochists), and not on the authority of personal experience or the privileged position of intuition and familiarity. To be sure, as I worked on this project I met a handful of masochists who after hearing me speak came up to tell me that my work corresponded well to their own intuitions, insights, and experiences. But of course it is impossible to know whether there were other masochists at the same lectures who simply shook their heads, shrugged, and walked away after finding my work off the mark.

This book, then, offers my best attempt to draw together the available evidence about masochism and offer a theoretical account of it. The evidence itself is often flawed or incomplete, but there is enough of it (and enough variety in sources) that one can have reasonable confidence when it converges. Put another way, I found that the different types of evidence about masochism have different flaws but they all point to the same conclusions. The conclusions themselves are therefore not a product of one type of bias or flaw in the evidence.

In closing, I wish to thank the numerous colleagues, students, editors, reviewers, and others who helped with this project by discussing my theories and evidence, reading parts of the manuscript, and challenging the ideas and interpretations.

Roy F. Baumeister

Chapter One

Why Is Masochism Interesting?

Masochism is one of psychology's greatest puzzles. Masochistic actions and pleasures fly in the face of common sense. Sexual masochists desire physical pain, bodily restraint, and humiliating or embarrassing treatment. They want their sexual partners to tie them up, blindfold them, and spank or whip them. They ask to be insulted, displayed naked to strangers, kept on leashes like animals, or dressed in humiliating costumes. They desire to be forced to kiss their partner's feet, to be subjected to various rules such as never looking their partner in the eye, and to other indignities.

Not only do they desire such things, but they apparently derive great satisfaction and even sexual pleasure from them. For most people, pain or embarrassment brings an instant end to sexual pleasure, yet for masochists these things stimulate it. For some masochists, these activities become almost indispensable to sexual enjoyment.

How could someone enjoy pain? Pain is the opposite of pleasure. Unpleasantness is the very essence of the sensation of pain. Yet masochists desire pain.

One way of understanding masochism has been the simple assumption that these people are mentally ill. In Western society, there is a long tradition of dismissing things that seem to make no sense as being produced by irrational forces. Some have argued that mental illness has replaced demons as an omnibus explanation for deviant behavior. The attitude behind these labels is, "We don't need to understand these things, for they are incomprehensible." Masochists and other deviants are simply exempted from all principles of normal human psychology, as if one should not even expect them to make sense.

This book attempts to make sense of masochism. It assumes that the behavior of these people is comprehensible—that in fact it conforms to many of the patterns and processes that guide the behavior of normal individuals in our culture. Whenever possible, we attempt to avoid explaining masochistic behavior as insane. It is not necessary to regard masochists as mentally ill in order to understand them.

Indeed, as we see here, there is increasing evidence that the majority of masochists are not mentally ill. They appear to be normal, capable individuals who are typical members of society in all respects except for their sexual tastes.

Most past theories about masochism have been based on clinical observations. The view offered in this book should be regarded not as a rival view but as a complementary view. There is little doubt but that some mentally ill people engage in masochism, and clinical observations and theories are the best way to go about understanding the dynamics involved in those cases. But if the majority of masochists are *not* mentally ill, it is necessary to develop some ways of understanding masochism on the basis of what is known about the behavior of normal, healthy individuals. The clinically based theories of masochism are presumably quite sound and accurate in explaining the appeal of these activities to mentally ill persons, but it may be wrong to assume that the appeal to healthy individuals is the same.

Masochism is worthy of study and explanation because on the surface it contradicts much of what we know about human behavior. Getting pleasure from pain is only the most obvious paradox of masochism. Let us take a closer look at some of the reasons to be interested in the psychology of masochism.

DEFINITION

Before proceeding further, it is necessary to furnish a definition of masochism. Psychology has furnished various definitions of masochism, and many psychologists have used the term without giving a definition of it, so one can easily become entangled just trying to decide what is masochism and what is not.

The term *masochism* was coined by the noted early sex researcher Krafft-Ebing. He used the term to refer to an unusual and deviant pattern of sexual activity involving pain and submission. Krafft-Ebing named the phenomenon after Leopold von Sacher-Masoch, a 19th century Austrian novelist whose writings portrayed men humiliated and tormented by beautiful women. Sacher-Masoch's interest in these activities apparently extended beyond his literary work; he seems to have spent much of his adult life trying to get women to dominate him, including having them whip him and having them betray him by having sex with other men (Cleugh, 1951).

Krafft-Ebing defined *masochism* as "the wish to suffer pain and be subjected to force" (1983, p. 27). He said that the masochist "in sexual feeling and thought is controlled by the idea of being completely and unconditionally subjected to the will of a person of the opposite sex; of being treated by this person as by a master, humiliated and abused" (p. 28). For a first attempt at definition, this was not far off the mark. To update his definition, it is necessary to change his stipulation that the master be of the opposite sex, for there is evidence that some people like to be dominated by members of their own sex.

The problem of defining masochism became much more complex with Freud. Krafft-Ebing had specifically defined masochism as a form of sexual behavior, but Freud began to use it to refer to nonsexual behaviors as well. Since Freud's time, many psychologists have often used the term to refer to nonsexual behavior patterns, based on their presumed resemblance to sexual masochism (see Glick & Meyers, 1988; Panken, 1983, for excellent reviews of recent Freudian treatments).

The danger in describing nonsexual behavior patterns as "masochistic" is that at present it is almost impossible to say what is a false analogy and what is apt. Without a solid understanding of the original form of masochism—sexual masochism—one cannot generalize to other patterns. For example, if one assumes that masochism is essentially the wish for injury, then one might label all self-destructive behaviors as masochistic. If one assumes that masochists desire intense sensations, then one might label all other sensation-seeking behavior as masochistic. If one sees submission to another person as the essence of masochism, then all submission to authority can be called masochistic. And so forth.

In simple terms, one cannot decide what *resembles* sexual masochism until one understands what sexual masochism is. Labeling nonsexual behaviors as masochistic is argument by analogy, and analogies cannot be constructed until the core phenomenon is understood. Accordingly, this book postpones discussion of nonsexual masochism until the nature of sexual masochism has been carefully examined. The important task is to understand the original, prototypical form of masochism, which is a pattern of sexual behavior.

To get started, therefore, it is only necessary to provide a working definition for *sexual masochism*. Krafft-Ebing's definition, suitably amended to include homosexual masochism, seems sufficient. To be more precise, one might define *sexual masochism* as a syndrome that associates sexual pleasure with one or more of the following three features: receiving pain; relinquishing control through bondage, rules, commands, or other means; and embarrassment or humiliation. Thus, not all masochistic sexuality involves pain, for example (Reik, 1941/1957), but at least one of the three features is necessary in order to label some sexual activity as masochism. Sex with any of these three features is masochistic; sex without any of them is not masochistic.

PREVALENCE

How common is masochism today? It is difficult to give a reliable estimate. Survey evidence is far from reliable, for many people may do such things but refuse to admit them to interviewers. One commonly quoted statistic comes from Kinsey's research. He asked people whether they ever experienced sexual arousal in response to stories or depictions of sadomasochistic activities. Kinsey and his colleagues found that 22% of American men and 12% of American women admitted such arousal (Kinsey, Pomeroy, Martin, & Gebhard, 1953).

The proportion of people who admit actually engaging in sadomasochism (S&M) is no doubt much smaller than the proportion admitting to fantasies. A handful of such surveys was reviewed in the early 1970s by Greene and Greene (1974). In one survey of American university students, whipping or spanking before sex was reported by about 5% of the females and 8% of the males. The highest figure was obtained in an international survey: 33% of English women reported having had such an experience (Greene & Greene, 1974, p. 42). At the low end, the frequencies approach zero. Again, however, one must be a bit skeptical of all such numbers, because many people may be reluctant to admit having participated in sadomasochistic sex. The number of people who report such activities is undoubtedly smaller than the number of people who do them. And the different rates found for different groups may reflect different willingness to admit such activities rather than different experiences.

Probably the most plausible guess is that 5%–10% of the population has engaged in masochistic activity for sexual enjoyment. Probably two or three times that many have enjoyed S&M stories or fantasies, and probably only 1% or 2% has actually done such things on any sort of regular basis. Still, each 1% of the American population represents between 2 and 3 million people, so small percentages quickly translate into large crowds. It is also important to note that many people probably have masochistic desires but never act on them, either because they are ashamed of their desires (cf. Cowan, 1982), because they cannot find a willing partner (cf. Spengler, 1977), or because they are afraid or shy (cf. Scott, 1983). In short, it is clear that most modern individuals do not show any inclination toward sexual masochism, but there is a fair-sized minority who have such interest or desires occasionally and a small group who actually engage in masochistic sex.

There is good evidence that many masochists are held back by fear, inner conflict, and other factors from acting out their fantasies. Prostitutes who advertise that they will dominate their clients have a large problem with no-shows. These professional dominatrices report that 80%–95% of the appointments they make with new (first-time) customers are broken (Scott, 1983). Typically, the client makes the appointment by telephone but simply never shows up. Apparently, many would-be masochists turn cowardly at the last minute, at least when dealing with a professional dominatrix. This suggests that many people have masochistic interests and desires but are reluctant to act them out. Thus, again, desires may be far more widespread than actual experiences.

The focus of this book is accordingly on the issue of masochistic desires and interests. Only a very small proportion of the population is regularly, actively engaged in masochism as a way of life or a hobby. A substantially larger group would like to engage in such activities, and even more have some interest in them. In any case, it seems clear that even the broadest definitions of masochism pertain to only a minority of the population. There is no basis for assuming that masochism is a part of the psychological makeup of everyone, or even of everyone in some broad category (such as women).

SELF

One major source of interest in masochism is the light it may shed on the psychology of self. Indeed, this is what led to my own interest in masochism, because much of my past research had been devoted to studying the self—and masochism posed a serious challenge to the psychology of self. Masochism apparently contradicts several of the most general principles about the nature of the self. Either psychology's views of the self are wrong, or else some way must be found to understand the relationship between those views and masochism.

Modern psychology has been extremely interested in the nature of the self, in recent decades. It has devoted considerable attention to studying the self and theorizing about the self (e.g., Baumeister, 1982, 1986, 1987; Carver & Scheier, 1981; Greenwald, 1980; Higgins, 1986; Markus & Wurf, 1987; Schlenker, 1985; Swann, 1987; Yardley & Honess, 1987). There is so much information and theory about the self that it has been impossible to generate a comprehensive, satisfactory theory of the self. There is not even general agreement about the multiple, overlapping terms that sometimes mean the same thing as *self* and sometimes have more specialized meanings—terms such as *ego, identity, proprium.*

Despite this lack of a general theory of self, there are several broad principles that most theorists would agree about. Here are three generalizations about the self that fit what is currently known and would probably be acceptable to most psychologists:

First, selves are developed for a good reason, namely to help the person reach the natural, primary goals of achieving happiness and avoiding pain. In a word, selves are useful. They help the person organize experience and guide action toward these basic goals.

Second, the self develops a strong orientation toward control. The self seeks to control its environment, which means to achieve a good fit between itself and its world. Control can take the form of changing the world to fit the self's demands, or of changing the self to fit the world's demands (Rothbaum, Weisz, & Snyder, 1982). The quest for objective control of the world begins with curiosity, that is, the self's quest for information about the environment. The self tries to learn how to manipulate its surroundings, often as a means of getting what it wants.

But even without a clear idea of what it wants, the self exhibits simple curiosity and other signs of the desire for control. In addition to the quest for *objective* control, the self seeks a *subjective* sense of being in control, that is, efficacy (e.g., Bandura, 1977). The self seeks to believe itself in control even when it is not. People tend to overestimate how much control they have, at least until something goes wrong (then, the self begins to deny responsibility). The self is prone to illusions of control, which are false beliefs of having control (Langer, 1975; also Alloy & Abramson, 1979). Deprived of control, the self immediately begins to fight back (e.g., Brehm, 1966). The self wants freedom, choice and multiple options.

Third, the self is strongly oriented toward maximizing esteem. There are many forms of this motive. People desire self-esteem, that is, they want to think well of themselves. They also desire public esteem, that is, they want other people to think well of them, to respect and to admire them. People want to preserve their esteem from loss, and so they react strongly to any threat to their esteem. They also desire to increase their esteem when they can.

These three basic principles about the self underlie most of the self's activities. Countless research studies have demonstrated them in innumerable contexts. People want to be happy and to avoid pain and suffering. They seek to maintain and increase their control over themselves and their surroundings. And they desire to maintain and increase their prestige, respect, and esteem.

Viewed from the perspective of these three principles about the self, masochism is a startling paradox. Masochism contradicts these broad, fundamental features of the self. The self is developed to avoid pain, but masochists seek pain. The self strives for control, but masochists seek to relinquish control. The self aims to maximize its esteem, but masochists deliberately seek out humiliation.

On the surface, then, masochism poses a severe challenge to psychology's knowledge about the self. No theory of masochism can be complete without explaining how masochism can run counter to the most basic facts about the self. Resolving this paradox will tell us a great deal about the essential nature of masochism.

GENDER

Another source of interest in masochism concerns its relation to gender. This relation has been a source of confusion and controversy. Freud associated masochism with femininity. He saw the women of his day as passive and submissive, and he concluded that passivity and submissiveness are feminine traits. These same traits are apparent in the behavior of masochists. He concluded that women are by nature masochistic.

Many of Freud's followers sustained this view of feminine masochism. Some noted that the woman's role in courtship is often passive and submissive, for the initiative is left to the man. Others suggested that woman's experience of sexual intercourse is masochistic, starting with the physical injury upon loss of virginity. Many other broad features of women's behavior were made to fit into this theory that women are masochistic (e.g., Deutsch, 1944).

Other theorists were far less certain that masochism was vitally linked to femininity. Theodor Reik debated the matter with himself and finally decided that women are not masochistic. In fact, he concluded that men are more masochistic than women, although he was not entirely consistent.

Feminists were outraged by the view that women are masochistic. They accused the Freudians of trying to blame women for their own inferior status, and they angrily contended that the theory of women's masochism could be used to justify the oppression and exploitation of women. Feminists sought to correct the many social injustices that victimize women, from wife-beating to salary discrimination. They feared that these injustices would be allowed to persist if people accepted the view that women desired to be victims because of their innate masochism.

The debate is far from over. Recent work has argued forcefully that most of the evidence for women's masochism is misleading and misinterpreted (see Caplan, 1984). For example, some have called women masochistic for being prostitutes or for remaining with abusive husbands, for these patterns seem like voluntary ways of bringing pain and suffering to the self. Yet prostitutes and abused wives are often simply making the best of a poor set of choices. They do not get pleasure from their suffering.

On the other hand, other theorists continue to spin out the theory of feminine masochism. One recent book reaffirmed masochism as a central feature of the psychology of women, using everything from menstrual cramps to social shyness as evidence for it (Shainess, 1984). Other recent papers have argued that women deliberately engage in self-defeating behaviors of many sorts, such as fearing and rejecting success at work (Horner, 1972).

The debate currently stands as follows. The more traditional members of the psychoanalytic community still believe that women are masochistic, although an increasing number of them are defecting from this view. There is substantial evidence that many men are masochistic, and the theories of feminine masochism struggle to accommodate this fact. For example, some of them simply say that masochistic men are feminine. Most psychologists are reluctant to label women in general as *masochistic,* partly because the term has acquired a very negative connotation. But many researchers still see aspects of women's behavior as carrying elements of masochism.

Part of the problem is that we do not have a good understanding of masochism, so the debate is carried on amid multiple, conflicting definitions. What does it mean to say that all women are inherently masochistic? Certainly not all women engage in masochistic sex, and the vast majority would immediately deny that they desire or enjoy pain. Does it mean that all women secretly or "unconsciously" wish that their husbands would spank them, as a prelude to sex? That they would spank them, not as a prelude to sex? Does it mean that women are passive? That they are self-destructive? That they submit to authority willingly? That they deliberately sabotage their own chances for success or happiness?

The relation between gender and masochism is complex, but it cannot be addressed until a clearer understanding of masochism has been achieved.

PATHOLOGY AND MORALITY

How should masochism be regarded? To many people, especially throughout the general public, masochism is proof of sexual perversion or mental illness, or both. For example, the anonymous author of *The Sensuous Woman,* a best-selling popular sex manual, encouraged her readers to explore all forms of sex play they could imagine—*except* masochism, and in fact she advised getting rid of any sexual partner with sadomasochistic inclinations. Popular advice columnists in the print media have periodically expressed similar views. All in all, the prevailing opinions of influential people condemn masochism (see Greene & Greene, 1974, for review of these views; also Cowan, 1982).

Many psychologists share this negative view of masochism, although many others dispute it. There is currently a great deal of controversy as to whether masochism should be listed as a form of mental illness. This controversy concerns masochism in social behavior, for *sexual* masochism is already classified as a sexual disorder. According to the *Diagnostic and Statistical Manual* (3rd ed.) of the American Psychiatric Association, anyone who engages regularly in masochistic sex is mentally ill by definition. But the attempt to include "masochistic personality disorder" as another form of mental illness met with severe protest and resistance (Franklin, 1987).

There is a long tradition of regarding masochism as the activity of mentally sick individuals. Freud (1938) described masochism as a perversion. His follower, Wilhelm Stekel (1929/1953), linked masochism to cannibalism, criminality, vampirism, mass murder, necrophilia, epilepsy, pederasty, and more. He actually said that all masochists are murderers, and in a temporary lapse of therapeutic fervor he described their company as the "kingdom of Hell" (p. 409). Boss's (1949) treatment was equally negative and sensationalistic. Reik (1941/1957) said that all neurotics are masochists (pp. 368-372). In short, clinical perspectives have regarded masochists as seriously disturbed.

Recent empirical studies have furnished a surprisingly different picture. Researchers portray masochists as remarkably normal people, at least when not indulging their sexual tastes. Thus, the anthropologist Gini Graham Scott (1983) described participants in the female-domination clubs on the West Coast as "better educated and from higher income and occupational brackets than the average American" (p. 6). Andreas Spengler (1977) surveyed practicing sadomasochists in Germany and likewise found them to be upper class, successful individuals.

A famous study of the "sexual profile of men in power" found, to the researchers' extreme surprise, a high quantity of masochistic sexual activity among successful politicians, judges, and other important and influential men. Prostitutes catering to such clients administered more sexual domination than any other sexual service or act. It appears that U.S. Congressmen and successful executives are more likely to be masochists than are high school dropouts or blue-collar workers.

The masochists who are found in psychotherapy are likely to be the least well adjusted, simply by the fact that they are in therapy. Even so, some clinical observers have found masochists to be relatively normal and well adjusted. Lyn Cowan (1982) described her masochistic therapy patients as "successful by social standards: professionally, sexually, emotionally, culturally, in marriage or out. They are frequently individuals of admirable inner strength of character, possessed of strong 'coping egos' and with an ethical sense of individual responsibility" (p. 31). Even Stekel (1929/1953) admitted that many masochists appeared to be "ideal whole men" (p. 51).

There is no way to integrate all these views. Masochists cannot be warped individuals with sick, twisted minds akin to mass murderers and necrophiliacs, if they are also strong, responsible, successful individuals with a strong moral sense.

To address this problem, it is first necessary to narrow the focus to sexual masochism. Some psychologists have used the term *masochistic* to refer to a wide range of behaviors having nothing to do with sex, but (as already explained) this tendency merely introduces a hopeless mass of confusion unless one is quite certain how to understand the core phenomena of masochism, which involve specifically sexual masochism. With sexual masochism, the question can then be phrased this way: Are masochists dangerous perverts and lunatics, or not?

Therapy patients do not make a good group on which to base such an answer. People in psychotherapy often have some form of mental illness. Therefore, it makes most sense to use the empirical studies of masochists in general. Among these, it appears that most masochists are not dangerous perverts or mentally ill individuals. They appear to be normal people, apart from their deviant sexual tastes. In fact, they appear to be a little above average in many respects.

One might make the analogy to homosexuality. For a long period, homosexuality was regarded as a form of mental illness. Observations of therapy patients supported this view, for many homosexuals in therapy were indeed ill. But more recent views have acknowledged that the majority of homosexuals are not mentally ill, something that could hardly be learned by focusing on therapy patients. Although there are undoubtedly some homosexuals among the mentally ill, homosexuality itself is not a form of mental illness. Moreover, it may be misleading to take what is known about mentally ill homosexuals and generalize to all homosexuals. The same could be said about masochism. Although masochism may appeal to certain groups of mentally ill individuals, it is likely that the appeal to normal individuals is different. This book suggests ways of understanding masochism without invoking theories of mental illness. This is not to suggest that the clinical theories are wrong, for they may be entirely correct in explaining masochistic dynamics among the mentally ill. Rather, this book offers ways of understanding masochism when it is not part of mental illness.

Next, we turn to the question of the masochistic sex itself. Is there something wrong with engaging in such activities? Obviously, there is no neutral position from which to answer this question, and one might ask the same question about any other sexual activity.

Our modern American culture tends toward sexual tolerance. The standard liberal view is that anything done between consenting adults is acceptable, at least if no one is hurt and no one's rights are abridged. In this view, masochism is borderline. It does occur between consenting adults, but the masochist does get hurt. Are people allowed to be hurt if they desire to be? Again, this depends on cultural attitudes. Many feel that the society should have laws to prevent people from doing things that might harm themselves, such as gambling or taking drugs. Others feel that people have a right to do what they want as long as they do not endanger anyone else.

Again, though, these are culturally relative views. Our Victorian predecessors had a more narrow and severe view of appropriate sexuality. To them, if you enjoyed masochistic sex (or many other forms of sex), you were sick as well as immoral. This view is equally viable. The definition of sexual morality and perversity is to some extent arbitrary, and each society sets its own boundaries.

Definitions of illness are likewise somewhat relative and variable, and masochism is once again in the gray area: It can be defined as healthy or sick, depending on prevailing attitudes. One refreshingly sensible view was proposed by Freud, who said that one should refer to *perversion* only if some activity (other than sexual intercourse) becomes absolutely indispensable to sexual pleasure. In other words, if you can only enjoy sex under some unusual conditions—such as oral sex, or watching others make love, or touching underwear—then you are perverted. But if you can sometimes enjoy sex without those activities, then they are not perversions. Applied to masochism, this means that someone would be a masochistic pervert if he or she were only able to enjoy sex in connection with being dominated. But if the person enjoys normal sexual intercourse and merely uses masochism to provide variety or novel excitement on an occasional basis, the person should not be labeled *sick* or *perverted*.

If masochists are normal individuals apart from their sexuality, then they must be held responsible for their actions and preferences, which raises some moral questions. Is there something immoral about masochism apart from its sexual pleasure? One group of feminists have argued strongly that the answer is yes, although other feminists have disagreed. The feminist critique of sadomasochism is based on the view that masochistic sex involves an implicit endorsement of interpersonal violence, oppression, and exploitation. Sadomasochism, in this view, expresses a subtle vote of approval of Nazi brutality, wife-beating, the Spanish Inquisition, genocide, and other objectionable practices (Linden, 1982).

How much do private sex acts invoke public political meanings, and what effects do these have? This is a difficult set of issues. Masochism is indeed loaded with symbolism, but few masochists seem to have any sense of making political statements by their sexuality. From the present perspective, the feminist critique is mistaken because masochism rejects any relation to political realities in the outside world—in fact, masochism is an attempt to remove awareness of the world altogether.

THINGS ARE NOT WHAT THEY SEEM

One reason for psychology's difficulty with masochism is that everything about masochism seems misleading. Masochism involves more fiction and illusion than nearly any other pattern of human behavior. Nothing about it is quite what it seems. As a result, observers and theorists have been repeatedly misled. If you take masochism at face value, you will probably miss some vital features about it.

A first illusion in masochism concerns the pattern of control. On the surface, the dominant partner is in control. The masochist appears helpless, often being tied up and blindfolded. All initiative, all decisions, are left up to the dominant partner, while the masochist merely obeys and submits. Yet often it is the masochist's wishes and desires that determine the course of the interaction. The script that is enacted is often written by the masochist. Indeed, prostitutes complain about the inordinate particularity of some masochistic clients. For example, some men desire to be verbally humiliated with a precise series of insults. If the prostitute deviates at all from her lines, even just forgetting a word or two, the men get upset and insist that she start over.

There are other ways in which the interaction is controlled by the masochist. Dominants sometimes imply that they are basically catering to their masochistic partners (e.g., Califia, 1983). They have to monitor the masochist's responses carefully and closely in order to ascertain exactly how much pain to administer, for too little makes for an unsatisfying experience, and too much ruins everything.

The very entry into S&M is often initiated by the masochist. In many couples, one partner wants to submit sexually but the other is reluctant to dominate, so the masochist has to convince the other to engage in these activities (Scott, 1983). Sacher-Masoch, the man for whom masochism is named, followed that pattern in his own life, constantly urging his reluctant lady friends to take the dominant role with him (Cleugh, 1951). The reverse pattern, in which one person desires to take the dominant role but the partner is reluctant to submit, is apparently quite uncommon.

In short, the masochist's lack of control may be more apparent than real. The masochist is in control in some ways, or is at least an equal partner in the decisions (e.g., Greene & Greene, 1974). It is a commonplace observation by participants in S&M that the masochist is "really" in control.

On the other hand, one must not be entirely convinced by such statements either. It would be misleading to suggest that masochistic submission is a means of exerting control. The masochist exerts control in order to provide him or herself with a satisfying experience of loss of control. Masochists desire to be helpless and vulnerable, and they exert their initiative to get themselves into that position.

Thus, the dynamics of control in masochistic sex are not what they seem. Another illusion in masochism concerns pain. Masochists desire pain and submit to it willingly. Does this mean that they enjoy the pain? Masochists often suggest that pain becomes pleasant in some way, but their remarks are suspect. Some masochists note that pain becomes pleasant in fantasy but they are surprised that in reality the sensation remains unpleasant (e.g., "J", 1982). One couple I interviewed suggested that the pain becomes pleasant, but when I asked them how this happened they quickly added that the sensation of pain remains painful and unpleasant. The pain is tolerable and there is something about it that appeals to the masochist, but it is simply not true that pain turns into pleasure.

It is important to note that the pain in masochistic sex games rarely reaches intense levels, by all accounts. People who engage in S&M speak of watching for the masochist's limits and ceasing when the pain starts to become really unpleasant. Masochists desire pain in small, very carefully measured doses. They may even help control the amount of pain. Some couples use "safe words," a pre-set verbal signal that the masochist can use to tell the dominant partner to stop inflicting pain.

Nor is it true that masochists simply enjoy pain in general. Masochists dislike many forms of pain as much as anyone. In one case, a masochistic woman had a strong dislike of going to the dentist because she found the treatments painful. Her boyfriend suggested that she try to enjoy the pain as a masochistic experience. Her efforts were unsuccessful, however, and she continued to loathe dental work, even though she continued to enjoy masochistic sex (Weinberg, Williams, & Moser, 1984). Masochists only enjoy pain in certain contexts.

Pain has a natural, biological function, which is to warn of injury and thereby enable the individual to prevent damage to the body. Loss of pain sensitivity, which might seem appealing, tends in fact to put the person in serious danger. For example, leprosy tends to reduce the body's sensitivity to pain, especially in the fingers and toes. As a result, the leper may fail to react if one of these digits is being crushed under a heavy object or burned in a fire. Many lepers end up missing fingers or toes, not because the disease itself causes these digits to fall off (it has no such effect), but because the loss of pain sensitivity undermines the body's readiness to protect itself from damage.

In everyday experience, pain and injury are highly correlated. Most injuries, from a cut finger to a broken bone, cause pain. And most pain occurs in conjunction with some bodily damage. That is presumably what pain is: nature's system for warning of bodily damage.

But masochists seek pain without injury. All reports and observations indicate that masochists are extremely careful to prevent any chance of injury. They take various, often extensive precautions to ensure that they are not harmed (e.g., Lee, 1983; Scott, 1983). Dominant partners who harm someone or whose practices even seem to risk injury are soon shunned by others. Manuals for S&M are essentially descriptions of how to administer pain without causing injury: where it is safe to strike a person, how to slap the face harmlessly, how to tie someone up without cutting off the circulation, and so on (e.g., Bellwether, 1982).

The key point is that masochism deprives pain of its natural, biological association with injury. Pain is divorced from injury. In a sense, masochists *fictionalize* pain. They make use of the sensation for some purpose other than its normal, natural function. Pain is cultivated, while injury is avoided.

The normal association between pain and injury has misled many theorists and observers about the nature of masochism. Masochism has often been seen as a form of self-destructive or self-defeating behavior. Some psychologists use the label *masochistic* to refer to any pattern of seeking harm to the self (see Franklin, 1987, for review and discussion). But it is clear that masochism is not self-destructive. Masochists do not want to be harmed. They want *safe* pain.

In short, masochistic practices are highly misleading. One can easily draw mistaken conclusions from casual observation of the masochistic quest for pain or the masochistic negotiation of control. This web of fiction and illusion pervades most masochistic activities, so it is necessary to be careful and thorough in reviewing masochistic practices before constructing a theory to explain masochism.

METHODS AND EVIDENCE

At present, there is no fully valid or reliable source of evidence about masochism. There are several types of evidence, but each is flawed in some way. The best one can do is to look for converging patterns among the different sources of evidence, keeping the limitations and qualifications in mind.

The confusing mixture of past theories about masochism is partly due to this problem in getting valid evidence. It is hard to get any reliable facts about masochism. Consequently, theorists have constructed their ideas almost in an empirical vacuum. The result has been an odd assortment of theories. Some have valid insights, whereas others seem quite far-fetched.

The most common basis for past theories about masochism has been clinical observations. These observations have serious drawbacks as evidence. One problem is that contented, well-adjusted, satisfied masochists would not show up in psychotherapy (see Reik, 1941/1957). Clinical impressions of sexual dysfunction and general pathology may thus reflect the sampling bias inherent in a clinical sample. The case parallels that of homosexuality. For a long time, clinical psychology regarded homosexuality as a form of mental illness, for they only saw homosexuals who were mentally ill. Finally some observers pointed out that it is quite possible to be a homosexual and enjoy normal mental health. Homosexuality is no longer regarded as a form of mental illness, but that is a recent development. The long tendency to see homosexuals as sick individuals was a natural consequence of basing theory on clinical observations—for clinicians only saw sick homosexuals. The same is probably all the more true for masochism.

A second problem with basing theories of masochism on clinical observations is that the appeal of such activities for mentally ill people may well be entirely different from the appeal to normal people. After all, the mentally ill buy guns, accost strangers, and wash their hands for reasons that are quite different from the reasons normal people have for those acts, and a comparable difference probably applies to deviant sexual activity. In particular, clinicians have argued that masochism is derived from sadism, that masochists are self-destructive, that masochism results from severe difficulties with sexual functioning, and that being beaten is a viable means of achieving a sense of self. All of these arguments could well apply to mentally ill people who are drawn to sadomasochism, but they are contradicted by the evidence about normal people who participate in such activities.

A second source of evidence is first-person writings about masochism. Masochists sometimes write about their views and experiences, and their writings often attempt to offer a theory about what masochism is (e.g., Califia, 1983; Greene & Greene, 1974). These accounts are useful, but one must keep in mind that there may be a desire to justify one's behavior patterns. Such a tendency would lead to some self-serving biases that might rationalize their activities. After all, masochists are engaged in bizarre, deviant, socially stigmatized activities, and it is not surprising that some of them would want to present these in a positive light in order to win approval or tolerance. Moreover, most masochists lack knowledge of psychological theory and may therefore rely on whatever psychological concepts they have picked up from the popular culture. These may be a poor basis for a theory.

Probably it is best to regard masochists' explanations for masochism as an important source of information about masochism—but not as psychological theory. We can learn much from what masochists tell us, but we must not confuse them with trained researchers and theorists.

There have been a handful of surveys of people who participate in masochistic activities. Surveys of practicing masochists furnish some useful data, but there are several drawbacks. First, there may be a severe sampling bias: People who respond to these surveys may not be typical of masochists. Indeed, several survey researchers have said they found it practically impossible to obtain responses from female masochists (e.g., Spengler, 1977; Weinberg & Falk, 1980). Because masochistic sexuality carries a negative stigma (cf. Greene & Greene, 1974), many people may be reluctant to admit such activities to researchers. Moreover, responding to surveys may be contrary to the spirit of masochism. Being an active "subject" whose opinions and experiences matter, and especially giving an accurate account of one's life and identity, may contradict the self-negating tendencies of masochism.

A few researchers have engaged in participant observation, which means that they entered into the sadomasochistic subculture, took part in its activities, and recorded their impressions. The sampling biases are probably less extreme here than with the surveys or clinical data, although strictly private masochists (and couples) will probably not be included. Also, it is possible that taking part in sadomasochistic sex games with groups of people over a period of many months may gradually undermine the detached objectivity of a scientific observer. Still, the participant observation studies are probably the best evidence about masochism that has been published so far.

This book attempts to review and integrate all the available evidence from the sources just listed. It also adds new evidence of two sorts. The first of these is historical and cross-cultural evidence about masochism. Historical evidence about sexuality cannot be fully conclusive, for we have no firm way of knowing about the sex lives of our ancestors. Still, there is considerable information about sex in history, and several historians have been able to assemble it and make some very educated guesses about the sexual practices of previous eras. Historical evidence offers the opportunity to test several theories about masochism. We can determine whether masochism is a natural phenomenon that occurs in all cultures and eras—or is a product of certain cultural factors. If the latter, we can see what social conditions produce masochism, what conditions increase or decrease the incidence of masochism, and so forth.

The second form of new evidence about masochism is an original study of masochistic cognitions. These were culled from letters to sex-oriented magazines in which masochists have written about their experiences and fantasies. Based on Scott (1983), I selected the best-selling magazine of this genre (*Variations*), obtained 3 years' worth of issues (36), and coded and analyzed the epistolary self-reports. In this way, over 200 letters were obtained. These were coded on a variety of content dimensions; interrater agreement was .933, which seems adequate (Baumeister, 1988a, 1988b).

The letters are authentic communications from masochists, although they have been subject to editing to remove bad grammar and unpublishable material. The editors have vouched for the authenticity of the letters (McCarty, Personal Communication, 1987; Springer, 1976). Authors are not paid, so there is no incentive to write apart from interest in sharing one's sexual experiences and desires. In particular, the magazine staff does not write the letters.[1]

There are several drawbacks to using published letters as evidence about masochism. First, there may be a tendency to write about good experiences more than bad ones, so the bias will be opposite to the bias in the clinical observations. People who try masochism and have a terrible experience are unlikely to write about it for a sex magazine. Even if they did write, the editors might not publish such letters. The editors want to publish what their public wants to buy and read. A magazine that caters to masochists is unlikely to sell many copies if it portrays masochism in an undesirable, unpleasant light.

Second, a sample of letters will include only masochists who can read and write, thus leaving out the lowest part of the socioeconomic spectrum. This may be only a minor problem. Evidence suggests that most masochists are drawn mainly from the middle and upper socioeconomic classes (e.g., Scott, 1983; Spengler, 1977), where most individuals do know how to read and write. Still, it is important to remember that anyone who is illiterate is unlikely to be found in a magazine letters column. Also, people who dislike writing about their experiences for personality or other personal reasons will similarly be omitted.

Third, the published letters may not reflect a representative sample

---

[1] *Variations* belongs to the *Penthouse* group of magazines, all of which include reader letters reporting alleged sexual experiences. These letters have contributed significantly to the popularity and visibility of these magazines over the years. It seems safe to assume that if *Penthouse* secretly fabricated its own letters, it would have been discovered and exposed by *Playboy* (or some other major competitor). It is implausible that the magazine staff could have sustained such a fraud over two decades, especially in a field so closely related to investigative news reporting (which often forms a substantial part of the nonsexual content of these magazines).

The high visibility of the *Penthouse* magazines is an important assumption of this argument. Obviously, the argument does not apply to the variety of less successful competitors, which may or may not secretly generate some or all of their own letters.

of masochists. In my view, this is the most serious problem. The editors of *Variations* have informed me that the letters they publish can only be taken as a profile of the masochist as he or she is tolerated in print by the community (McCarty, personal communication, 1987). They refuse to publish references to illegal actions, presumably including especially drug use and perhaps activities involving children. They also suppress reports of dangerous and harmful activities, such as use of feces in games (cf. Scott, 1983).

Beyond these restrictions, one may assume that the editors try to publish the most entertaining letters and try to publish a balanced assortment of letters, for repetition becomes boring. The desire to publish the most appealing or entertaining letters is not a problem, for one can argue that whatever sorts of letters have the broadest appeal reflect the most prevalent forms of masochistic desires. The bias toward balance and variety suggests that any statistical differences obtained are probably underestimates of the true differences. For example, if there are far more letters from men than from women, the editors may publish a higher percentage of letters from women in order to achieve a greater balance. In considering statistical findings, therefore, it may be useful to recall that the true differences may be somewhat larger than they appear.

It is also important to note that the letters in *Variations* focus mainly on heterosexual couples. Some homosexual experiences are reported, but the vast majority of letters refer to heterosexual activities. It will be necessary to look elsewhere for evidence about homosexual masochism.

A fourth problem is that there is no way to verify the accuracy and veridicality of the letters. How do we know whether the people really had the experiences they describe? Some letters are clearly labeled as fantasies. Others claim to be authentic experiences but seem implausible for various reasons. These may be based on actual experiences but embellished by fantasy, or they may be outright fantasies. Other letters may indeed be accurate reports of actual experiences.

For example, in over 250 sexual episodes described in these letters, many of which lasted an hour or more, no one reported being interrupted by a telephone call, which seems to defy the odds. Of course, if people only write about their best or favorite experiences, this might explain why things generally went so smoothly. Still, it may be that there was some retrospective selection, distortion, and fabrication in describing these events.

There is simply no basis for assuming that these letters are thorough, honest, accurate, and representative accounts of actual behavior. All of this is not a problem, however, if the letters are regarded as cognitions (mental events) rather than as behavioral self-reports. Indeed, if embellishments and distortions have occurred, they may *improve* our insight into the mind of the masochist. It seems likely that masochists would embellish their reports by adding details to make it seem a more perfect experience, according to their own private view of the perfect masochistic experience. From reading them, therefore, one may learn about how masochists envision perfect or ideal experiences. These letters make it possible to see what masochists imagine and desire, only partly constrained by the practical issues and exigencies of everyday reality.

Indeed, it could be argued that these letters are a better means of studying masochistic desire than actual behavioral evidence would be. Empirical studies of overt masochism have repeatedly found that the actual behaviors of masochists are often constrained and restricted by lack of opportunity (especially lack of willing partners), by misunderstandings or inadequate communication between participants, by the need to maintain secrecy, and by various other mundane obstacles (e.g., Greene & Greene, 1974; Lee, 1983; Scott, 1983; Spengler, 1977). Data about actual behavior are thus a problematic and degraded guide to knowing the underlying motivations and wishes. In contrast, reports of favorite experiences, embellished experiences, and fantasies may offer a good means for examining the structure of masochistic desires.

Thus, the sample of letters may provide a good way of finding out what masochists like to think about. The letters report their favorite or ideal experiences, in many cases probably embellished with fantasy. They cannot be taken as reliable evidence about what masochists do, but they do tell us about what masochists imagine and desire. They reveal the scripts and schemas that define the masochistic imagination.

Last, I have interviewed a handful of masochists. These were individuals who heard about my research, mostly through my public lectures, and volunteered to talk with me. These interviews were not carried out in a systematic fashion, nor was the sample constructed to be representative, so they are to be considered merely a source of impressions and a way of getting personal reactions to these ideas.

Once again, there is no source of empirical evidence about masochism that is free of flaws. The best one can do to get a reliable picture is to look for converging patterns of evidence from multiple sources. In my view, there is such a convergence: All the different sources of evidence (except the Freudian clinical observations) point toward the same theories and conclusions. We may therefore be cautiously confident about these views.

Chapter Two
Overview of Main Ideas

This book presents two main theoretical views of masochism. That is, masochism should be understood in two basic ways. Masochism is too complex to fit easily into one theory or pattern; not all participants in masochism get the same things out of it. There is some overlap between the two theories, but they are independent. This chapter provides an overview of those two theories, and later chapters flesh them out and provide the basis and evidence for them.

PRIMACY OF MASOCHISM

Before embarking on a theoretical account of masochism, it is necessary to settle one important matter, namely its relation to sadism. Most past theories of masochism have argued that masochism and sadism are closely related, even to the extent that all sadists are masochistic and vice versa. Moreover, the majority of these past views have treated masochism as derived from sadism. These views may once have been plausible and tenable, but they are difficult to reconcile with current knowledge.

Relation Between Sadism and Masochism

The prevailing theory since Freud has been that sadism is the fundamental, original pattern, and masochism is derived from it. In this view, masochists are sadists in disguise, so to speak. People supposedly want to hurt and dominate others, but because of guilt feelings and other inhibiting factors they convert this desire into its opposite, namely the desire to submit to hurt and domination at another's hands. As Freud put it, masochism is turned around sadism—that is, turned around and directed against the self. Theodor Reik (1941/1957) was even more explicit about this. He said the masochist's message is "What you do to me, I want to do to you" (p. 200). Masochistic submission was a disguised way of expressing one's secret desires to dominate and hurt others.

More recent theoretical views have tended to preserve the assumption that masochism is derived from sadism. Some scholars have abandoned the distinction altogether and simply speak of *sadomasochism,* saying that sadism and masochism are simply "two sides of the same coin" (Weinberg & Kamel, 1983).

Strictly speaking, there are two separate points here. The first is that sadism and masochism always occur together: Wherever one occurs, the other may be assumed to exist also. The other point is that sadism is the basic and fundamental pattern, whereas masochism is the secondary or derivative pattern. This makes sadism the more important one to study and to understand psychologically.

From the present perspective, both of these points are wrong. Sadism and masochism do not always occur together, as far as current evidence goes. More important, when the two are related, masochism seems to be the more important and fundamental pattern.

If past theorists erred, perhaps their mistakes were understandable and forgiveable. In particular, some past theorists may have been misled by overreliance on clinical observations. Such observations may tell us about what attracts mentally ill people to sadomasochism, but they may furnish a misleading picture of sadism and masochism among normal people. It may well be that the mentally ill are sometimes drawn to cruelty. It may also be that when they get involved in deviant sexuality, it is out of a desire to inflict pain rather than to receive it. But in these cases, the sexual activity is a symptom of something quite different, some deeper mental illness. Masochistic activity among the mentally ill is probably quite different from masochistic activity among normal individuals.

In short, the mistaken assumptions of past theorists may have been quite reasonable conclusions based on their evidence, but unfortunately the evidence was misleading. It may well be that sadism is more fundamental and important than masochism among mental patients. But even if that is true, the facts may be quite different among normal people.

The traditional view holds that sadism is the fundamental pattern, which means that masochism is of secondary importance. Ample evidence appears to contradict this view. Empirical studies of normal people provide strong evidence for what may be called the *primacy of masochism,* that is, the view that masochism is more widespread, fundamental, and theoretically important than sadism. If anything, sadism appears to be the derivative pattern.

One source of evidence is the sheer frequency of sadism versus masochism. All signs indicate the masochism is far more common than sadism. In the present sample, the number of letters written by submissives was more than double (in fact, almost triple) the number written by dominants. (An additional few described episodes in which the partners exchanged roles.) More people want to write about submissive experiences than about dominant experiences. If sadism were the main form or the more common pattern, there should be a relative surplus of letters written by dominants, but instead there is a relative shortage, and a rather large one.

The same pattern obtains elsewhere. A collection of writings on lesbian sadomasochism (Samois, 1982) contained 11 contributions by submissives, as compared to only 3 by dominants. True, this collection and my sample both have been selected by editors, but one would think editors would strive either for equal numbers of both or for a balance reflecting the actual interest. In particular, it seems unlikely that editors would emphasize the perspective opposite to that of the majority of their contributors and readers. The relative surplus of masochistic accounts probably reflects the primacy of masochism.

Other sources avoid the problem of editorial selection, and the same conclusion emerges. Nancy Friday (1980) has spent much of her journalistic career collecting sex fantasies of all varieties, from anyone who would send them to her. In her discussion of sadism and masochism she agreed with the standard view that the two are closely linked and that sadism is the more important and fundamental pattern. But she reported that in her mail, masochistic fantasies outnumber sadistic ones by about four to one.

Prostitutes cater to the sexual tastes of men who cannot find willing partners, and in recent decades prostitutes have found themselves doing more and more S&M. Do prostitutes' clients consist more of sadists or masochists? Xaviera Hollander (a.k.a. the "happy hooker"), the renowned media spokesperson for prostitutes, said that roughly 90% of the clients who purchase sadomasochistic services prefer the submissive role (Greene & Greene, 1974). A famous study of prostitutes catering to rich and powerful clients in Washington, DC found a similar pattern: Requests to be beaten outnumbered requests to inflict a beating by about eight to one (Janus, Bess, & Saltus, 1977).

On the West Coast, there are various clubs for people who wish to engage in S&M. An anthropologist who studied these clubs found once again a hefty preponderance of submissives, ranging from double to quadruple the number of dominants (Scott, 1983). On a more individual basis, she said that a common pattern in couples is that one partner wants to submit masochistically but the other person is reluctant to take the dominant role. The reverse pattern, in which one partner wants to dominate but the other is reluctant to submit, is apparently quite rare. In the early 1980s, the novel and movie *9 1/2 Weeks* featured an eager dominant and a reluctant submissive, but this pattern is apparently uncommon, and so the book and movie must be regarded as atypical or unrealistic.

A review of the research literature turned up only one study that failed to find a substantial majority of submissives. This study was done by mail in Germany, and it found about equal numbers (Spengler, 1977), with a substantial majority of respondents who liked to take both roles. Again, this can hardly be taken as a sign that sadism is more common or widespread.

In short, the weight of statistical evidence points to a substantial numerical superiority of masochists over sadists. Based on current knowledge, masochism is simply far more common than sadism.

Further evidence for the primacy of masochism comes from studies of how people get involved in S&M. In general, it appears that people start out as masochists. For example, one study examined the S&M subculture among male homosexuals (Kamel, 1983). It found that almost all participants had started out as submissives. Some of them had later moved on to begin taking the dominant role, although others had not. Another study of male homosexual sadomasochists likewise found that they had all started out as masochists (Lee, 1983). The same pattern has been found among heterosexuals (Scott, 1983) and lesbians (Califia, 1983).

Thus, behavioral evidence suggests that masochism comes first, and sadistic or dominant role taking comes only later, if at all. Given that masochism precedes sadism, it is illogical to argue that masochism is derived from sadism. Rather, sadism must be considered to be the secondary, derivative pattern.

Another sign of the primacy of masochism comes from the way sadomasochists describe their activities. Apparently, in the majority of sadomasochistic encounters, it is the wishes and desires of the submissive rather than the dominant partner that form the basis for the scene that is enacted (e.g., Scott, 1983). Some first-person writers claim that the submissive partner is "really" in control during S&M, because it is the submissive's needs and desires that initiate, shape, script, and limit the sex play. This is important, for it seems to indicate that in many couples the impetus for S&M activity comes from the masochistic partner.

Although no statistical data are available, the present sample of observations likewise suggests that it is the submissive person who is mainly responsible for starting and guiding the S&M activities. From reading numerous accounts of S&M sex written from both dominant and submissive perspectives, one gets the clear impression that the masochists are more strongly motivated than the dominants. Indeed, it often seems inappropriate to call the sexually dominant partner a *sadist,* for often these individuals do not seem to derive great satisfaction or sexual pleasure from inflicting pain (see also Lee, 1983). Many of them write as if they regard the activities as a pleasant, somewhat weird, new form of sexual play. As Scott (1983) suggested, many of them may have been talked into participating by a partner who desired to submit, and they are simply enjoying a good time with some kinky fun. The intense cravings described by many masochists are largely (although not completely) absent from the writings of dominants.

One sign of the lesser involvement of dominants is the frequency of sexual orgasm from S&M. A fair number of masochists report having orgasms without direct sexual contact (that is, without stimulation of the sex organs), but dominants almost never do. In receiving a spanking, for example, some masochistic women and occasionally men report sexual arousal even to the point of orgasm, but almost no one reports receiving an orgasm from inflicting a spanking on someone else.

The point here is simply that masochistic desires appear to be stronger than sadistic ones, in many reports. Masochists are more likely to speak of their "needs" for such activities than are dominants. This also seems to suggest that masochism is the more important pattern psychologically.

Are Masochism and Sadism Always Related?

"There is no sadism without masochism, and no masochism without sadism," said W. Stekel (1929/1953, p. 138).

Clearly, some people exhibit both dominant and submissive patterns in sexual behavior. But *all?* Given the rarity of universals in social behavior, one must be skeptical of such generalizations even on an a priori basis.

What sort of evidence could one use? Researchers sometimes point to the fact that many participants in S&M switch roles. But "many" is not "all," and this evidence in fact falls far short of universality. There is ample empirical evidence of individuals who do not switch roles.

Indeed, even the fact that some people switch roles is not conclusive proof of their desire to do so. As already noted, there appears to be a substantial shortage of dominant partners in the S&M community, and many people who desire masochistic submission are unable to find a partner to dominate them (e.g., Scott, 1983; also Spengler, 1977). It is hard enough to find anyone at all interested in S&M, because the social stigma of deviant sexuality makes these people quite secretive. And given the surplus of submissives, when a masochist does manage to find someone else interested in S&M, the odds are that this person will also be masochistically inclined. As a result, many pairs of individuals who engage in S&M consist of two masochists, who must somehow find a means of satisfying their shared interests despite their incompatible role preferences. Various researchers have suggested that these pairs of masochists sometimes resolve their dilemma by taking turns. Thus, they end up switching roles, but not from any desire to do so. Taking the dominant role is a compromise of sorts. They may be purely masochistic in their desires, but they periodically take the dominant role in fairness to the partner.

Probably the best compilation of research on S&M is the work by Weinberg and Kamel (1983). These researchers periodically repeat the usual conclusion that sadism and masochism are inevitably, always related. But each time they make that claim, their evidence is one-sided. Their evidence repeatedly shows that the majority of sadists also have had masochistic experiences. Thus, as noted earlier, most masters and mistresses have started out as submissives. Weinberg and Kamel do not furnish evidence of the reverse; that is, they never claim that all (or even most) masochists have had dominant or sadistic experiences. Maybe all sadists are, or were, masochists; but this does not mean that all masochists are sadists. It may simply be that everyone starts out as a masochist, and some of them later become dominant or sadistic, whereas others never do.

In short, it is an open question whether sadistic and masochistic desires always coexist. There is fairly convincing evidence that most people who take the dominant role have previously taken the submissive role. On the other hand, it appears that many people engage in masochistic activities without desiring or trying out the dominant role. And even if they do switch roles sometimes, masochistic submission may be their primary interest and desire.

Conclusion

Masochism should not be dismissed as a minor derivative of sadistic desires. Rather, masochism is more important than sadism. Masochism appears to be more common and widespread than sadism, masochism precedes sadism when both appear in the same person, and there is some evidence to suggest that masochism is more strongly desired than sadism. Claims that masochism and sadism always coexist may be severely exaggerated. Masochism should be the main focus of theory and research, because it is the fundamental and primary pattern.

ESCAPE FROM SELF

The concept of *self* has taken a central place in psychology during recent decades. In its broadest usages, it encompasses all familiar and colloquial meanings—thus, it means the same thing as when it is used in ordinary speech. This book uses it in much the same way. More precisely, the self consists of one's physical body and the set of meanings that are elaborated around it (identity). Social and interpersonal roles, commitments and obligations, memberships in groups and institutions, personal values and goals, personal history, concepts of one's own personality, and conceptions of one's potential identity—all these are added on to the body to form the notion of self.

One central argument of this book is that masochism essentially involves escape from self. The preceding chapter explained that masochism challenges our prevailing ideas and theories about the self. Normally, the self seeks pleasure and tries to avoid pain—but masochists desire pain. Normally, the self seeks control—but masochists desire to relinquish control. Normally, the self seeks to protect its dignity and maximize its esteem—but masochists desire humiliation.

Masochism thus has a paradoxical nature, as seen from the perspective of the psychology of self. This paradox reveals the essential nature of masochism. Masochism is an all out attack on the self, an attempt to remove the main features of the self. Masochism represents an unusually powerful and probably effective means of escape from self.

A more precise rendition of "escape from self" is the motivated loss of self-awareness. During the masochistic episode, the person forgets his or her normal identity. In a sense, the person's identity temporarily ceases to exist. The ongoing activity and reality of the self are suspended. The self is deconstructed, that is, reduced to its bare minimum.

Masochism resembles an engrossing game or drama, in which normal identities are suspended by the players or actors. It is no accident that masochists typically refer to their activities as *games* or as *scenes*, for these terms indicate the suspension of normal reality that is essential to masochism. During these activities, masochists cease to be their normal selves and may even seem to become someone else.

It would be misleading, however, to say simply or categorically that masochism removes the self or eliminates self-awareness altogether. Some features of masochism, such as embarrassment or the presence of an audience, seem to promote self-awareness. Some recent theoretical

Levels of Self

Several recent theories have emphasized that human thinking and awareness have multiple levels, and that people move systematically among these levels. These theories may be extended to the self.

According to the theory of *action identification* (Vallacher & Wegner, 1985, 1987), people can think of any given action in different ways. For example, the same activity can be described as "moving my fingers," as "writing," as "preparing a report," as "meeting a deadline," as "working," as "pursuing my career," and as "supporting my family." There are high and low levels of describing actions. High levels have more abstract, symbolic meaning, less mechanical detail, and a broader temporal focus than low levels. To tell them apart, one uses the "by-test," based on the word "by." Higher levels are accomplished "by" lower levels. For example, you work by preparing reports, you prepare reports by writing, and you write by moving your fingers. The reverse does not make sense: You don't move your fingers by writing, rather, you write by moving your fingers. Writing is thus a higher level of action identification than moving your fingers.

These different levels correspond to different ways people have of thinking about what they are doing. Sometimes people think about the high levels, and sometimes they think in terms of the low levels. There are personality differences, for example: Some people think in high-level terms more often than others.

Several key theoretical points about these different levels must be noted. For one thing, people generally prefer the higher levels. They like to think about what they are doing at high levels, and they move up to higher levels whenever possible. Learning enables one to move up to progressively higher levels. When learning to play tennis, the novice focuses on the lowest levels. The instructor says to pay attention to how one grips the racket, how one position one's feet, how to move one's arm, and so forth. It is doubtful, however, that people would find tennis enjoyable if they remained at that level of awareness. Fortunately, once one masters the low levels, they become removed from awareness (i.e., they become automatic), and one begins attending to the higher levels. In tennis, higher level thinking concerns knowing the score, deciding on strategy, and so forth. In general, then, low levels are important for learning, but people prefer high levels.

What are the benefits of low levels, apart from the necessity of starting there when learning something new? Several factors attract people to low levels. First, when something goes wrong, one shifts to lower levels to correct a problem (see Carver & Scheier, 1981). For example, when things start to go wrong in work or school, the individual commonly begins to examine the details of procedure to seek a solution.

A second benefit of low levels is that they allow one to escape the high-level implications of actions that may be undesirable. Several studies have investigated how criminals can commit crimes without feeling guilt or remorse or concern about their victims (Wegner & Vallacher, 1986). It appears that criminals tend to focus their minds on their actions at the lowest levels. When breaking into someone's house, they are not thinking of their actions in high level terms, such as "violating the law," "taking another person's possessions," or "destroying someone's happiness." Rather they think in low-level terms: getting the window open, checking for dogs or alarms, avoiding fingerprints. The broader implications never cross their minds, for they are immersed in the details. The avoidance of broad meanings by immersing oneself in procedural details has been documented in other contexts (e.g., Lifton, 1986).

A broader way of stating this second benefit of low-level thinking is that low levels have less emotion attached to them. With a minimum of symbolic or abstract meaning, there is little basis for strong emotions. This means that a person can escape from anxiety or other bad feelings by shifting to lower levels. Consider the case of a student taking an important exam for which he is very poorly prepared. He might think about his actions in high-level terms, such as "failing a test," "flunking out of school," or "ruining my career plans." All those meanings have strongly negative emotions associated with them, and someone who dwells on them is likely to be very unhappy and perhaps even paralyzed with anxiety. In contrast, one could think about the same activity in low-level terms, such as "writing" or "moving my hand," and these low-level descriptions are not generally associated with negative emotion (which is why the criminals prefer them, as just noted). Thinking in low-level terms may not help the person do any better on the test, but at least it will provide an escape from unpleasant emotions. Sometimes that is enough. People often desire an escape from bad emotions, and in such circumstances low levels of thinking are very appealing (Pennebaker, in press).

Another important feature of low-level thinking is that it is often a vital step in changing from one high-level interpretation to another. Psychotherapy often seems to operate by taking people who have one maladaptive high-level interpretation for their actions, getting them first to focus on the low levels (the details) of exactly what they are doing, and then bringing them up to a new high level. In other words, there is a down-and-back-up movement involved in changing one's high-level way of viewing one's actions.

The down-and-back-up transition process was illustrated in a research study done with newlyweds (Vallacher & Wegner, 1985). Researchers consulted the local newspapers in several Texas cities to find wedding announcements. They telephoned the individuals about 1 month before their wedding and asked them to describe what they were doing by this wedding. The answers came back in high-level terms: Expressing my love, starting a family, and so forth. The researchers then called back the day before the wedding with the same question. This time, the answers came in low-level terms: Checking on the caterer, buying shoes, making telephone calls.

Two months later, the researchers called these people one more time with the same question. They received answers that were phrased in high-level terms, but this time the answers were different from what people had said 1 month before the wedding. The most common answers at this point, unfortunately, were often of a less attractive nature: People described the wedding as acquiring in-laws, messing up my life, getting problems. Still, the key point is that the intervening low-level thinking at the time of the wedding was a vital step in the switch from one set of high-level meanings to another.

Thus, one can be aware of one's actions at high or low levels, that is, in a meaningful and integrated fashion, or in a fragmented and relatively meaningless fashion. This distinction corresponds to what has more generally been described as deconstruction, that is, the breaking down of meaningful thought into fragmentary awareness (e.g., Baumeister, in press; Culler, 1982; Scarry, 1985). Meaningful construction means elaborating and synthesizing an assortment of phenomena into an integrated whole. Deconstruction means abandoning these broad, integrative interpretations in favor of a narrow focus on immediate events and parts.

The terminology of high and low levels is satisfactory when discussing action, but when applied more broadly it becomes misleading. Indeed, "deep" meanings would be the same as "high-level" ones, so broad integrative interpretations might be described as an upward or a downward movement in meaning. Accordingly, for discussing masochism we favor the terminology of *deconstruction,* but readers familiar with action identification theory should simply understand the deconstructed awareness as low-level thinking.

For understanding masochism, a key point is that self-awareness can occur at different levels (Carver & Scheier, 1981). Highly constructed self-awareness involves knowing oneself as a individual involved in various projects and relationships, with multiple goals, ambitions, responsibilities, and so forth. At high levels, one is aware of one's identity, in the sense of a symbolic or abstract definition of self that extends far into the past and future. The high level self thinks, plans, and makes decisions. It is associated with personal values and even with its own value and worth, as in self-esteem and reputation.

In contrast, it is possible to be aware of oneself in a deconstructed or low-level fashion. This form of self-awareness involves little in the way of abstract meaning or symbols. Instead, one is aware of oneself as a physical body experiencing sensations and movements. Sense of time is focused narrowly in the immediate present, without any clear connection to the ongoing, long-term self and its extensive past and future. The plans, worries, and other factors that go with meaningful self-awareness are absent, for they require a great deal of meaning and interpretation. Deconstructing entails reducing meaning and interpretation to a minimum, so deconstructing the self converts the self into merely a locus of movement and sensation.

To put it another way: A person's identity is an elaborate construct, that is, an integrated network of definitions and concepts, all added onto the original, minimal basis of self, namely the body. Deconstruction removes all those complex, meaningful definitions of self from awareness, leaving the self as little more than a body.

Masochistic Deconstruction of Self

The concept of deconstruction, based on the distinction between high and low levels, enables us to see what masochism does. Masochism is a deconstruction of self. It is essentially an escape from the high levels of self. It systematically removes or prevents high-level self-awareness. When masochism promotes self-awareness, it is at the lowest levels. Masochism contradicts and undermines the meaningful definitions of self, replacing these with a mere awareness of the body. In some cases, an entirely new definition of self is constructed to replace the old (removed) identity.

The deconstructed self consists of a physical body, existing in the immediate present, experiencing movements and sensations. These are what masochism focuses attention on. Pain makes the body aware of sensation, as does sexual stimulation. The person's sense of time is constricted to the short-range, immediate here-and-now. The body is treated as an object of pain, or scorn, or sexual desire. It is reduced to a mere thing, to be used in whatever way the dominant partner wishes.

The higher levels of self involve extended time perspective, long-range goals and involvements, and abstract or symbolically constructed identity. It includes things such as one's career, one's family roles, ones standing in the community, and one's major projects and obligations. These are carefully and systematically denied in masochism. The maintenance of self-esteem and reputation, normally one of the self's most important functions, is rendered impossible by humiliating treatment. The self ceases to be a decision maker, for the masochist is often bound and gagged, and the masochist's actions are decided by the commands and whims of the dominant partner.

Indeed, masochism seems to consist essentially of a series of steps that make it impossible for the person to "be" his or her normal self. Pain undermines many of the mental processes that normally occupy the self. While being whipped, for example, one cannot engage in abstract, complex thought, nor in long-range planning. The denial of dignity and self-esteem by means of humiliating treatment makes it impossible to sustain the normal identity. The masochist's actions are deliberately designed to be incompatible with a normal adult identity: For example, adults do not normally kiss each other's feet, submit to spankings, or beg permission for sexual acts, and in order to do these things the normal identity must be suspended. Last, making choices and exerting initiative are impossible for the masochist, such as when tied spread-eagled to the four corners of a bed.

Masochism thus prevents the person from being aware of many meaning aspects of his or her self-concept. Awareness is confined to a minimal, relatively meaningless, deconstructed version of self. The self is stripped of its civilized, human properties, and it ceases to be a complex, symbol-using, decision-making, valued entity. It is reduced to a body or even a mere thing. Masochism replaces identity with body.

Sometimes masochists carry the escape from normal, constructed identity one step further. Not only do they remove their normal identity from awareness, they may even construct an entirely new identity, at least in play or fantasy. In a sense, this is the ultimate escape from self, for one replaces the normal definitions of self with an entirely new identity. The most common form of this in masochism is the wish to become a full-time slave. In practice, this is often quite difficult, but it seems to be an appealing fantasy to many masochists (cf. Scott, 1983).

The creation of a new high-level identity sheds further light on the nature of masochistic escape. Becoming a full-time sex slave is, after all, a meaningful (high-level) construction, in that it extends into the past and future, includes symbolic definition and commitment, and so forth. Thus, one must conclude that masochism is not simply the desire to escape all possible forms of high-level self-awareness. Rather, the masochist wants to escape specifically the particular, actual high-level identity that he or she normally has. Put another way, the masochist wants to lose awareness of his or her normal everyday self. This can be accomplished either by reducing self-awareness to the lowest levels or by being aware of self as someone new and different.

Why would masochists desire to escape from meaningful awareness of self? Such awareness is not always pleasant; indeed, it can become a difficult burden. The various demands to make decisions, to accept responsibility, to cope with pressure and crises, to prove one's worth, and so forth are all part of the maintenance of one's identity. They can easily lead to fatigue, anxiety, stress, and other unpleasant feelings. As noted earlier, many of these unpleasant feelings are clearly associated with high levels, and by deconstructing the self (that is, escaping to low levels) one can be free of them for a while. The appeal of masochistic escape is described in more detail in a later chapter. For now, it is sufficient to say that we should not be surprised that people sometimes desire powerful techniques for removing their ordinary awareness of self.

RELATIONSHIP AND JUSTIFICATION

A second perspective on masochism in this book concerns its relevance to meaning in life. People in modern Western culture have certain typical problems in constructing meaningful lives for themselves. Masochism represents one form of solution to these common problems. It may be only a temporary or partial solution, but it is still appealing.

Life-Interpretation Theory

Elsewhere, I have developed a conceptual structure for understanding meanings of life. A brief summary of that structure is provided here, for it furnishes a basis for understanding part of the potential appeal of masochism.

The basic idea is that people have certain needs for meaning, which means that they require their lives to make sense in certain ways. These needs for meaning can be grouped into four basic types. Any given meaning of life can be broken down and analyzed in terms of these four types of needs for meaning.

The first type is the need for *purpose* in life. People want their lives to have some sort of purpose. Two major types of purposes are goals and fulfillments, which correspond to intrinsic and extrinsic motivators. Goals are particular things one strives to accomplish. Fulfillments are potential states that promise the person a sense of satisfaction and well-being upon reaching them. Goals and fulfillments are not all in the future, of course. People want to be able to look back on their past and see it as leading toward certain goals or as providing certain fulfillments. As people grow older, if they look back on their lives and feel that they have not reached any important goals nor experienced sufficient fulfillment, they are likely to feel that their lives have been wasted and meaningless.

A second need is for *efficacy*. A person achieves a sense of efficacy by exerting control over one's environment (or over oneself). Without efficacy, people feel useless, helpless, and alienated. They tend to get ulcers and other illnesses. Control should be understood here in the broad sense of bringing the world and the self into harmony. This can be accomplished either by changing the world to make it suit oneself, or by changing oneself to fit in to one's world (Rothbaum, Weisz, & Snyder, 1982). Either way, people need to feel that they have some effective means of adapting to their lives and having some influence over what happens to them.

The third need for meaning concerns *justification*. Justification refers to feeling that one's life and actions are justified, that is, that they are right and good. People need to have some way of knowing what is right versus what is wrong, and they need to feel that they have been able to do what is right. Morality is the most common source of justification, although there are others. Indeed, any source of value or any set of rules that distinguishes good from bad can help people justify their actions. Justification depends on having a value base, which is a fundamental source of value that can justify other things without needing external justification itself. Religions often furnish value bases, for example. People feel justified if they are doing something for God's will or for Jesus' sake—they do not ask "Why should I do what God wants me to do?" God's will does not require further justification. God's will is an end in itself, an ultimate value, in that scheme.

The fourth and final need is for a basis for *self-worth*. People need to feel that they are important and valuable. Self-worth may be accomplished by feeling superior to others, and it may arise from being associated with some group or important cause. Self-worth often seems to depend on validation by others.

Clearly, these four interpretive needs overlap to some extent. For example, one's sense of self-worth tends to be low if one lacks efficacy or if one is making no progress toward one's goals. And if one lacks control, one cannot be held responsible for what happens, so justification becomes irrelevant. And if one cannot justify one's actions, self-worth may be low.

The Modern Dilemma

One can use this set of interpretive needs to understand how the people of a given culture or group understand their lives. Of special interest, of course, is how people in our society today construct their lives. It is apparent that many people today are uncomfortable with questions about the meaning of life, yet it is also clear that many of them are able to live reasonably happy and full lives. They find sufficient meaning to get by.

Modern Western culture is quite effective at satisfying some of the needs for meaning, but it does not effectively provide for others. More precisely, modern life provides individuals with plenty of goals but not with clear, viable models of fulfillment; it offers abundant sources of efficacy and bases for self-worth; and it presents difficulties with respect to justification. Let us consider these more closely.

Goals are everywhere. People today have numerous and widely assorted goals. Deadlines, promotions, paying the rent, getting an education for oneself or one's children, making a sale, and numerous others pervade modern life. Modern Western individuals are an extremely goal-oriented lot.

On the other hand, there is a shortage of viable, satisfactory ideas about human fulfillment, as well as a shortage of accepted techniques for reaching fulfillment. For over 1,000 years, Christianity dominated nearly every phase of Western culture, and it taught people to have high expectations for fulfillment. The Christian model of fulfillment consisted of permanent, divine, unspeakable bliss, which was expected to occur some time after one's death. When Western culture began to shift away from Christianity, people began to seek fulfillment in this life rather than the next, but no earthly satisfactions ever really measured up to salvation in heaven as an ideal of intense fulfillment. People look to love, work, money, creativity, and entertainment to provide fulfillment, but people wonder if these are really enough. The popularity of the ideal of self-actualization during the 1960s reflected the wish for a new, better model of fulfillment. Everyone wanted to be self-actualized, even though no one knew quite what that meant or how it was to be achieved. In short, in modern life there is a pervasive restlessness and dissatisfaction with available modes of fulfillment (Baumeister, 1986).

Efficacy is abundantly available in our society. Modern technology has given Americans an unprecedented capacity to adapt the environment to their needs and wants. An endless variety of interpersonal and occupational endeavors enables the individual to make a difference, to have an impact, to exert control. Americans believe that if you have faith in yourself you can accomplish great things.

Justification became problematic along with fulfillment, when Christianity lost its central place in Western culture. Westerners have not found any source of value and goodness that can really compare with sacred, divine truth. Morality had had enormous force when it was strongly rooted in Christian faith and God's will, but deprived of this religious foundation morality gradually lost a lot of its power. These developments in our cultural history are too complex to summarize adequately in this brief space. For present purposes, the important point is merely that the modern individual has trouble finding an unimpeachable criterion for justifying his or her actions and knowing that they are right. It is hard to create a new value base, especially a sufficiently strong one that can replace religion. In another work, I have described this modern shortage of value bases as the "legitimation gap."

Last, criteria of self-worth are amply available in our society. There are numerous and remarkably precise means of comparing oneself against others and against external standards of worth. From salary to career accomplishment, from correct and desirable affiliations to fame and esteem, the modern individual knows how to evaluate self-worth. Moreover, most people manage to convince themselves that their own worth is impressively high. A standard finding of psychological research is that most people consider themselves above average, and that by any reasonable criterial measure most people's self-esteem is high or moderately high. Indeed, researchers sometimes complain that it is difficult to find large enough samples of people with low self-esteem. As individuals, Americans think quite well of themselves.

Masochism as Life-Scheme

Masochism can thus be examined from the perspective of human interpretive needs. What sort of meaning does masochism give to human life? It appears that masochism is relevant to all four interpretive needs, although it makes a strong positive contribution to only two of them.

Efficacy is undermined in masochism, for the masochist submits to loss of control in various ways, including bondage and obedience to external commands. Some masochists have a chance for efficacy in minimal ways, usually described as being a "good slave," such as in pleasing the dominant partner sexually or in doing various menial tasks for the partner. For the most part, however, masochism revolves around loss of control, thus depriving the individuals of any opportunity for efficacy.

Likewise, masochism tends to undermine the individual's self-worth. The masochist submits to various humiliations and degradations. In some cases these reduce the masochist to something less than human, such as in cases where the masochist is treated like a dog or other animal. The only positive source of self-worth offered the masochist is through being a good slave to an esteemed master, but this is minimal. Slaves, by definition, have low self-worth, and achieving self-worth merely by means of affiliation to someone else seems to deny that one has any worth in one's own right.

On the other hand, the masochist does gain an effective means of justifying actions. The masochist does not have to make difficult judgments about what is right or wrong to do. The wishes and commands of the dominant partner are the ultimate source of rightness and goodness for the masochist. For the masochist, the right course of action is always to please, satisfy, and obey the dominant partner, and that is all there is. The relationship to the dominant partner thus takes over as the major value base for the masochist. These relationships are extremely important to masochists; masochism is far more relationship oriented than many other sexual activities. One main reason for the importance of this relationship is that it represents an ultimate, solid value base that can justify actions without question or doubt. Even submitting to pain is justified, as long as it pleases the dominant partner. The person is willing to suffer for the sake of the partner, because the relationship justifies it. In short, all problems of right and wrong are resolved for the masochist, and the anxiety and guilt and doubt that accompany such moral dilemmas are removed. The masochist need only submit and obey.

Finally, the masochist gains a powerful and seemingly viable model of fulfillment. The masochist achieves the utmost in intimacy by blending him or herself completely with the partner's will. The masochist also derives strong sexual satisfactions. Thus, sexually and emotionally, masochistic submission provides intense fulfillment.

Masochism can thus be seen as a tradeoff. One sacrifices efficacy and self-worth, and in exchange one acquires justification and fulfillment.

It is noteworthy that the benefits of masochism are precisely in the areas that are most problematic in modern life. The masochist gives up what the modern individual has a surplus of—self-worth and efficacy. In exchange, the masochist receives two scarce and rare interpretive commodities—justification and fulfillment.

Furthermore, we see that some masochists get the best of the tradeoff by minimizing the sacrifices. Some patterns of masochism downplay the loss of self-worth and efficacy, placing greater emphasis on the relationship as a source of justification and fulfillment. For these masochists, the tradeoff is an especially good bargain, and one may assume that this theory of masochism applies especially to them.

CONCLUSION

This chapter has briefly sketched the main themes of this book. Masochism is a complex and misleading phenomenon that has been misunderstood in past work. Instead of being viewed as a secondary, derivative pattern that is an offshoot of sadism, it should be accorded primary importance, because it is apparently far more prevalent and fundamental than sadism.

Probably no single explanation of masochism is fully sufficient. Two distinct (but overlapping) theories were proposed. For some masochists, perhaps especially masculine ones, the escape from and denial of self form the essential features of masochism. For others, the appeal of masochism emphasizes meaningful and symbolic benefits, including a firm knowledge of right and wrong and an intensely fulfilling form of intimacy.

On the surface, these two theories of masochism seem almost contradictory, for one emphasizes the removal (deconstruction) of meaning, whereas the other involves the creation of meaning. They share, however, the removal of the familiar definitions of self from awareness. In one case, the deconstruction of self is the main focus, and self is simply reduced to its bare minimum. In the other case, the familiar identity is not only removed but replaced.

Chapter Three
Masochism, Culture, and History

Is masochism a normal, common part of human sexuality, found at all times and in all cultures? Or is it peculiar to certain kinds of social and cultural conditions? This chapter takes a close look at the cultural context of masochism. There are several reasons for the importance of knowing the extent to which masochism is limited to certain cultures or historical periods.

First, several past views of masochism have linked it with instinctive desires and processes. Freud's views portrayed masochism as a basic part of the psychology of women and a viable solution to instinctual conflicts in anyone, male or female. Stekel (1929/1953) argued that masochism is the product of the natural conflict between instinctive drives to dominate and to submit. He suggested that people have a "will to pain," implying that the desire to suffer is innate. The innate endowment of human beings is generally the same across culture and history, by definition, so its manifestations should be relatively constant. If masochism derives directly from instinctual processes, masochism should be found in most cultures and most historical periods.

Thus, modern Freudian approaches need to regard masochism as essentially universal. Glick and Meyers (1988), for example, assert that "masochism, both sexual and characterological, has most certainly existed for eons" (p. 2), although they report no evidence to back up this strong assertion.

Second, if masochism varies across cultures or across historical eras, this variation provides a good way of finding out about its causes. The variations presumably reflect the different influences of different cultural and social conditions. In this view, masochism is largely the product of learned, culturally conditioned appetites, rather than innate ones. Theories about the causes of masochism can be tested by seeing how well they fit the evidence about the presence versus absence of masochism in various cultures.

For example, a widely cited article by Paul Gebhard (1969) argued that masochism is a product of a cultural environment that contains dominance relationships. That is, the culture teaches people to think in terms of dominance and submission, and they carry these lessons over into their sexual practices. This view would predict that there would be a relationship between social organization and masochism, such that the more a society is based on dominance and authority, the more masochistic activity there should be. Obviously, nearly all societies have always had some degree of dominance and power relationships, so Gebhard's view might predict that masochism should be evident in most societies. But there should still be variations in degree. If cultural emphasis on dominance is a cause of masochism, then the more cultural dominance there is, the more masochism there should be, at least approximately.

This book has offered theories of masochism that fit clearly into the second category, that is, views that portray masochism as a product of cultural conditioning and socialization. Masochism has been portrayed as a product of the desire to escape from self and as a quest for meaning, particularly involving a model of fulfillment and a value base for providing justification. Before looking at how masochism is distributed across culture and history, let us look briefly at the historical trends relating to self and meaning in our own culture.

SELF IN HISTORY

If masochism is an attempt to escape from the burden of selfhood, then masochism should show up most where that burden is most severe. This section surveys Western history to ascertain the points at which demands for autonomy, uniqueness, and individual agency were highest or showed the greatest increases. These periods should be associated with increases in masochism.

In an earlier book, *Identity* (1986), I traced the development of identity and its problems through Western history. The ancient world apparently had little in the way of identity crises or problems, as we know them today. For the most part, it seems, people in the ancient world knew who they were. The one possible exception would be the latter periods of Greek civilization and of the Roman empire, in which there were some individualistic trends. These trends are hard to verify, and there is little reliable evidence of anything like the modern concern with self or identity crisis.

The long period of the Middle Ages appears to have been relatively free of identity problems. People's identities were defined through standard, stable, and straightforward means. Each person's identity was clearly known to self and to others. Moreover, there was little emphasis on individuality (see Weintraub, 1978), in the sense of trying to be unique or different. Most people planned and measured their lives according to standard, ideal patterns. The value of each life was in how well it resembled these ideals rather than in its unique features. The writing of lives, in biography, discussed people according to these standard patterns (most of which were based on religion), and such writings seemed remarkably indifferent to factual accuracy or personal insight. Autobiography was almost nonexistent. People simply did not write about themselves.

The Renaissance brought a major change. People began to think and act in more individualistic terms around the end of the Middle Ages. The period following the Middle Ages was thus a vitally important one for identity and individuality.

The three centuries following the Middle Ages are commonly described as the "early modern period," covering the approximate years 1500–1800 (e.g., Stone, 1977). It was during these three centuries that identity problems began to take shape. Most important, it was at this time that Western culture became heavily individualistic.

Individuality can be defined on the basis of two criteria (Weintraub, 1978). The first of these is placing value on unique characteristics or experiences of individuals. That is, what is important about someone is how he or she is different, rather than how he or she is the same as everyone else. The second criterion is belief in unique destiny or potential. In other words, it involves the belief that each person has something special or unique that he or she can accomplish, create, experience, or be. Your fate is your own, and if you fail to fulfill it, no one else can fully substitute for you.

The first of these two criteria, namely placing value on individual differences, became apparent at the beginning of the early modern period (Weintraub, 1978; also Baumeister, 1986; Trilling, 1971). In the 16th century, people began writing about themselves in much greater detail than ever before, emphasizing their personal traits and experiences. This century became fascinated with the difference between the way someone seemed or acted and the way that person really was underneath. The belief in the inner self became important during that time.

The second criterion of individuality, namely belief in a unique destiny for each individual, was satisfied in the 18th century, toward the end of the early modern period (Weintraub, 1978). The Romantic emphasis on creative art, passionate love, inner character, and related notions shows their emphasis on fulfilling one's own special potential. By the early 19th century, individuality and individualism were common concepts and they underlay the way people approached life.

Thus, the early modern period was the critical one for the development of new attitudes about the self. Before that period, the culture treated differences among individuals as undesirable and somewhat unimportant, it took people at face value, and it expected everyone to conform to a few standard, ideal patterns. Choices were to be guided by Christian faith and morality, supplemented by various social obligations.

By the end of the early modern period, however, all that had changed. The culture was greatly interested (one might say obsessed) with how people were different from each other. People were not taken at face value; in fact, there was an escalating interest in how to learn about the inner self. Moreover, the culture was coming to accept the view that each person was a unique, special individual, with his or her own capacities and potentialities, having perhaps a special mission or destiny for life. Choices were increasingly to be made by searching inside oneself for the answers. Christian morality was merely an advisor or guide for this inner search, and social duties were often regarded as objectionable restrictions and as oppressive, intolerable constraints.

The 19th century saw the full flowering of the individualism that had emerged during the early modern period. By the end of the 19th century, the culture had come to regard values not as objective reality—instead, people were allowed to have "personal" values, which they formed by searching inside themselves for ways to choose among the assorted, conflicting set of values offered by the culture. People (or at least males) were expected to be strong, capable individuals, who asserted their autonomy and initiative in their life activities. The inner self was viewed as a vast, complex, and highly developed region that was rich with extensive contents.

Finally, the 20th century has continued the same views of the self but has posed some new problems and difficulties for it. Thus, we still place value on being independent and autonomous; but it is much harder for a modern office worker to be independent and autonomous than it was for a self-sufficient farmer of a century ago.

In Western culture, then, the early modern period was the one during which the society came to demand that each person be unique, autonomous, and capable of independent action. The culture came to accept the belief that every person has a unique inner self and a special fate (which the person might or might not fulfill). The individual thus came to be seen as the captain of his or her own fate, constrained only by duty to self, by the moral obligation not to hurt or infringe on others, and by the vagaries of social conditions.

The burden of selfhood should be thus associated with the early modern period. During those three centuries, society came to demand a lot more of each individual self than it had in the past. One may assume that individuality spread in part because many people were attracted by it and were pleased with it. On the other hand, as individuality became too widespread, some people may have found it not to their liking and may have suffered under its demands. Even people who enjoyed the new individuality and thrived on it may have occasionally found its pressures to be excessive. In short, probably not everyone wanted always to be unique, autonomous, self-promoting, and so forth. As a result, the desire for escape from the burden of self should have increased markedly during the early modern period, especially perhaps toward the end.

Based on this overview, it is possible to make a simple prediction. If masochism is indeed a form of escape from self, it should have increased substantially toward the end of the early modern period. We should expect to find a significant and substantial increase in masochistic activity around the 18th century.

Other theories, of course, would make different predictions. If masochism is a product of a cultural emphasis on dominance and submission, then we should expect a decrease in masochism during the early modern period, for Western societies were becoming more egalitarian and democratic. And if masochism is a direct result of instinctual processes inside the individual, then it should be relatively constant, for the influence of broad cultural shifts would be relatively unimportant.

JUSTIFICATION AND FULFILLMENT

The second view of masochism I have espoused portrays masochism as a response to a need for certain kinds of meaning in one's life. Specifically, masochism offers the individual a new way of justifying behaviors and suffering, plus an ideal of fulfillment and a means to achieve it. One can examine this view historically also, by considering the history of justification and fulfillment.

Western history has been dominated by Christianity since that religion became dominant in the waning centuries of the Roman empire. Ever since then, most Westerners have been Christians, which is true even today. For devout Christians, all questions of justification were matters of Christian doctrine and faith. Christian morality spelled out in fairly precise detail what was right and what was wrong. Christian morality itself was justified on the basis of God's will and commands. Indeed, Christians believe that God has communicated his commands to humanity directly, even printing some of his rules on stone tablets, and later sending his son to earth to explain things to us.

Not only justification, but also fulfillment was a matter of Christian faith and doctrine. According to the Christian view, the individual should expect fulfillment after death, in heaven. Salvation in heaven was the main form of fulfillment that Christians wanted. Christianity also spelled out the means of reaching this state of fulfillment. Virtuous action, pious faith, and participation in Church rituals were the main means by which Christians attained salvation. Some Christian sects deviated from these views, but by and large these were the principal beliefs.

When Western society began to live by more secular attitudes, people ceased to be fully satisfied with the Christian versions of justification and fulfillment. It was no simple matter for the culture to turn away from official, pervasive Christianity; rather, this was a major and fundamental upheaval. This shift took place during the period called the Enlightenment, in the 17th and 18th centuries. Most people still believed in Christianity, but it ceased to be the center of their lives. Many others were frankly agnostic, Deistic, or even atheistic. Regardless of their professed faith, however, the managers and workers in the new society that followed the Industrial Revolution did not base their lives and actions mainly on Christianity.

As people turned away from their religion, some basic questions surfaced regarding the meaning of life. Morality had based its rules on the will of God, but now it needed a new source of justification. Beginning with Kant, moral philosophers scrambled to find a new foundation for morality. They sought a new way of justifying moral rules as coherent logical, and compelling, but they were not terribly successful (MacIntyre, 1981).

By the Victorian period (the latter part of the 1800s), many people were plainly worried that morality was in decline. Intellectuals debated things like "Can morality survive without religion?" (Meyer, 1976). In short, people saw that Christianity was losing its hold on society, and they feared the consequences (Houghton, 1957; Howe, 1976).

Thus, ample evidence shows that during the 18th and 19th centuries society felt its primary value base to be eroding, and that justification was becoming a problem as a result of this erosion.

With fulfillment, the picture is about the same. One of the biggest consequences of the gradual turn away from Christianity was the quest for fulfillment in the present, earthly life. For centuries, people had accepted life as unsatisfying because fulfillment was supposed to be deferred until after death. Now people began to desire fulfillment in this life. But what did fulfillment mean, and how was one supposed to achieve it?

It was obvious to all that people were massively unhappy and that social conditions were to blame. Rousseau's philosophy was terrifically appealing, for he said that modern society was rotten and that a return to nature would make people happy. Translated into action, this meant political violence to overthrow various governments and establish individual freedoms. For others, it meant starting new communities that were supposed to be enlightened, perfect societies. People were able to remove many of the principal obstacles to their happiness by changing the structure of government and reforming the old (or inventing new) political systems.

But removing a few obstacles to fulfillment was not enough to bring fulfillment, as it turned out. This raised a problem; it was difficult to decide what else was necessary for fulfillment. After all, it is easy to understand freedom *from* oppression and tyranny, but it is harder to form a clear idea of what to use this freedom *for*. Westerners had not generally tried to think of models of fulfillment on earth. Suddenly they were free to do so, and in fact it became *urgent* to do so. The result was a kind of cultural groping around for new ideas of fulfillment, and this experimentation has continued down to the present (Baumeister, 1986).

The first few attempts at generating new ideas of fulfillment created quite a sensation. The Romantic period (roughly 1775–1850) is remembered as trying especially hard to solve the question of fulfillment. The Romantic fascination with the creative process, especially the inner lives of the famous Romantic poets, far surpassed anything of the sort that had preceded it. Passionate, "Romantic" love also came to be viewed as a vital ingredient of a fulfilled life, in sharp contrast to earlier views (cf. Stone, 1977). The "work ethic" explored the idea that one's own inner adaptation to work would edify and satisfy the individual (Rodgers, 1978). Cultivation of one's own personality was seen as a means of becoming unique and fulfilling one's own special destiny.

Thus, Western society embarked on a massive search for new means and models of fulfillment by the late 18th century. The concern about the loss of the Christian value base and the resulting dangers to moral justifications were also apparent around that time. By the middle of the 19th century, much of society was facing these problems in one way or another.

Chapter 2 suggested that the appeal of masochism is in part that it offers the individual a convenient value base to use for justifying acts, as well as a model and means of fulfillment. It follows that the appeal of masochism would increase when society began to lose its other means of satisfying those needs. Once again, the 18th and 19th centuries are the prime focus. Masochistic activity should have shown a substantial increase during those two centuries, according to this theory of masochism.

HISTORY OF MASOCHISM

The history of sex is not without controversy, and many conclusions lack full evidence. We simply have no way of knowing with certainty what medieval peasants or ancient Assyrian nobles did in bed. Still, there is a substantial amount of evidence about the history of sex, and historians have been able to make some very educated guesses about the sex lives of our ancestors. Several important works have examined the history of sexuality in detail, notably those of Vern Bullough (1976a), Reay Tannahill (1980), and G. Rattray Taylor (1954/1970). All these have examined the history of masochism, but probably the most earnest and thorough attempt to document this history was that of Havelock Ellis (1905/1936).

There are several obstacles to using this work. For one thing, some of the historians have been misled by psychologists to label as *masochism* anything that seems submissive, or self-destructive, or anything that involves willing acceptance of pain. Others have referred vaguely to masochistic *attitudes* in discussing any sort of submission. These interpretations simply cloud the issue. For present purposes, the best approach is to hold to a strict definition of sexual masochism. Thus, we survey the history of sex to search for signs of erotic response to pain, bondage, or humiliation.

The general conclusion from this research can be stated quite simply. It appears that sexual masochism has been mostly absent throughout Western history until the early modern period. There are a first few hints of it around 1500. Then, abruptly in the 18th and 19th centuries, there is abundant evidence of sexual masochism. Thus, sexual masochism is a modern phenomenon, spreading through society during the 1700s and 1800s. Moreover, masochism is quite unusual in this respect. Most varieties of sexual practices have been amply documented throughout our history. That makes it all the surprising that masochism is associated so strongly with the modern period.

The Ancient World

Sexual variety was well known to the ancient world. Most of the modern sexual practices, including many that would be considered deviant today, were familiar to the ancients (Tannahill, 1980). One of the few missing ones, however, was masochism.

It is hard to be certain that masochism was completely unknown. The best one can do is note its absence when it might have been expected. For example, one scholar concluded that the sex manuals of the ancient Chinese were as complete and detailed as any modern sex manual, except that masochism was conspicuous by its absence (Tannahill, 1980). Likewise, ancient Greek literature was full of sex scenes, which have been carefully documented and catalogued. But there was apparently no reference to sadomasochism (Licht, 1934). The Latin erotic literature enjoyed by the Romans likewise ignored sexual flagellation (Ellis, 1905/1936). The closest they came to masochism was a scene in Petronius' *Satyricon* involving a mild whipping to the front of the body. But this was not done for the erotic enjoyment or stimulation, but rather as part of magical cure for impotence (Ellis, 1905/1936).

There are some ambiguous phrases in ancient poetry that express a desire to submit to one's beloved or to worship one's beloved. Some scholars have taken these as an indication of a masochistic attitude, although they certainly do not involve actual masochistic activity. The best example, apparently, is an Egyptian poem written about 1200 B.C. in which the writer fondly imagines himself as servant to his beloved, provoking her anger in order to hear her angry voice (Ellis, 1905/1936, p. 112f). That is all. The submissive attitude is clearly suggested and punishment is even hinted at. Still, it is an isolated example, and it is a long way from masochistic sex.

A few other scholars have noted that ancient religious rituals sometimes involved self-mutilation and have used these as evidence of masochism (Bullough, 1976a; Taylor, 1954/1970). Sometimes this argument is bolstered by the lame suggestion that these religious rituals had a sexual component. Because these few practices are the only behavioral evidence anyone has produced for sexual masochism in the ancient world, they are worth examining closely. Considered carefully, they are not a valid indication of masochistic activity.

In the first place, there is a wide gap between sexual activities and religious activities, even when some superficial similarity exists. Some people burn candles and incense to facilitate sexual seduction, but it would be absurd to suggest that that proves that people who burn candles and incense in church ceremonies are engaged in sexual seduction. Likewise, some people may kneel to perform oral sex, but his does not prove that people who kneel in church are engaging in a sexual activity. Religion and sex are very different contexts that lend very different meanings to behaviors. Submitting to pain and harm in a religious context is not necessarily (not even likely) the same thing as doing it during sexual play.

Second, and more important, the self-mutilation that may have occurred during certain religious ceremonies does not resemble modern sexual masochism, even superficially. As noted earlier (also see chapter 4), masochists carefully avoid harm to themselves. They seek pain but take great precautions to avoid injury. Their actions bear no resemblance to the actions of religious initiates who gouge their skin with knives or even cut off parts of their bodies.

Third, there is simply no sign that any sexual arousal occurred in connection with the religious self-injury. In these rituals, people submitted to pain and perhaps experienced exalted states of religious consciousness, but evidence of sexual arousal is utterly lacking. In contrast, research on modern masochists shows extensive evidence of sexual arousal.

In short, modern masochists do certain things in a sexual context and for the sake of sexual arousal. Ancient religious initiates did different things, in a religious (and nonsexual) context, and apparently without a dimension of sexual feeling. It seems safe to dismiss these bits of alleged evidence of sexual masochism in the ancient world.

Again, it would be wrong to be too critical of the historians who confused these religious activities with sexual practices, for they were probably honestly misled by psychologists. Freudian theory often treated religious matters as simply disguised sexuality. Furthermore, Freudian approaches took a broad view of masochism as any activity that causes harm or pain or injury to the self, whether sexual or not. The historians probably accepted this too-broad, misleading definition. Moreover, they may have expected to find evidence of masochism too, because there is relatively clear behavioral evidence of most other varieties of sex play. Unable to find anything reliable in terms of purely sexual masochism, they may have fallen back on the Freudian equation and used the religious activities as evidence of masochism.

Given that these religious activities are the best (and apparently the only) evidence of sexual masochism in the ancient world, and given the reasons to doubt that the religious activities really qualify as sexual activities, it seems reasonable to accept the conclusion that sexual masochism was unknown in the ancient world. Possibly there were traces of masochistic feelings, and perhaps some day some scholar will find a clear sign of actual masochistic behavior. But if genuine sexual masochism existed at all, it was quite rare.

One last piece of evidence about ancient sexual practices is revealing. The notion of domination was not totally absent from ancient attitudes about sex. Anal sex may have occasionally carried some symbolic message of domination. Specifically, penetrating someone's anus may have symbolized dominance over that person. This has been suggested by a few bits of evidence in colloquial expressions and even in one ancient myth (Bullough, 1976b).

The myth comes from Egypt. Seth expresses a desire for anal sex with Horus. Horus' mother Isis advises him to trick Seth by putting his hand between his buttocks to prevent anal penetration and catch Seth's semen. Horus does this and then surreptitiously throws the semen into a river. Later, Isis tells Horus to masturbate. She takes Horus' semen, spreads it on some lettuce, and feeds it to Seth.

Some days later, Seth goes before the court and demands that the gods recognize his supremacy over Horus because of having penetrated him anally. Horus denies that he has submitted to anal penetration. The presiding god Thoth calls to the semen of both men. Seth's semen replies from the bottom of the river, whereas Horus' replies from inside Seth. The gods reject Seth's claim and recognize Horus' supremacy.

This myth does seem to indicate an awareness of anal sex as an expression of domination over another person. But it is quite apparent that there is no masochistic interest in that symbolism. *Rather, the interest is entirely on the dominant side.* Both characters are trying to dominate the other; both tried their best to avoid being penetrated anally and thus dominated. Likewise, the colloquial expressions cited by the same scholar also express the desire to dominate, not the desire to submit. One may conclude from all of this that some men may have wanted to penetrate others in order to symbolize domination. Perhaps, then, a few of the ancients had desires to dominate others sexually. But there is no sign of interest in sexual submission.

Thus, sexual masochism seems utterly absent from the evidence that survives about the ancient world. Again, it is not as if the ancients were sexually prudish or simply avoided all variant or deviant sexual practices (Bullough, 1976a, 1976b; Tannahill, 1980). There is abundant evidence of male homosexuality in the ancient world. Prostitution was well known. Masturbation, anal intercourse, oral sex, incest, and pederasty (sex with children) were also familiar. Sex with animals was quite well known; indeed, ancient Mesopotamia had separate laws dealing with sex with cattle, sheep, and pigs. Mutual masturbation, cunnilingus, and fellatio were known, as was lesbianism. There is some evidence of transvestism. The extent of sexual activity in the spectator galleries of the Roman arenas, where deliberately excessive cruelties were routinely staged, has suggested a mixture of voyeurism and sadism to at least one authority (Bullough, 1976a). Furthermore, the ancients have left records of their concerns and debates over sexual issues including adultery, mistresses, contraception, transsexualism, abortion, penis size, potency, obscenity, venereal disease, and other questions that are still troublesome today.

Thus, the ancient world lived a relatively full sex life and was quite familiar with a broad spectrum of sexual practices and concerns. The lack of evidence about masochistic sexuality in the ancient world is therefore all the more surprising. Although masochism may not be the only sexual practice to be missing from the ancient world, it is one of very few.

The Middle Ages

The Middle Ages left extensive writings about sex. In particular, the theologians and commentators of the Christian church establishment wrote extensively about sexual practices. They were hardly writing sex manuals, of course. For the most part, they were debating the relative sinfulness of various sexual practices. Still, their debates furnish ample evidence about medieval sexual practices and attitudes.

Once again, the historians who have surveyed this material have recorded little or no trace of sexual masochism (Bullough, 1976a; Bullough & Brundage, 1982). Homosexuality was a major and ongoing concern, as was sexual infidelity. Seduction, rape, and fornication were perennial issues. Masturbation, abortion, contraception, prostitution, and adultery were endlessly debated and condemned. Sexual deviations such as bestiality, coprophilia, transvestism, and anal sex were also discussed and deplored. But masochism was apparently absent.

Other sources give a similar picture of medieval sexuality (Bullough, 1976a). Male and female homosexuality, oral–genital contacts, masturbation, and many other practices can be found in medieval writings, but not masochism. Thomas Aquinas listed the sexual sins in order of severity, starting with having sex with animals (the worst), then homosexuality, then use of artificial devices in sex, which was roughly equal in sinfulness with oral and anal sex; then followed masturbation, incest, adultery, seduction, and finally plain fornication (Tannahill, 1980, p. 272). But masochism was not included on his list.

There are two main explanations for the absence of masochism in all these writings. Masochism was omitted either because of its rarity or because it was tolerated without comment. Several reasons make the latter hypothesis (that the medieval authors knew of sexual masochism but found it so acceptable that it needed no discussion) extremely implausible. First, so many other sexual activities received comment and discussion that it is unlikely that sexual masochism would be left out if it existed. Second, the Church's hostility toward most forms of sexual activity, especially deviant sexual activity, was extremely strong, and it is absurd to suggest that masochism would be tolerated simply or easily.

The only viable conclusion is that sexual masochism was largely unknown to the medieval writers. Possibly the theologian writers had never heard of it. If they had heard of it, either they did not believe it, or they knew it to be extremely rare. Either way, the implication is that sexual masochism was not practiced very much in the Middle Ages, if at all.

Once again, it is worth mentioning that there were occasional religious activities that had some vague resemblance to sexual masochism. The most important of these was probably religious flagellation, which broke out in cult movements from time to time. Flagellants marched around while whipping each other. The main goal of these sects was to appease God and convince him not to send further woes to earth. When times were especially bad, people would conclude that God was angry, and so they would make themselves suffer in the hope that God would be satisfied and let up (Eliade, 1985). There was nothing sexual about this, and indeed any sexual arousal or pleasure from such activities would almost certainly have been considered counterproductive. Flagellants sought to reenact the suffering of Christ, and some of them felt they had to be punished for their sinful nature. They were not engaging in kinky sex, which (indeed) would have increased their sins rather than removing them.

The fact, monastics sometimes whipped themselves in order to help conquer their sexual desires (Ellis, 1905/1936). The pain of self-flagellation was regarded as one antidote to carnal weakness. Thus, pain was used to combat sex, not to promote it.

Toward the Modern World

Thus far we have reviewed the historical research covering periods up through the Middle Ages and have found no clear evidence of actual sexual masochism. There have been a few hints of masochistic attitudes and of religious activities that vaguely resemble masochism, but most of these evaporate on close inspection. Our ancestors apparently included very few masochists, if any at all. This lack of evidence ends abruptly in the early modern period. Isolated mentions of masochistic sexuality begin to appear in the 16th and 17th centuries, and by the 18th century there is an abundance of such evidence.

Most of the historians begin to report sexual masochism in the 17th century. The one exception is also the one who searched most thoroughly for any scraps of evidence of masochism: Havelock Ellis. He concluded that the first actual report of sexual masochism was recorded shortly before the start of the 16th century (Ellis, 1905/1936, p. 132). Two further cases are mentioned during the 16th century. Thus, by 1600 there were at least three authors who claimed to have known or heard of some man who liked to be whipped as a prelude to sexual intercourse. Although masochism was almost certainly extremely rare at this time, it had at least begun to exist.

Literature first began to treat masochism during the 17th century (e.g., Bullough, 1976a). The first work to contain an actual flogging scene was the tragedy *Venice Preserv'd,* by Thomas Otway, written in the middle of the century. Scholars have found a few other references to flogging in the literature of that century (e.g., Ellis, 1905/1936; Bullough, 1976a). Still, these were a mere trickle in contrast to what the next two centuries brought.

Pornography dealing with flogging began early in the eighteenth century. The earliest surviving work of that sort was called *A Treatise on the Use of Flogging*, published in 1718 (Bullough, 1976a). By the end of the 18th century, a great deal of such pornography was available (Bullough, 1976a; Tannahill, 1980). In addition to the purely pornographic works, there was a fair amount of masochistic discussion in poetry and other literary forms (Falk & Weinberg, 1983). Indeed, there were even some clubs formed for the express purpose of sharing literary efforts on such themes.

Interest in masochism went far beyond reading and writing, of course. There were allegedly private clubs whose members engaged in masochistic activities, chiefly flogging, as a major form of recreation (Bullough, 1976a; Falk & Weinberg, 1983). The evidence for actual masochistic behavior is convincing. For example, there were prostitutes who catered to masochistic tastes (see later). The autobiography of the influential philosopher Rousseau described his masochistic enjoyment of pain and shame upon being whipped by a servant girl. He said that these incidents occurring when he was 8 years old determined his sexual tastes and desires for the rest of his life, although for the most part they were confined to imaginary acts (cf. Ellis, 1905/1936, pp. 146–147).

Sexual masochism has been abundantly documented from the 18th century to the present. Possible there is somewhat more evidence of it in the 19th century than in the 18th, but this difference is not fully convincing. The drastic increase in such evidence occurred in the 18th century. This abundance of evidence of sexual masochism stands in sharp contrast with the utter lack of any such evidence prior to the Renaissance.

Chapter 1 presented evidence about the prevalence of masochism today. It continues to exist throughout our society, although it is clearly a minority pattern. Recent decades have seen increasing attention given to masochism in books, magazines, and movies, but it is difficult to determine whether this reflects an increasing prevalence of masochism or simply increasing tolerance of unusual sexual tastes.

History of Prostitution

To confirm the validity of conclusions about the historical pattern of masochism, one may consult histories of prostitution. Prostitution has existed throughout recorded history. Sometimes it has enjoyed social and legal tolerance approaching full acceptance, whereas at other times it has been rigidly outlawed and suppressed. But prostitution has nearly always existed. For present purposes, the key question concerns whether prostitutes provided sadomasochistic services.

Prostitution has been well documented throughout the ancient world, and the services of prostitutes extended well beyond normal sexual intercourse. It is quite clear that prostitutes have long catered to a variety of sexual tastes. Thus, in the ancient Middle East, there were both heterosexual and homosexual prostitutes for male customers, as well as male prostitutes catering to female clients. (The only missing category was lesbian prostitution.) There were even "animal prostitutes" catering to clients who desired sex with animals (Benjamin & Masters, 1965). But historians have found no evidence of sadomasochistic prostitution.

Likewise, ancient Greece and Rome had varieties of prostitutes, including both homosexual and heterosexual ones. Rome had prostitutes catering to clients with special tastes for pederasty or fellatio. Again, though, there is no mention of professional domination (Benjamin & Masters, 1965).

The medieval Church went through several major changes in its attitudes toward prostitution (Otis, 1985). At first it tolerated prostitution as a necessary evil, even repeating the old argument that prostitution reduced the frequency of rape by giving lustful males a sexual outlet. Later, the Church became less and less tolerant. The transition to this more negative stance was marked by discussions of which particular forms and aspects of prostitution were most problematic. These included homosexuality, bestiality, concubinage, and adultery. Once again, though, there seems to have been no discussion of flogging or domination provided by prostitutes (see Otis, 1985).

Things changed abruptly in the 18th century. Historical records from that era contain ample evidence that prostitutes catered to masochists. There are numerous references to prostitutes who specialized in flogging. Indeed, in large cities there were entire brothels devoted to flagellation (Benjamin & Masters, 1965; Bullough, 1976a). Evidence of dominant prostitution is generally continuous from the 18th century up to the present.

In short, historical treatments of prostitution only begin to contain evidence of masochistic clients and services during the 18th century (see also Bullough & Bullough, 1964). Earlier prostitutes catered to various sexual requests, desires, and tastes, but apparently not masochism. Given the lack of evidence that prostitutes flogged or spanked customers before the 18th century, one must assume such practices to have been either quite rare or nonexistent. In contrast, by 1800 there was a definite and stable market for such services.

Conclusion

The historical evidence about masochistic sexuality is not totally solid. Still, there is no mistaking the major shift. Prior to the 17th century there is practically no evidence of sexual masochism in any source.

Literature and pornography do not mention masochism, religious and legal treatments of sexuality omit it, autobiographical accounts fail to mention any such activity, and there is no indication that prostitutes dominated or flogged their customers for money. There are three brief mentions of individuals who engaged in masochistic sexuality; these are all hearsay and all occurred shortly before the 17th century. In short, sexual masochism was nearly or even completely unknown until the Renaissance, and it was almost completely nonexistent through the 16th century.

In contrast, starting in the 18th century, sexual masochism is evident in many forms of evidence. Masochism appears in serious literature and in pornography, in prose and in verse. Manuals describe how to administer floggings. Autobiographies and legal proceedings contain references to masochism. Some prostitutes thrived by flogging their customers.

The dramatic increase in evidence of masochistic activity suggests rather strongly that masochism increased sharply during the 18th century. The current evidence could be summarized this way: Sexual masochism first began to appear in isolated cases around 1500, it began to spread during the 1600s, and it became a widespread and familiar feature of the sexual landscape during the 1700s.

It would be premature to conclude that no one ever practiced masochism before the early modern period. But if sexual masochism did exist before then, it was rare and obscure. In contrast, it has been a recognized and durable part of Western sexuality since the early modern period. This is not to say that a majority of the population engages regularly in bondage and spanking, or anything of the sort. Masochism is apparently confined to a distinct minority of the population. Still, it is a sizable minority, apparently including millions of people.

In the West, then, masochism must be recognized as essentially a modern phenomenon. It was rare or even completely unknown in the ancient world and in the Middle Ages. It appeared and spread during the early modern period and has been around ever since.

CROSS-CULTURAL PERSPECTIVES

Research on sex practices in other cultures offers another way to learn about the conditions under which masochism appears. If masochism is natural or is psychologically innate, then it should appear in most cultures. In contrast, if it is a reaction to a cultural emphasis on individuality, then it should be found only in the most individualistic societies and cultures, such as our own. And if the appeal of masochism is based on offering a value base and a mode of fulfillment, it should appear mainly in cultures that have some uncertainty in their values—for example, societies in which there are multiple, conflicting systems of values, or societies in which people lack a satisfactory concept of personal fulfillment.

The problem of defining masochism plagues the cross-cultural studies just as it did the historical studies. If one defines masochism loosely, as any acceptance of pain or any submissive attitude (especially not restricting it to sexuality), or as any use of painful stimulation during sex, then one finds masochism in many other cultures. On the other hand, if one adopts a strict and conservative definition of masochism as sex play essentially linked to pain, loss of control, or humiliation, then one finds almost zero evidence of masochism outside of modern Western culture.

Biting and Scratching During Sex

The use of minor pain to spur romantic passion during coitus is widespread. Many people bite and scratch each other during sex, and these practices have been recorded in many cultures (Davenport, 1976; Ellis, 1905/1936; Ford & Beach, 1951). Biting and scratching during sex have even been recorded in lower species of animals (Ford & Beach, 1951). Cultures that are sexually permissive are especially likely to foster such practices (Ford & Beach, 1951). This may be because sex without love is most likely to occur in a permissive society. Love contributes strongly to sexual passion. Without love, people may be more likely to resort to physical sensations to intensify sexual passion.

Thus, sex is sometimes associated with minor pain in many cultures. Some theorists have used that as evidence of masochism in other cultures. They acknowledge that biting and scratching falls short of full-fledged sexual masochism, but they consider it a first step in that direction (e.g., Ford & Beach, 1951).

In our culture, many people probably enjoy being bitten or scratched during sex without considering themselves masochistic. As we shall see here, pain thresholds are raised during sexual arousal, so a fingernail scratch on the skin during intercourse may not even be felt as directly painful.

The most reasonable conclusion is that biting and scratching during sex are not sufficient to speak of masochism. They indicate a preliminary association between pain and love or sexual desire, but they do not constitute full-fledged sexual masochism.

Nonsexual Activities

Other researchers have noted that people in many cultures show submissive attitudes or submit to pain. For example, initiation rites associated with adolescence (especially male adolescence) often involve some pain. These experiences seem, however, to have religious and cultural significance that bears little clear relation to sex, if any (e.g., Gebhard, 1971). The pain in such ceremonies may signify a symbolic test of the boy's readiness to become a man, or it may serve to cement his attachment to the tribe or group in some way, but it does not lead to sexual arousal or pleasure. Also, the adolescent may endure the pain, but there is little sign that he desires or enjoys it.

Submission to authority figures is a necessary part of power relations in any society, and calling that "masochism" does little except generate confusion. In nearly every culture, a woman is required to submit to her husband's authority and power, and often she may seem to do so willingly. But that is simply an acknowledgement of the reality of her situation. It does not mean that she is masochistic.

In many cultures, it is customary to speak in modest, self-deprecating terms. This may be a form of humor, such as when someone makes jokes about him or herself, or it may simply be the norm for polite speech. Again, though, it seems misleading to call this masochistic, as some researchers have done (Davenport, 1976).

Full-Fledged Sexual Masochism

If one adheres to the strict, conservative definition of sexual masochism, the cross-cultural evidence becomes much clearer. In this book, full-fledged sexual masochism has been defined as the systematic use of pain, loss of control, and humiliation to enhance sexual arousal and pleasure. I have been unable to find any evidence of this in other cultures.

Compilations of sexual practices in other cultures generally report no evidence of full-fledged sexual masochism (e.g., Marshall & Suggs, 1971). Some researchers specifically state that there is no sign of sexual masochism in the particular culture they are studying (e.g., Marshall, 1971). More commonly, the topic of masochism is ignored altogether. If researchers do try to speak of masochism in another culture, the evidence is usually either scratching and biting during intercourse, or nonsexual activities such as religious rites.

One important article summarizing the cross-cultural evidence drew the following conclusions. First, it reviewed the evidence of biting and scratching and noted that such evidence is found all over the globe. Likewise, pain is accepted in various nonsexual contexts. But genuine sexual masochism has not been documented in any culture outside our own. "Well developed sadomasochism, where pain is a necessity for sexual performance, seems absent [from other cultures]" (Gebhard, 1971, p. 216).

Conclusion

Surprising as it may seem, the evidence clearly points to the conclusion that full-fledged sexual masochism is mainly confined to modern Western culture. It is not found in other cultures. Some other cultures use scratching and biting during sexual intercourse, but beyond that there is nothing to indicate sexual masochism. In particular, the use of loss of control or of humiliation as a sexual stimulant has not been recorded in other cultures.

The lack of sexual masochism in other cultures cannot be explained by saying that Western culture is the most sexually permissive or sophisticated. Many sexual variations are tolerated in other cultures; indeed, they often appear to be tolerated elsewhere better than in Western culture (e.g., Gebhard, 1971; Tannahill, 1980). And there are certainly other cultures whose overall attitude toward sex is more tolerant and permissive than that of our own Western culture (Suggs & Marshall, 1971; Tannahill, 1980).

Moreover, sexual masochism spread through our culture with seemingly little relation to the sexual permissiveness of the times. Masochism apparently spread through the culture during the 18th century, which was a time of sexual tolerance and even license. It continued to spread during the 19th century, when Victorian attitudes regarded sex in a very negative, repressive fashion. And it has continued in the 20th century, as society has moved out of the Victorian repressive phase and back toward a permissive phase. In short, both culturally and historically, sexual masochism seems independent of broad attitudes of sexual tolerance and permissiveness. This raises further doubts about theories that link masochism to sex guilt.

It seems likely that sexual masochism exists somewhere outside of Western culture. Probably some researchers will eventually find some evidence of it, at least on an occasional basis. But it appears to be extremely rare. The only culture that shows substantial evidence of a sizable number of sexual masochists is the modern Western culture.

This conclusion is consistent with the view that sexual masochism depends on how society constructs the individual self. The emphasis on individuality is unusually high in modern Western culture, and so the desire to escape from self should be strongest in our culture.

The absence of masochism in other cultures is harder to reconcile with the second theory of masochism (based on finding meaning for life). Although few societies have reached the state of value pluralism and ideological chaos that Western society has, there are certainly others in which values are in crisis or in conflict, and there must be others that do not offer the people a compelling ideal of fulfillment. The life-interpretation theory of masochism would expect that some other cultures would show sexual masochism, at least during periods in which the culture has no single set of meanings and values to offer the individual.

Thus, the cross-cultural evidence appears to be most consistent with the view of masochism as escape from self. If so, one may predict that as other societies become increasingly individualistic, either through their own natural evolution or through contact with the individualistic West, real sexual masochism will begin to appear there too. As other cultures evolve to place increasing burdens of autonomy, uniqueness, and self-promotion on the individual, the desire to escape this burden will also spread. Some individuals will eventually discover sexual masochism as a viable means of escape.

IMPLICATIONS

The historical and cross-cultural evidence points strongly toward a couple conclusions. First, it appears that masochistic sexual activity is far from universal. It has not been practiced with any equality or regularity in most phases of our history. Instead, it seems safe to conclude that sexual masochism is a product of Western modernity. There is some question as to whether the modern West can claim to have *invented* (or discovered) sexual masochism. But there is little doubt that sexual masochism has been far more common in our recent past than at any previous time.

Thus, sexual masochism is historically relative. One important implication is that masochism is a product of culture. It reflects appetites and desires that are created by certain social conditions and structures. It is not natural in the sense of a tendency that is an innate part of human nature, for natural tendencies should be universal in human life, that is, they should be found in a wide variety of cultures and settings. Sexual masochism is a cultural phenomenon, not a natural one.

Some theorists have sought to view masochism as arising out of the instinctual nature of human beings. Freud described some types of masochism as innate, and Stekel likewise spoke of instinctual needs. These arguments must be regarded with some suspicion in light of the cultural relativity of masochism. All human beings presumably have largely the same basic instincts, so the evidence of historical and cultural variation raises some serious problems for the instinctual theories. Possibly these can be resolved by suggesting that the instinctive motives behind masochism were always there but were only expressed under modern, Western social conditions. Still, such an approach seems dubious.

The most likely conclusion from the evidence is that masochism is a product of culturally created appetites (cf. Gebhard, 1969). The simplest and most parsimonious explanation for the recency of masochism is that masochistic desires are a product of modern times. More specifically, something about modern Western society instills in people certain feelings and desires that can take the shape of masochistic sexuality.

In the West, masochism showed a substantial increase during the early modern period, especially the 17th and 18th centuries. To understand the cultural causes of masochism, then, one should look at what was new about Western culture at that time. Elsewhere, I have proposed two of the biggest changes of that period. First, the culture came to emphasize individuality, and second, it began to seek meaning in life outside of the Christian scripts and prescriptions. To be sure, there were other changes around that time, especially the Industrial Revolution and the reappearance of political democracy. But these two main changes seem most relevant to the various theories of masochism. Indeed, other cultures have had industrial manufacture and political democracy without sexual masochism.

The cultural shift toward individuality was a broad, fundamental pattern, and it could well have helped lead to sexual masochism. Just when the individual self took on a vastly augmented scope and importance, evidence of masochistic sexuality proliferated. Unless this is some kind of remarkable coincidence, it provides important support for the view of masochism as escape from self. The culture began to prescribe that everyone be unique, autonomous, self-promoting, and responsible. No doubt many people were quite happy about these new demands, but it is unlikely that everyone would be equally comfortable with the new selfhood. As a result, there may have been an increased need to escape from self periodically. Sexual masochism represented one powerful and important form of such an escape. The culture's increased construction of self led to increased interest in techniques for deconstructing it.

The turn toward secular life, of which the Industrial Revolution was one part and one cause, was also an important feature of the era that produced masochism. This too seems more than coincidence. When people ceased to be fully satisfied with the Christian views of the meaning of life, they soon encountered several major gaps. In particular, no source of value and justification emerged with the power religion had held, and forms and means of fulfillment became a troublesome problem. The Romantics searched high and low for value and fulfillment, with uneven success. It is certainly plausible that some of them turned to masochism as at least a partial or temporary solution.

Thus, the historical record of masochism is entirely consistent with the two main theoretical views suggested in this book. First, masochism is a means of escaping high-level self-awareness. This view fits well with evidence that masochistic sex spread when Western culture drastically increased the burden of selfhood. Second, masochism offers some aid in placing meaning on one's life and activities, notably in offering a value base for justification and a form (and means) of fulfillment. This view fits well with evidence that masochistic sex increased when Western culture became dissatisfied with the system that had furnished it with value, justification, and fulfillment for centuries.

The historical evidence should not be overstated. Evidence about the history of sex is incomplete and in some respects controversial, although the increase in evidence of masochism in the 18th century seems beyond dispute. More important, it is quite hard to draw firm causal conclusions about broad historical changes, especially perhaps changes in something as murky as patterns of sexual desire. It is possible that the 18th century increase in sexual masochism was caused by some historical development unrelated to the emphasis on individuality and decline of Christianity. My interpretations are not the only possible ones. But it is certainly incumbent on any theory of masochism to explain these cultural and historical variations, and instinctual theories (among others) seem to have considerable difficulty doing this.

It is worth adding that the historical evidence is consistent with the present theories in an important way. A different historical pattern might have raised serious doubts about these views. For example, suppose it had turned out that masochism was absent in the ancient world, extremely common in the Middle Ages, uncommon from the Renaissance to the Victorian periods, and slightly more common today. Such evidence would be quite hard to reconcile with the theory portraying masochism as escape from self.

Fortunately, however, the historical evidence appears to strengthen the case for the theoretical views advanced here. If the historical evidence were all that supported these theories, there might be reason to be skeptical. But because the historical evidence points toward the same conclusions as the evidence to be presented in the next few chapters, one may be reasonably confident.

The cross-cultural evidence about masochism is also quite consistent with the view of masochism as an escape from self. The burden of selfhood is especially pronounced in modern Western culture, and sexual masochism is far more common and apparent here than elsewhere. The cross-cultural evidence provides only weak support for the life-interpretation theory of masochism. True, the modern West has particular problems with life's meaning, but somewhat similar problems have probably occurred in other cultures as well. If these problems cause sexual masochism, then one would expect to find sexual masochism in at least a few other cultures.

Once again, it must be kept in mind that there is no form of evidence at all that provides a fully reliable understanding of sexual masochism. Given that all sources of evidence have flaws, the best one can do is look for converging patterns. The historical and cross-cultural evidence converges in important ways with the other forms of evidence reviewed in this book.

Chapter Four
Essentials of Masochism

Having sketched the main theories and examined the historical and cultural distribution of masochism, it is now appropriate to look more closely at the phenomena of masochism. In the opening chapter, masochism was defined by three main features: pain, loss of control, and embarrassment or humiliation. This chapter examines each of these three features. The desires and activities of masochists are examined in relation to possible explanations of the consequences that could potentially account for their appeal.

PAIN

The issue of pain immediately brings up the paradoxical nature of masochism. How could someone enjoy pain? Pain is an unpleasant, aversive sensation, so almost by definition it seems impossible that anyone would like it or want it. Yet masochists apparently desire pain.

Past theories have experimented with various means of dodging the issue or explaining away this paradoxical enjoyment of pain. Some have argued that pain is not really an essential part of masochism. Reik (1941/1957), for instance, said that masochists enjoy the anticipation of pain and the consequences of it, but they do not enjoy the pain. That is, the thrill of fear and the relief of guilt (but not the actual sensation) form the appeal of pain. He downplayed the role of pain in masochism, as if thereby hoping to avoid the problem. But it cannot be dismissed so easily. The majority of masochists do seek out and submit to pain (although not all of them). Pain is a principal criterion of masochism, and for many it is the focal aspect of the experience. Pain is undeniably a vital part of masochism. "Pain is great," as one masochist told me simply.

Another approach was tried by Cowan (1982). She proposed that people learn important things from pain. She held that learning about oneself is sometimes painful, so seeking pain may be a viable means of gaining self-knowledge. But where are these alleged insights? Neither masochists nor researchers have found any evidence of specific things that people learn about themselves from being spanked or tied up.

Yet another approach was tried by Caplan (1984). She disputed the labeling of various groups of women as masochistic, on the grounds that they never really enjoy the pain. For example, some psychologists have regarded battered women who remain with abusive husbands as masochists. Caplan argued, however, that these women often lack viable alternatives, and so they remain with their husbands because to them it seems the best of a poor set of options, not because they enjoy pain. Caplan's arguments are thorough and compelling, and gradually she demolishes the stereotypes. Eventually, Caplan comes to doubt that anyone ever directly enjoys pain. I doubt it too. But does that mean that masochism does not exist?

There are two plausible ways that pain could be appealing. Either the sensation of pain becomes pleasant itself, or pain becomes appealing on the basis of something other than its sensation. Both of these possibilities need careful examination in order to understand the masochist's paradoxical quest for pain. Before reviewing the explanations, however, it is necessary to be clear about what is being explained. We begin, therefore, with an examination of the use of pain in masochism.

Varieties of Pain

Although the history of the human race has seen the invention of elaborate and exotic means of administering pain, most masochists seem to show little imagination and variety in the techniques they use. Among the letters in my sample, pain was administered chiefly by spanking, paddling, or whipping, usually on the buttocks. The whipping was most commonly done with a riding crop or belt. Usually the flagellation was kept rather mild. People were spanked or whipped until the pain reached some particular level, and the administration of pain ceased long before it became intolerable.

There were occasional reports of other varieties of pain. Some referred to using clothespins or other clamps to pinch the skin, especially on sensitive areas such as the nipples. Some reported slaps in the face. That was about all.

Other researchers confirm that these are the most common patterns. Some additional (but uncommon) techniques for giving pain involve piercing the skin lightly with needles, tying the person tightly so as to inflict pain, and dripping melted wax from a candle onto the skin (Scott, 1983). Use of knives or razors has been noted, although the practice is apparently quite rare (Spengler, 1977). Scratching with fingernails and biting are also mentioned, although these seem to be popular with many lovers who do not consider themselves masochists and do not engage in any other masochistic activities.

Prostitutes' techniques for inflicting pain on masochistic clients depend on whether it is necessary to avoid leaving any marks on the skin. Many clients apparently insist that no marks be left. The reason, presumably, is that they are married to women who find sadomasochistic sex objectionable (else the man would do it with his wife rather than a prostitute). These women would probably take a dim view of having hubby come home with welts on his back from a prostitute's whip. In contrast, other clients *like* the prostitute to leave marks. Some reportedly will later masturbate while looking at their welts, because the marks remind them of the masochistic experience (Janus et al., 1977).

It appears that most masochists do not like to be whipped to the point of drawing blood. Some masochists accept red marks or bruises on the skin, but that is apparently the upper limit. As noted in chapter 1, most masochists are very careful to avoid injury.

There is a little evidence that some masochists, perhaps especially males, take pride in how much pain they can endure (Scott, 1983; also Janus et al., 1977). Ordinarily, they still stop long before there is any injury, but they want to "take" as much as possible until it becomes intolerable. Pride in enduring pain is particularly interesting because in most respects masochists are denied any basis for pride. As we see here, masochists submit to humiliation in many ways. Yet some take pride in the quantity or intensity of their pain.

Undoubtedly there are many levels and degrees of pain. It is clear that masochists desire only the milder levels. They are extremely careful to stop long before injury. Even without injury, however, there is apparently a point at which the pain ceases to be sexually or emotionally stimulating and becomes unpleasant. Masochists want a carefully limited quantity of pain.

Dominants speak of pushing a submissive to his or her limit, and then *a little bit beyond,* as an important feature of sexual dominance (e.g., Califia, 1983; Lucy, 1982; also see Linden, 1982). The limit is presumably the point at which the masochist wants to stop because the pain is becoming too much. Apparently, these couples enjoy having the dominant partner continue just a little past this point. One can infer that a common pattern is for the couple to continue the pain until the submissive wants to stop, then they continue a bit longer, and then they stop.

Four reasons can be suggested for this tendency to continue just *past* the point at which the masochist wants to stop. First, it might help preserve the illusion that the dominant is fully in control. After all, sadomasochistic couples are typically pretending that the pain is being administered for the sake of the dominant, when in reality it is often the submissive who desires it. If the dominant stops spanking as soon as the submissive signals to stop, it may become too obvious that the masochist is giving orders and controlling the situation. Once the illusion is spoiled, the game breaks down and loses some of its appeal. Fantasy and illusion are vital ingredients in masochism, and this continuation of pain past the submissive's limit may be one concession to sustaining the fantasy and illusion.

Second, it is plausible that people can take a bit more pain than they think they can. They may signal when they think they are nearing their limit, but in fact the limit is somewhat farther off. There is some research evidence that people will "anticipate" their pain thresholds by signalling before they reach the true threshold (Lepanto, Moroney, & Zenhausern, 1965). Another way of putting this is that there is a substantial gray area between mild, acceptable pain and severe, intolerable pain.

This explanation is the one favored by the dominants themselves. They say that they help the masochist discover that his or her true limits are higher than previously thought.

A third possible explanation is that continuing the pain past the limit may greatly intensify the thrill of fear. If the masochist is certain that the dominant will stop as soon as the masochist signals, then the masochist may feel in control of the situation. On the other hand, if the masochist signals to stop and the dominant refuses, even if just for a moment, the masochist may feel in danger of much greater pain or even harm, and this feeling may be quite appealing (cf. Reik, 1941/1957). The results may be especially important for the next episode. If the masochist knows that last time the dominant stopped as soon as the masochist wanted, then the masochist may feel safe and secure. But if the dominant previously continued past the signal to stop, the masochist cannot be absolutely sure what will happen this time, and so the entire experience may become more arousing. Thus, the extra pain is used to intensify the masochist's feelings of *loss of control,* an important feature of masochism that we discuss shortly.

The fourth possible explanation is that the dominant partners really do derive pleasure from inflicting pain. Their desire may therefore not be satisfied by giving pain to the masochist as long as the masochist wants it. But once the masochist wants to stop, then it becomes pleasant and stimulating for the dominant.

There is unfortunately little empirical basis for deciding which of these four theories is correct. The fact that couples go only a little bit past the masochist's limit seems to fit the first three more than the fourth one. The fourth explanation is based on true sadistic pleasure, which is rarely evident, although in principle it is plausible. Given that masochists seem to like being punished slightly beyond their limits, however, the wishes of the sadist cannot be the only factor, so at least one of the first three must be correct. Possibly they are all true.

It is also important to note that pain thresholds may change during periods of sexual excitement. Cross-cultural studies as well as surveys of American sexual behavior show that many couples bite or scratch each other during intercourse without any other signs of sadomasochism. Biting and scratching would cause pain under normal circumstances, but in a sexual context they are apparently arousing and even pleasant (e.g., Davenport, 1976). The implication for masochism is that sexual arousal may increase the masochist's tolerance for pain. The same level of chastisement that normally would hurt a great deal may be only slightly unpleasant to the sexually aroused masochist. In other words, masochists may often be experiencing less pain than a simple consideration of the spanking would suggest. This underscores further the point that masochism remains at mild (although real) doses of pain.

The notion that pain tolerance thresholds rise during sexual arousal is particularly consistent with the second explanation, for it contributes to the notion of the gray area between anticipated and actual tolerance for pain. The second explanation was also supported by the remarks of people who engage in S&M, so it must be considered the most likely of the four, although more than one could be true.

Pain into Pleasure?

There is a theoretical rumor—one cannot really call it a theory—to the effect that intense pain becomes pleasant, or at least that intense pain cannot be distinguished from intense pleasure. There is very little proof for the belief that pain becomes pleasant. Victims of torture, women who give birth without anesthesia, and sufferers from migraine headaches tend to contradict any assertion that pain turns into pleasure. Still, the rumor persists.

What do masochists themselves have to say? Their reports give slight support to the notion that pain becomes pleasant. The majority of masochists' writings do not describe the pain as directly pleasant in any way. A few do make references to "pleasure/pain" or some such mixture, suggesting that there can be some connection. Still, some of these must be suspected of being fantasies. (In fantasy, pain *is* capable of turning into pleasure). The more reliable sources (e.g., Greene & Greene, 1974; Samois, 1982) tend not to make any such claims.

The direct conversion of pain into pleasure may indeed be a fantasy of masochists. Some researchers have suggested that masochists enjoy the idea and the anticipation of pain more than the actual sensation of pain (e.g., Reik, 1941/1957), which would be entirely consistent with the view that masochistic fantasy blends pain and pleasure. One illustration of this connection in fantasy was provided in a first-person account by "J" (1982, p. 42). She said that as she gradually developed an interest in masochism, she became fascinated by the idea of submitting to a whipping, and finally she decided to try it. When properly tied up for the first time, she was still wondering what it would be like. The first strokes came, and she gave a yell of protest. Her thoughts: "I am surprised at how much it stings... So, it really does hurt!" Thus, her masochistic fantasy had downplayed the pain, to the extent that she was actually surprised by the fact that it hurt.

Perhaps, then, the masochistic imagination does like to think that the pain will somehow become pleasant. Once the actual experience begins, however, the masochist finds that the pain is indeed unpleasant. Still, in most cases the masochists apparently enjoy the experience enough to want to repeat it.

In general, it is implausible that the appeal of pain lies in its becoming pleasurable. Masochists apparently do not enjoy painful sensations as a rule. Thus, they dislike headaches, dental work, and getting their fingers smashed in a car door, just like anyone else (e.g., Weinberg, Williams, & Moser, 1984; also Reik, 1941/1957; Scott, 1983).

More important, the pain-into-pleasure argument is based on intense pain becoming pleasant—but masochists rarely venture into intense pain. Even if severe pain could become pleasurable, this would not explain masochism, because masochists stay with mild, carefully limited doses of pain.

The masochist's pain is therefore probably not pleasure. It is genuine, if relatively mild, pain. The appeal of pain in masochism thus must lie in something other than its sensation, for the sensation remains painful, not pleasant.[1]

---

[1]Once again, it is worth noting that what would normally be painful may be less so during sexual arousal. A small bite on the shoulder or a finger's scratch on the back would normally be unpleasant, but apparently many people find these pleasant and arousing during intercourse. This is not actually the conversion of pain into pleasure; rather, it is the raising of pain thresholds so that a certain stimulus is not painful. This stimulus can then contribute to pleasure, unless it becomes too strong (and therefore painful). Still, this may be what causes people to think that pain can be converted into pleasure. Probably this threshold effect is involved in masochism, but it is only a small and theoretically unimportant part of the process. Although the masochist's pain threshold may be raised, it does not raise far enough to make a spanking or whipping pleasant. Masochists report these things as genuinely painful, although usually only mildly painful.

Pain as Symbol of Submission

Another possible explanation for the appeal of pain is that it symbolizes one's submission to the partner. Accepting pain without reason, without protest, might well serve as a powerful sign that one belongs to the dominant partner. Indeed, many of the letters in the present sample referred specifically to *arbitrary* chastisement. The whipping and spanking was administered not because the masochist had done anything wrong or deserved to be punished, but merely because of the random whim of the dominant partner. Masochists seem to regard such arbitrary punishment as one of the ultimate proofs of their submission and commitment.

This emphasis on the symbolic nature of pain is plausible because it allows the sensation of pain to be unpleasant (i.e., painful). The masochist dislikes what the pain feels like, but he or she enjoys what the pain symbolizes.

Western culture has a long history and tradition behind the idea of suffering for the sake of love (e.g., de Rougemont, 1956; Fiedler, 1966/1982; Tannahill, 1980). Modern individuals are well acquainted with the idea that making sacrifices or enduring suffering are acceptable ways of expressing one's love for another (e.g., Cowan, 1982; Gilligan, 1982). Masochists are part of this culture, and they feel the same connection. One researcher described a particular masochist's attitude by saying that "enduring the pain was his way of showing Misty he cared" (Scott, 1983, p. 105).

The symbolic appeal of pain is indicated in various bits of evidence about masochism. For one thing, masochists do not enjoy accidental pain; they prefer intentional pain. That is, they insist that the partner deliberately inflict the pain on them, or else they do not enjoy it. This is an important fact, for it shows that masochists are not responding to the sensation alone, but rather to its meaning and context. Masochists desire to suffer by the express intention of the partner, which means that they desire to suffer for the sake of the partner's wishes and pleasure. If the partner does not enjoy administering the pain, the masochist does not enjoy it either.

Ample evidence for this requirement of intentional pain is provided in Scott's (1983) research. She recorded that one common pattern is for a masochistically inclined husband to persuade his reluctant wife to dominate him. To please him, she ties him up and begins spanking or whipping him, but because of her inhibitions and reluctance she keeps stopping to ask him if she's doing it right. Scott said that this ends up being quite disappointing to the masochist. If it is too apparent that the dominant partner is merely following the wishes of the submissive, the pain apparently loses its appeal.

Curiously, the need for the pain to be intentional can cause minor problems even with in the masochistic episode. The dominant women interviewed by Scott described their dilemma of what to do when they might accidentally inflict pain on a submissive partner. For example, they might have the man tied up and then accidentally step on his toe. Such pain is not sexually stimulating to the masochist, and one's normal impulse would be to say "Sorry" or "Excuse me." Yet to apologize would break the spell or the mood of the game, in which the submissive is supposed to be fully at the dominant's mercy. As one woman put it, "Being dominant is never saying you're sorry" (Scott, 1983, p. 153). The only satisfactory solution, apparently, is for the dominant to pretend that she meant it—that is, she intended to step on the masochist's toe. By making it seem deliberate, she incorporates it into the scene.

Thus, masochists do not merely want pain. They want their partners to *want* to hurt them.

A few signs suggest that masochists want to be desired and even loved because of their submission. "To want someone to want me precisely because I'm submissive—my submissiveness is a gift to them," is the way one masochistic lesbian put it (Zoftig, 1982, p. 93; note, however, that there are no systematic or extensive data on this point). They want their submission to strengthen the bond of relationship. Thus, again, the attraction of pain seems to consist partly in that the masochist finds it an effective means of proving his or her love and cementing the attachment to the partner.

Later, we return to the importance of the relationship context in masochism. For now, the important point is that masochists seem to desire that pain be administered in such a context. Thus, for example, many masochists are reluctant to use a professional dominatrix, because they want to submit to someone with whom they have an ongoing relationship (Scott, 1983). And those who do visit prostitutes tend to be steady, repeat customers much more than other clients of prostitutes (Janus et al., 1977). This implies that they start to form relationships of a sort with the prostitute.

The significance of the relationship context for the present argument is that it points again to the symbolic nature of pain. What a context does is to furnish meaning. So if masochists require a particular sort of context for their pain, it is probably because they want the pain to have a particular sort of meaning. To the extent that this is true, it points to the following conclusion: It is the meaning of pain, not the sensation of pain, that attracts the masochist.

Specifically, masochists seem to want the pain to signify that they are pleasing the dominant partner and carrying out the partner's wishes. The masochists' acceptance of pain symbolizes their inferior, submissive position in the relationship, and it expresses their love and commitment to the partner. They want to suffer as a way of expressing their love, and they want this gift of suffering to strengthen the partner's love for them.

How thorough and satisfactory is this explanation of the appeal of pain based on its symbolic message? It is quite plausible, because it allows the pain to be unpleasant—which fits the nature of pain. It is consistent with evidence about how such couples actually use pain, especially evidence that the meaning and context appear to make a difference in whether the pain excites the masochist or not.

On the other hand, it is probably not a complete explanation. There are many ways of demonstrating one's love, and some explanation is needed for why masochists would prefer that one over the others. Moreover, masochists seem not simply to endure the pain for the partner's sake, but they actively desire it and seek it out. And, last, in many cases the pain is presented without any interpretation at all. Sometimes pain is appealing despite little or no meaning.

Thus, the most reasonable conclusion seems to be this. Pain does function as a means by which the masochist can symbolize his or her submission to the partner and love for the partner. Indeed, this may be a very important aspect of the masochistic desire for pain. But it is probably not the full explanation. Masochists do like the symbolism of pain, but a thorough understanding of pain's appeal requires further explanation.

Pain as Punishment

Symbolizing love and submission is not the only meaning that pain can have. Another important potential meaning of pain is punishment. It is conceivable that masochists desire pain as a form of punishment for their wrongs and misdeeds. Indeed, many past theorists have taken this approach, and it seems at least superficially plausible, because spankings and whippings are normally used as forms of punishment. Normally, of course, people do not *desire* to be punished by spanking or whipping. But one might suggest that masochists have done something wrong, so they feel guilty, and they anticipate that being punished will relieve them of guilt. Therefore, they desire the punishment as a means of relief from guilt.

There are two principal forms of the hypothesis that masochism is essentially punishment for guilt. One form emphasizes feelings of sexual guilt, and the other emphasizes guilt in general. The theory of sex guilt is critically examined (and rejected) in a later chapter on why masochism is sexually stimulating. Here, we concern ourselves with guilt in general.

The guilt hypothesis is extremely difficult to evaluate. One approach would be to search masochistic accounts for evidence of guilt. The letters in the present sample were sorted into three categories of guilt. One category included clear evidence of guilt. These writers referred to pain delivered specifically as punishment for particular offenses or misdeeds. Thus, some couples said they used spankings as part of a plan to help one spouse lose weight (sort of an "S&M diet") or give up smoking. Suitable resolutions were made, and backsliding was punished. Others described spankings that were delivered for embarrassing the spouse in public, for not fulfilling one's obligations or household chores, and the like. Several letters described incidents in which spouses were spanked for flirting, necking, or petting with others.

A second category was designated as "trumped up" guilt. In these, the spanking was administered as punishment, but the offense was clearly invented to serve as a pretext for punishment. Thus, the couple would commence an S&M game, and the submissive would be punished for failing to undress fast enough, for breaking some arbitrary rule (for example, for having an orgasm without permission), or for inadequate performance of oral sex. It is hard to take these seriously as evidence of guilt motivations, for apparently neither partner really feels that the offender has done something wrong outside the context of the game.

The third and final category involved administering pain without any implication of punishment or guilt. Indeed, sometimes there is an explicit denial of such meaning, such as when the dominant says that the punishment is done arbitrarily to prove "that you belong to me and I can do whatever I want with you." Some masochists seem to find this arbitrariness an appealing proof of their submission.

The letters were about equally distributed among the three categories, except for a slight tendency for female masochists to report more punishment based on actual guilt than other authors. (Data and statistics are reported in the Appendix.) Thus, some masochists are drawn to contexts involving guilt and punishment, whereas others are indifferent to it and even avoid such implications. Overt guilt is evident in some letters and not in others. It may explain the appeal of pain to some masochists, but not others.

But perhaps overt guilt is not the true cause. Some theorists have argued that masochists have *unconscious* guilt feelings that impel them toward submission and punishment. In other words, perhaps they feel guilty but do not know it. This hypothesis is almost impossible to evaluate, for by definition there would be no evidence that could prove or disprove it.

A further difficulty in evaluating the guilt hypothesis concerns the fantasy nature of masochism. It is quite clear that masochists like to enact scenes or games involving fantasy. Punishment for misdeeds might be a convenient script for a spanking—so even if there is evidence of guilt, it could be merely a superficial fiction irrelevant to the masochist's true motivations. This is most obviously suggested in instances of trumped-up guilt, but it may even apply in cases involving actual guilt. Thus, for example, the majority of normal couples do not use spanking to enhance compliance with dieting or no-smoking resolutions, and most people do not spank their spouses for neglecting household chores. One must suspect that a couple who chooses to use spanking in that way may have had inclinations toward masochistic sexuality in the first place. In short, it may be that the guilt did not really cause the spanking; rather, the masochistic inclinations led the couple to seize on the guilt as a reason to engage in spanking.

Given the lack of direct evidence about the role of guilt in sexual masochism, it seems worth stepping back and trying to evaluate the hypothesis on its own merits. Does guilt cause people to desire punishment? Research has not found this to be true, although there are not many studies. There is evidence that feeling guilty makes people want to do good deeds, in order to make themselves feel better (Freedman, 1970; Rosenhan, Salovey, Karylowski, & Hargis, 1981). But there is little or no evidence that feeling guilty makes people want to suffer. On this basis, one may doubt that masochists are motivated by a desire for punishment to relieve guilt.

Another problem is that it seems simply implausible that masochistic chastisement might actually help relieve genuine guilt. If someone has done something seriously wrong, such as breaking the law or deliberately injuring another person, would this be rectified by engaging in unusual forms of sexual play? It seems unlikely. The secret sex games of masochists are kept well separated from ordinary life, and they probably have little power to change circumstances in real life. Imagine someone who committed murder or embezzlement and was caught several years later, and who then asked for mercy because he had submitted to a series of spankings in his sex life. It is doubtful that anyone would take seriously his claim to have atoned sufficiently for his guilt. Masochism simply does not work as genuine, legitimate atonement or restitution for real guilt.

On the other hand, it is plausible that masochistic submission enables the person to escape from guilty feelings. In this view, masochism does not expiate guilt, but it does provide a temporary escape from it by taking one's mind off of troublesome aspects of the self. In the next chapter, this aspect of guilt is examined more closely.

In conclusion, then, it is difficult to draw firm conclusions about whether pain appeals to masochists on the basis of being a symbolic punishment for misdeeds. In terms of clear, direct evidence, the best that can be said is that some masochists do like the pain to signify punishment, and others do not. Punishment is thus at best a partial explanation. There is little clear or direct evidence about whether guilt causes people to desire punishment, and there is no way of getting good evidence about unconscious guilt.

Psychology of Pain: Unmaking the World

So far, we have examined various ideas about the possible meanings and implications of pain. Perhaps a better understanding will emerge from taking a close look at the psychology of pain. What are the effects of pain on the mind?

The natural, biological function of pain is to serve as a warning of injury. Pain *seizes one's attention* and signals that the body is in danger of being damaged. As we have already seen, however, masochists are careful to avoid injury. So they are not using pain in its normal function. They do not want pain for the sake of alerting them to possible injury, for they have already taken care of removing the danger of injury. Masochists divorce pain from injury.

That leaves the attention-grabbing effect, however. The warning effect may be irrelevant to masochism, but that does not mean that the attentional effect is also irrelevant. Pain focuses the mind on a particular, immediate sensation. Could this explain the appeal in masochism of pain?

A deep and extensive analysis of the mental effects of pain was recently furnished by Scarry (1985). As she put it, pain "unmakes the world." That is, the sensation of pain removes one's broader awareness of the world. Likewise, pain undermines the awareness of the self in symbolic terms—self enmeshed in the world by means of interpersonal commitments and relationships, personal values and opinions, and so forth. Pain shrinks awareness to the here and now. It deconstructs self and world.

Many of Scarry's ideas are based on a careful analysis of the process of torture, based on actual accounts and descriptions by victims. Torture typically begins with the imprisonment of an individual whose actions and views oppose those of the captors. The person enters the prison as a symbolic, complex individual, with strong beliefs and attitudes, with various loyalties and ambitions and obligations, involved in various relationships, and having strong feelings about the past, future, and present circumstances in the world (such as political trends in the country). This individual is then systematically subjected to pain. Eventually the person will renounce or betray all those attitudes, loyalties, relationships, and so forth. The torture victim will make statements renouncing or rejecting all the basic beliefs and attitudes that formed the basis for the person's struggle. The victim will give away secret information that may endanger friends and colleagues, even putting the individual's cause at risk. In short, the torture victim will act contrary to the beliefs and values that form the core of his or her identity.

How does this change occur? Psychologically, the key is a re-focusing of awareness. The pain in the body takes precedence over the symbolic aspects of the self. The person will betray relationships, values, obligations, hopes, beliefs, and the rest, in order to bring about an end to the pain. It is not a process of rational deliberation or calculated tradeoff; rather, the pain makes those other things seem unreal and irrelevant. In sufficiently severe pain, the world shrinks to the immediate surroundings (the room and the people in it), to the present moment, and to the sensations in the body. Pain obliterates all psychological content except for itself.

Pain thus empties the mind of its meaningful contents. The complex, symbolic self that entered the torture chamber is eliminated. All that is left is a physical body, a locus of movement and sensation. The awareness of past and future melt away, and the mind focuses on the immediate present—on the presence or absence of pain at the present moment. Pain fosters an extremely low-level, deconstructed awareness of self.

For masochism, the implication is that pain has great potential as a narcotic. (By narcotic, I mean something that can affect the mind and remove certain thoughts from awareness.) Pain blots out high-level thinking, along with complex and symbolic self-awareness.

Obviously, torture victims submit to pain unwillingly, but it is possible to imagine someone who would *want* to forget certain high-level concerns and aspects of self. For example, someone might want to stop worrying about the future (or past), or someone might want to be free of constantly thinking about plans and ambitions, about obligations and commitments, about responsibilities and other high-level meanings. Pain might appeal to such a person as an effective way of focusing the mind on the here and now, away from troubling concerns and abstractions.

If pain is an effective narcotic, one might ask why it is not more popular. There are two main drawbacks to using pain to blot things out of the mind: Pain is inherently unpleasant, and it usually accompanies injury (which may have severe practical drawbacks). These drawbacks would seem sufficient to keep people in general from using pain in this way. But masochists manage to get around these drawbacks. They seek out carefully controlled doses of pain, administered by an intimate partner, so the aversiveness is kept within acceptable bounds. (Also, they generally follow it up with sexual pleasure, which may also overcome the unpleasantness.) And they carefully and thoroughly separate pain from injury, thus eliminating the second problem.

The emphasis on suspense and anticipation instead of actual pain is entirely consistent with the use of pain as a narcotic, for it completely gets around the unpleasantness of pain. Anticipating pain may focus the mind on the here and now almost as effectively as the actual pain, and perhaps even more effectively. One dominant woman aptly described the attention-grabbing effect of anticipated pain this way: "A whip is a great way to get someone to be here now. They can't look away from it, and they can't think about anything else!" (Califia, 1983, p. 134). It may indeed be hard for the mind to wander to abstract ideas, long-range plans, distant worries, or high-level concerns when someone is standing over you with a whip.

Thus, masochists circumvent the drawbacks of pain, presumably enabling them to enjoy its narcotic effects. Moderate pain, in a context of fantasy role playing and sexual stimulation, may be a powerful escape from the everyday world.

The first-person reports of masochists are consistent with this view. When describing what goes through their mind during a whipping, they almost never refer to high-level thoughts or distant concerns. They describe simply the awareness of their sensations of pain, the heat in their buttocks, and so forth. It is also noteworthy that they do not even report thinking about past misdeeds or faults, contrary to the theory that masochistic pain is essentially punishment based on guilt. In some cases, they describe the narrowing of attention as almost trancelike (e.g., "J", 1982). More generally, it simply seems as if the mind becomes empty of all contents except the pain.

When I asked masochists what goes through their minds during a masochistic scene, they often had difficulty answering. They described the intensity of sensations, and the emotions that occurred afterward, but they had trouble describing their mental state during the episode. As one put it, "You get so wrapped up that you're not even aware of any of your surroundings." This captures the narrowing of attention and the cessation of broadly meaningful thought that accompany masochistic pain. Indeed, this woman insisted that masochism intensified intimacy, for she felt that she and her lover became aware only of each other during S&M. "You get totally lost with each other," as she put it, suggesting that this produced a feeling that the two people blended into each other.

One vivid articulation of this reduction of awareness was by a masochistic lesbian: "The bubble of my self, the prison of my mind, exploded, expanded . . . I was hurtling forward on deep, sobbing currents of my breath, waves unleashed from the bottom of the sea. Then long throbbing seconds of liberation and silence and obliteration" (Califia, 1982, p. 177). The image of silence and obliteration at the bottom of the sea captures the escape from self and world that seems to form the heart of the masochistic experience.

Two additional implications of Scarry's work deserve comment. First, she noted that torture involves a heavy dose of fiction and illusion. For example, she said that torture is usually disguised as interrogation, with a persistent alternation between questions and pain, even though in fact the torturers generally care little for the information disclosed. The victim, meanwhile, is portrayed as "betraying" colleagues or ideas, as if the victim does something morally wrong by succumbing to the torture. Thus, the moral responsibility of the torturers is concealed and disguised, whereas that of the victims is fabricated and elaborated. Numerous other examples indicate that the world of torture is full of illusions and false meanings.

The pervasiveness of illusion in torture is entirely consistent with the argument that masochistic pain works as a narcotic. After all, there is just as much illusion in masochistic sex games as in torture. Pain removes many high-level meanings from awareness, bringing the person down to low levels of meaning.

Earlier, in discussing action identification theory, I noted that change (reinterpretation) of meanings generally followed a pattern of deconstructing one set of meanings and then elaborating new meanings—in action identification terms, first shifting down to low levels and then back to high levels (Vallacher & Wegner, 1985). Thus, deconstruction is a first step in the creation of new meanings, including illusory meanings. Pain obliterates high-level meanings, leaving a psychological vacuum that can be filled by other interpretations. In torture, pain produces a narrow, immediate focus that makes room for fictional, illusory interpretations of what is going on. In masochism, pain removes the high-level awareness of the person's normal identity and involvements, making room for fantasy and illusion. As we already saw, masochists sometimes take on new identities during their sex games (such as becoming a full-time slave). Such identity change is probably made easier by pain's ability to deconstruct identity—by shifting attention to the immediate physical events, away from broader meanings and definitions of self.

The second implication is that pain does actively *promote* awareness of self at a low level. Not all forms of self-awareness are removed by pain. In pain, you become acutely aware of your body, or at least of a small part of your body. This is of course an extremely low level of self-awareness. There is no extension of self-awareness into the past and future, no symbolism or abstract identity. One becomes self-aware in the immediately present moment, as a body in pain. Thus, although pain removes high-level self-awareness, it promotes low-level self-awareness.

A standard philosophical argument makes a similar point. According to this argument, pain is *incorrigible,* which means that you cannot be mistaken about it. It makes no sense to say that someone thinks he or she is in pain but is wrong, or (conversely) to say that someone is in severe pain but does not know it. There is something absolutely certain and unshakable about knowledge of one's own pain. And no one else can be sure about your pain. Only you can be sure.

Philosophically, then, pain provides a sort of minimal proof of subjective existence. If you know something for certain that no one else can know for certain, then that proves you must exist separate from others. I hurt, therefore I am. Pain thus functions to affirm the bare minimum of existence. It does not prove a great deal about the self, but it does contribute at the lowest level.

How, then, should we evaluate the theory that masochistic pain serves to blot out the world and facilitate the escape from self-awareness? This theory is inherently plausible and there is ample evidence outside of masochism that it is correct. It fits much of the evidence about masochism, and it parallels the processes that we find with control and humiliation. On the negative side, it does not provide any explanation for the symbolic issues surrounding masochistic pain, especially the masochists' desire that the pain be administered intentionally. Thus, this theory is probably correct in its own right but is not a full explanation by itself for the masochistic interest in pain.

Conclusion: The Appeal of Pain

We have considered four theories about the role of pain in masochism. One of these, holding that pain turns into pleasure, was rejected as implausible and unsupported.

Two other theories seem to fit the available evidence and make sense. First, submitting to pain may serve as a symbol of the masochist's love and submission vis-à-vis the dominant partner. Second, pain functions as a kind of narcotic stimulus that blots high-level self-awareness out of the mind, thus providing an effective escape from many thoughts and issues. More precisely, pain deconstructs awareness of self, which is an important step in escaping from self. Neither of these theories seems completely adequate by itself to account for everything about pain in masochism, but together they do seem adequate. It seems likely that the symbolic aspect of pain is more important for some masochists while the narcotic aspect is more important for others. And there are probably many masochists who are attracted by both effects.

The other theory treated pain as punishment, and it proved difficult to evaluate. Some versions of this theory could be rejected, while others could not be either supported or rejected. Evaluating this theory is especially hard because it overlaps with the others. Guilt might cause someone to want to escape from self by means of pain's narcotic effect, or it might cause someone to want to reaffirm one's love and commitment to a beloved partner. Thus, although direct examination of the role of pain in masochism provided no direct support for the importance of guilt and punishment, this theory cannot be ruled out. We return to consideration of guilt and punishment later.

LOSS OF CONTROL

The second essential feature of masochism involves loss of control. This takes various forms. With pain, there were only a few practices that masochists reported, but with control there is a wide assortment. The largest category involves bondage: The masochist submits to being tied up. Even in bondage, there is quite an assortment of techniques.

Bondage enthusiasts apparently love to explore novel, different, and even creative means of restraint. The most common forms involve tying the masochist up with ropes, scarves, stockings or pantyhose, neckties, handcuffs, and occasionally chains. They are tied to beds and chairs, or sometimes in a standing position. Some describe being suspended, such as from hooks in the ceiling. These last appear to be the most dangerous activities in all of masochism, for occasionally the masochist's body weight pulls the hooks loose, unceremoniously dumping the masochist onto the floor or furniture below (Lee, 1983).

Masochists also enjoy being blindfolded and gagged. Although binding the hands together is probably the most common single form of bondage, blindfolding is probably the next most common. Some S&M manuals caution that gags can cause bad experiences (e.g., Bellwether, 1982), and so it is difficult to estimate how frequently masochists use them. One letter in my sample was from a woman who said she desired to be gagged but could not abide the sensation of having something in her mouth. She hit upon the solution of having her husband put masking tape across her mouth. This solution was allegedly quite satisfactory and arousing to them both.

The most popular position for bondage is apparently to be tied spread-eagled to the corners of a bed. The combination of helplessness, passivity, and exposure is presumably what makes this position a favorite of the masochistic imagination. Sometimes this position is reported as face-up, other times face-down, presumably depending on what further activities are planned.

Loss of control extends beyond mere physical restraint, however. Masochists submit to the authority of the dominant in a variety of ways. The most obvious of these is the use of direct commands. The dominant partner frequently gives orders to the submissive, who is expected to obey them immediately and thoroughly. In my sample, common commands included undressing, performing sexual services (especially oral sex), serving the dominant in various ways (e.g., serving drinks or attending at a bath), masturbating as a performance for the dominant (and occasionally others) as audience, engaging in sex acts with others, and simple physical movement (e.g., lie down).

Many masochists describe ongoing relationships with intermittent or regular S&M activities. In these, there is often a set of rules to which the masochist must conform. For example, one author listed the following rules: He was required to dress in women's clothes at home; he was not to have an orgasm except as commanded by his mistress; he would not speak unless addressed by his mistress; he was never to look his mistress in the eye; and he was to do all the cooking and cleaning. Similar sets of rules are reported in many other letters. Thus, many masochists are allegedly required to address the dominant partner only with an honorific title, especially "Mistress" or "Master." Others are required to wear some badge of servitude, such as a collar or chain or (for male masochists) women's panties, even outside the house.

Even more elaborate sets of rules are sometimes reported. These may include remaining naked at all times when at home, being on one's knees at the door to greet the dominant partner, and keeping all pubic hair shaved. A few masochists say they are required to recite particular speeches, usually expressing their slavery and devotion (or even worship) to the dominant.

Rules, commands, and bondage have in common the denial of the masochist's freedom and control. The masochist cannot show any initiative, make and implement any decisions, or hold any responsibility. The self as an active agent is systematically denied. Passivity and subservience are enforced.

The fully bound masochist is required to be a totally passive participant in whatever activity the dominant partner chooses. Moreover, the masochist's bondage leaves him or her utterly at the mercy of the dominant partner. (It sounds as if the dominant has seized control, but again it is usually the masochist who desires this.) Thus, the feeling of helplessness and vulnerability is apparently very appealing—even sexually exciting—to many otherwise normal people.

Part of the explanation may be that the bondage relieves one from any responsibility for the sexual actions and desires. People who feel guilty about sexual desire may be attracted to bondage, for they can then engage in sex without feelings of guilt. There is some evidence for this, although only a little. One masochistic lesbian said, for example, that bondage appealed to her because "it gives you a chance to be sexual without any responsibility for your sexy feelings . . . 'it's not my fault, mommy' " (Zoftig, 1982, pp. 88–89). There were not many such remarks, however, and it is doubtful that this sentiment is widespread.

It is noteworthy that this one incident (Zoftig, 1982) involved homosexual sex. Our society still stigmatizes homosexuality. Most evidence indicates that most American adults do not have a great deal of guilt about heterosexual sex. (Also, those who do have substantial sex guilt tend to be least likely to engage in S&M.) In my sample, a substantial minority of letters reported first-time homosexual experiences in connection with submission and bondage. It is plausible that these individuals had desired homosexual sex but had been restrained by guilt or inhibitions that were removed by the masochistic abdication of responsibility. It could also be the other way around, however: Instead of the masochism being a means toward homosexuality, the homosexuality could be a means toward masochism. That is, engaging in such actions could serve as further proof of the person's submission and lack of control.

Also, as noted previously some masochists report rules prohibiting them from having orgasms without permission from the dominant. Such rules also seem to reflect the transfer to the partner of responsibility for one's sexuality and actions. This might appeal to people with sexual guilt or inhibitions.

More broadly, however, masochistic submission may appeal to individuals who periodically find control and responsibility burdensome. It is quite plausible that some people find themselves required to make many decisions, exert power, and take responsibility more than they like. Interludes of masochistic submission, during which they are not permitted to make any choices or take any initiative, may strike them as a welcome relief.

Some observations are consistent with this view. Several researchers have recorded that many masochists hold important and responsible positions in their working lives, and the masochistic activity is thus quite contrary to their normal roles (Scott, 1983; Smith & Cox, 1983). Prostitutes who cater to politicians, judges, and other powerful men in Washington and New York report that their most common request is to be dominated (Janus et al., 1977). In contrast, prostitutes who cater to the lower classes receive far fewer requests for domination (Diana, 1985). Thus, masochism appeals selectively to the most powerful and responsible men (see also Juliette, 1983; Symanski, 1981).

Some couples exchange roles, taking turns at who dominates and who submits. The partner who has had the more demanding day at work tends to prefer the submissive role (Scott, 1983, pp. 79-81; further research is needed). In particular, women who work in S&M professionally tend to desire the complementary role at home. For example, a professional dominatrix may often desire to take the submissive role at home with her boyfriend. Full-time submissive prostitutes are almost nonexistent, but there are some who switch roles. A prostitute who has several sessions of submission (that is, in which a male customer spanks her) may well come home desiring to take the dominant role (Scott, 1983, p. 20).

These observations support the suggestion that people may be drawn to masochism because they desire to relinquish control and escape from autonomy. More systematic data are needed, to show that masochistic desires occur most often after major exertions of initiative and responsibility, but at present the evidence does support that conclusion.

Exerting control and initiative is one of the most important and fundamental aspects of the self. The self as active agent is a common theme underlying much of what is known about the self. Extensive research has shown this in many ways. People desire to have control over their environments and over specific social situations (e.g., Rothbaum, Weisz, & Snyder, 1982). They prefer to have choices: Having many options is better than having a few options, and having a few options is preferable to having only veto power, which in turn is preferable to having no choice at all. When people are deprived of some freedom of choice, often they immediately try to reassert it (e.g., Brehm, 1966). Deprived of some particular option, people immediately begin to desire that option more (e.g., Rhodewalt & Davison, 1983). Lack of choice breeds physical illness, especially ulcers but also illness in general (e.g., Weiss, 1971a, 1971b).

Furthermore, people desire to believe they have control even when they do not. The illusion of control is a common, widely appealing illusion (Langer, 1975). People would rather roll the dice themselves than let someone else do it for them. They prefer a lottery ticket that they chose at random over one that someone else chose at random. Thus, not only does the self seek *objective* control over the environment, it also seeks *subjective* control, that is, the belief that it holds control. Control is a central, vital aspect of the self.

Thus, the masochistic abdication of control indicates a denial or removal of the self. Masochists are attracted to an activity that is based partly on removing their control. In eliminating personal control, masochism denies a major aspect of the self. Unless one argues that this is mere coincidence, it appears that part of the appeal of masochism is denying one of the self's vital and basic tendencies.

For example, one woman with a demanding, responsible job in management described the appeal of masochism this way: "One of the greatest things about being the [masochist] is that you only make one decision: Here I am. Do with me what you will" (Santini, 1976, p. 47). She described her submission as peaceful. The masochists I interviewed likewise spoke about how easy it was to take the submissive role. Of course, it would be even easier not to engage in these sex games at all. What strikes masochists as "easy" or "peaceful" is simply the absence of any need to exert initiative or control. The self can be dormant.

Specific comments by masochists support the belief that bondage and loss of control help remove high-level self-awareness. In one woman's words, "when I wear the collar and the blindfold, I can set aside my usual thoughts and feelings about how I look or how well I'm doing. The collar and blindfold help me surrender to the moment" (from the sample of letters). Thus, bondage helps her escape from concern over evaluation and self-presentation, immersing herself in the immediate present. In this respect, the removal of self-awareness caused by bondage parallels the effects of pain.

Before concluding, it must be noted that there is a small amount of control that is left to the masochist. It occurs at an extremely low level, but it is nonetheless a form of active agency.

Oral sex provides a good illustration. Oral sex is reported by a majority of couples who engage in S&M (according to my sample). Moreover, it is far more common for the masochist to be giving than receiving oral sex. In my sample, submissives were three times more likely to be performing oral sex than to be receiving it. (And even when the masochist received oral sex, this often occurred after the S&M session was over, rather than being part of the scene itself.) By far the most common pattern, then, was for the masochist to perform oral sex on the dominant partner.

Receiving oral sex is a passive activity, whereas performing it is the active role. Thus, masochists are generally assigned the *active* role in oral sex, contrary to the passivity usually associated with submission. Superficially, at least, the pattern of oral sex thus runs counter to the main trends and patterns of masochism.

To resolve this, it is necessary to consider again the high versus low levels of thinking about actions. The active role in oral sex occurs at a very low, deconstructed level. The masochist's initiative is merely a matter of moving the mouth and tongue in a variety of ways, presumably seeking what elicits the most favorable response from the dominant partner. The time perspective of initiative in oral sex is extremely narrow: One's decisions are merely momentary movements of one's mouth. Likewise, the range of choices and the criteria of decision are quite narrow, and the degree of planning or of high-level, responsible initiative are minimal. This is especially apparent in light of the fact that the dominant was usually the one who decided upon the sexual activity in the first place and commanded the submissive to perform it. Thus, the masochist retains an active, agentic role only in an extremely deconstructed fashion.

Other forms of masochistic initiative follow the same pattern, in which the dominant makes the plans and gives the orders, and the submissive takes the active role only with regard to carrying out these orders and making small adjustments. Thus, some masochists are told to do the housework, and they exert low-level initiative in carrying out these tasks. Or they are told to masturbate themselves, so they take a sexually active role in caressing themselves.

Masochists relinquish control and responsibility at high, meaningful levels. The self as active agent is systematically denied in masochism in all meaningful and complex respects. The self makes no decisions that involve responsibility, an extended time perspective, or integrative (constructive) thinking. But at the lowest, most deconstructed levels, masochists retain or even gain control. The self is denied as a thinking, choosing, deciding entity, but it is emphasized as an active mouth or as a functioning set of hands and feet. Just as with pain, the dynamics of control in masochism deconstruct the self—removing its broadly meaningful aspects while emphasizing it at its lowest, most minimal aspects, especially immediate physical presence.

HUMILIATION

The third essential feature of masochism is the pursuit of humiliation and embarrassment. Masochists report an impressive range and variety of humiliating experiences. Apparently, masochists and their partners expend considerable effort and imagination in devising humiliations.

It is worth repeating that the humiliation is apparently desired more strongly by the masochist than by the dominant partner, in most cases. It would be wrong to argue that the sadistic or dominant partners are imposing their desires to inflict humiliation on hapless victims. Rather, people seem to desire to be humiliated. One sign of this is the fact that many prostitutes have clients who pay them to administer verbal insults (e.g., Juliette, 1983). Prostitutes are obviously responding to a market that is already there.

The present sample of letters provides further evidence that humiliation is more important to the masochist than to the dominant partner. To examine this, one can compare the frequencies with which such activities are reported in letters by dominants as opposed to letters by submissives. If some activity is reported more frequently in one group than in the other, it is reasonable to conclude that the activity is of greater interest to that group. And, assuming that the letters report favorite experiences and fantasies, one may infer that that group *desires* that activity more than the other.

Humiliation was reported more commonly in letters written by submissives than in letters written by dominants. In particular, half the letters by male dominants made no reference to humiliation of any sort, and those who did report humiliation often used only the mildest forms, such as displaying the slave nude or making her beg. Combining male and female-authored letters, a third of the letters by dominants reported no humiliation at all. Only half that many submissives omitted humiliation entirely. The implication is that the desire for humiliation resides in the masochist rather than the dominant.

Categories and techniques of humiliation varied widely. Many masochists are apparently attracted to the embarrassment of being displayed naked for the dominant partner and even for others. Sometimes this feeling is created by having the masochist strip while others remain fully clothed. Some remarks suggest that being nude in the presence of fully dressed people creates a feeling of vulnerability and subservience. Other couples achieve this embarrassment by having the masochist adopt a revealing pose. For example, one woman was required to sit naked on top of the television set, with legs apart, while her boyfriend watched a show.

Reik (1941/1957) reported a vivid example of a "display" fantasy. "A young girl derives her pleasure mainly from the idea that she is lying naked and at full length on a long table . . . with her legs spread wide so that her vagina is distinctly visible. A man, whose face is only dimly distinguishable, stands at her feet and scrutinizes her genitals" (1941/1957, p. 236). He said that this fantasy is typical of masochists and is extremely exciting even for very bashful women. Similar observations are made by Shainess (1984), who described masochistic fantasies (or dreams) of being naked in a room full of fully dressed strangers, and so forth.

Embarrassing costumes are sometimes used instead of nudity. In particular, male masochists are sometimes humiliated by being displayed while wearing women's lingerie. Last, some couples use actions rather than poses or costumes to create embarrassment. The most common of these is apparently having to masturbate for an audience. Apparently, both men and women are curious enough to enjoy watching a member of the opposite sex masturbate, and most feel inhibited about putting on such a show, so this procedure effectively entertains the dominant while providing an exciting humiliation for the submissive.

Verbal humiliation is also quite common. One variety of verbal humiliation consists of being insulted in various ways. Another variety is being required to beg, whether for a spanking or for an orgasm. Sometimes spanking is embellished verbally by having the masochist count the strokes aloud or thank the punisher afterward.

Other masochists report humiliations that emphasize degradation, that is, lowering the person's status. Some masochists like to be treated as animals, especially dogs. They are kept on leashes and sometimes required to perform dog-like behaviors, such as fetching with their mouths, drinking from a bowl on the floor, and going around on hands and knees. Some masochists like to be treated as babies. They submit to being dressed in diapers, kept in playpens, given bottles to suck and baby toys to play with, and typically at spanked at some point.[2]

Receiving an enema is a form of humiliation that has a limited but

---

[2]There is apparently a category of adults who desire to be dressed or treated as babies, for sexual pleasure, without any other signs of masochism.

enthusiastic following. To be sure, humiliation may be only part of the appeal of enemas, for some people seem to enjoy the sensations directly. Indeed, one researcher reported that enema devotees like to experiment with different substances, ranging from wine to Perrier water (Scott, 1983).

Masochists who desire intense humiliations sometimes wish to be urinated or defecated on, with the latter being especially rare, presumably for health reasons. Scott's (1983) characterization of urination as "the ultimate insult" among masochistic practices is probably correct.

Symbolic humiliation is sometimes achieved by cuckolding the masochist, that is, having the dominant partner have sex with someone else. Male masochists in particular are sometimes drawn to the reportedly powerful humiliation of having their wives have intercourse with another man. Sometimes the humiliation is compounded by having the masochist watch the incident or even help out, such as by helping the woman dress or undress, or by cleaning up afterward. The life of Sacher-Masoch, for whom masochism is named, included a number of such incidents. He reportedly arranged assignations for his wife and helped her prepare for them, all the while suffering intense humiliations. In fact, his wives and girlfriends (he had a series of relationship, which is perhaps not surprising in view of his unusual tastes) were often reluctant to have sex with other men, and he had to pressure them into doing it. In one case Sacher-Masoch pouted for years at several "missed opportunities," especially when it was his wife who backed out. After 10 years of marriage, his wife finally accommodated him by having sex with another man in their living room while Sacher-Masoch watched from the kitchen through a keyhole. He served them wine afterward. His wife did not find the experience particularly enjoyable, let alone thrilling, but apparently Sacher-Masoch himself loved it (Cleugh, 1951).

Last, there is a relatively mild and popular category of humiliations involving symbolic insults to the face and mouth. Women masochists report being humiliated by having their male partners ejaculate on their faces. Male masochists report having the dominant women's panties stuffed in their mouths. Other masochists report being told to kiss or lick various parts of the partner's body, especially the feet and anus. And some report having to lick up sexual fluids, a practice that is usually described as having the masochist clean up after some sexual contact.

These, then, are the explicitly humiliating practices used by masochists and their partners. It must be noted that various other masochistic activities have some degree of embarrassment or humiliation about them. Several writers comment on how embarrassing and humiliating it is for an adult to receive a spanking. Additionally, it is plausible that submitting to anal penetration, or even performing oral sex, has a symbolic message of submission, at least for some individuals (e.g., see Bullough, 1976b).

What are the effects of these humiliating practices? One obvious effect is that they temporarily lower self-esteem (and public esteem). Normally, the self exerts considerable effort to bolster and increase its esteem. An endless series of research studies has demonstrated this motive in countless contexts. But the humiliation in masochism must seemingly make the maintenance of self-esteem impossible, at least for a brief period.

The humiliations of masochism probably go beyond self-esteem and attack identity itself. The systematic assault on the masochist's dignity may make it difficult to sustain the normal, everyday identity. Indeed, masochists seem deliberately to seek out actions that will be incompatible with that identity. For example, some of the practices described in research on the sex lives of powerful men seem deliberately chosen to contradict the normal, prestigious identities of these men (see Janus et al., 1977). A male U.S. senator is not supposed to dress up in women's underwear, submit to being handcuffed and spanked, and afterwards kiss a prostitute's feet or genitals. While engaged in such activities, a man would probably have considerable difficulty sustaining his identity as a senator. This may be precisely why these activities appeal to some people: These practices effectively remove the normal identity. They may be the only way the man can "turn off" being a senator.

The denial of self is apparent in the practice of having the masochist beg. In terms of social exchange, having to beg signifies that one has nothing to offer. The self is reduced to zero as a negotiator. When masochists beg, therefore, they sacrifice not only their dignity, but also their very identity as a participant in the social world. The beggar is without power or resources and therefore cannot share in a community based on social exchange.

Power, resources, and status are especially important features of the masculine identity, for men define themselves in those terms more than women. It is thus no coincidence that men are more likely than women to seek masochistic experiences that emphasize loss of status and other forms of degradation. For men, masochistic humiliation revolves around the denial of the male ego and identity.

Humiliation strikes at female identity too. The feminine fantasy of being displayed naked is quite probably something that runs contrary to the woman's normal self and dignity. As Reik (1941/1957) and others have observed, women are generally brought up to be sexually modest, to conceal their genitals and even their underwear from the view of others. To be displayed naked would thus run contrary to one's identity as a self-controlled, sexually proper, and modest woman. Likewise, being required to beg for sexual pleasure would run directly counter to the way that women are typically socialized in our society.

The emotional effects of humiliation probably have some mental effects that may resemble those of pain—that is, they prevent awareness of self in broadly meaningful terms, while promoting an acute awareness of self in the immediate present. Intense humiliations and embarrassments may have the capacity to focus the mind at low levels and impair abstract, symbolic thought. Being the center of attention is alone enough to impair one's mental processes. Research has shown, for example, that being the token male in a group of females (or being the token female in a group of males) makes the person less able to recall the discussion, presumably because the attention to self impairs cognitive processing (e.g., Lord & Saenz, 1985).

To apply this to masochism, consider the woman who is lying naked on a table while one or two well-dressed men look at her genitals. Her capacity for abstract, symbolic, or long-range thought would probably be impaired. Her mind would probably become focused on her exposure and embarrassment. Thus, humiliation and embarrassment may focus the mind here and now, just as effectively as pain. Stripping the body of clothes symbolically strips the self of meaning, and her awareness is drawn to the most deconstructed aspect of self: the immediate, mere presence of her naked body.

Perhaps the most direct evidence that humiliation involves denial of identity is the frequent assimilation of masochist to slave. *Slave* was the most common term for masochists in my sample, and nearly all other sources report the same. Submissives define their roles as slavery.

The inherent and original meaning of slavery is *social death,* that is, the death of the persons' social identity (Patterson, 1982). Slavery originated, in ancient civilization, as a substitute for being killed in war. Becoming a slave was originally a symbolic replacement for physical death. Socially, slaves have almost always been treated as if they were dead or nonexistent. The slave is treated as someone without family ties, without social rank or status, without human rights, without opinions or beliefs or values, without ideology, without ancestors, and so forth. When a free person becomes enslaved, that person's social identity comes to an abrupt end. Even the 19th-century American slaveholders tended to regard (and treat) their slaves as less than fully human. In short, the essential meaning of slavery is *loss of personhood.*

The masochist's desire to be a slave must be understood as a desire for the symbolism of slavery. This symbolism is precisely the removal of one's permanent social identity and even of one's full-fledged membership in the human race. Slavery nullifies identity. The masochist's wish to be a slave is a desire for the removal of the social self.

Thus far, we have emphasized how masochistic humiliation makes high-level self-awareness impossible. By doing things that are grossly incompatible with one's normal identity, the individual makes it impossible to be aware of self in normal terms. But masochistic humiliation, like pain and loss of control, does also foster self-awareness at the lowest, most deconstructed levels. This is apparent in several ways.

First, some masochists report pride in their submission. They say they are proud of being good slaves or of being slaves to an important or desirable dominant partner. They may take pride in pleasing the partner. As noted earlier, some masochists take pride in how much pain or humilation they can accept (e.g., Reik, 1941/1957, p. 134, on "masochistic tests"; also Scott, 1983, and Janus et al., 1977). Thus, although the esteem connected with the normal identity is systematically and thoroughly undermined, there is a limited possibility for low-level esteem as a good slave.

Likewise, the embarrassed reaction to humiliating events may engender a deconstructed awareness of self. The woman who is displayed bound and naked on the dining table may be unable to think of herself as an upper middle-class, educated woman, with career and family roles. But she is probably quite aware of herself as a set of genitals to be viewed and desired by males. Her identity as a civilized, social being is removed, but her identity as a sex object is affirmed.

Thus, the self is denied and removed at high levels, but it is strengthened and focused at low levels. The dignified, respected, normal identity is deconstructed as the person performs actions that are incompatible with it. Yet the masochist is made aware of self as a body, as a nonperson, as a mere slave or sex object.

CONCLUSION

Despite the wide range and variety of masochistic practices, there are only a few main themes, and these all seem to involve the self in the same ways. In each case, it appears that the self is deconstructed: It is denied or removed from awareness at meaningful, high levels, while it is enforced and promoted at low levels.

The psychological effects of pain include a re-focusing of awareness on the here and now. Masochistic pain temporarily blots out the broader concerns and involvements that define the self, specifically those that extend across time and involve symbolic meanings and abstract relationship. Awareness is focused on the self as a physical body—as an object existing at the present moment and immediate location, experiencing certain immediate sensations. Thus, the complex, long-range, contextualized, symbolic identity is removed from awareness and replaced with a deconstructed awareness of self as a physical body.

Masochism involves relinquishing control, which is carried out through physical restraint (bondage) as well as through commands and rules. All initiative, responsibility, autonomy, and choice are prevented. The self as an active agent is thus denied in masochism, at least at high levels. Some minimal amounts of control and agency are left to the masochistic self, such as in initiating one's body movements while carrying out the dominant's commands, or as in performing oral sex. The self is reduced from responsible planner and decision maker to hands, feet, and mouth. Thus, the denial of control affects the complex, long-range, symbolic self but does not apply to the lowest levels of self, as a physical body.

Last, humiliation prevents the self from maintaining its esteem. The humiliating actions are deliberately chosen to be so incompatible with the person's normal identity that it probably becomes impossible for the masochist to continue to think of him or herself in normal terms during the masochistic episode. On the other hand, some limited amount of esteem and respect is available to the masochist at low levels, such as in being a "good slave" or performing menial duties effectively. The mental effects of humilation may likewise focus attention on the self as a physical body or sex object. Thus, humiliation too attacks the complex, long-range, symbolic identity but affirms and emphasizes the self in low-level, physical terms.

There are perhaps other meanings and effects to these masochistic practices. Submitting to pain may be a way of expressing love and submission to one's partner. Regarding oneself as guilty could contribute to a desire for punishment, to a willingness to relinquish autonomy and responsibility, and to acceptance of humiliation. Still, the deconstruction of meaningful aspects of self appears to be constant, pervasive theme in masochistic practices.

Chapter Five
Satisfactions of Masochism

This chapter explores what appeals to masochists about the practices described in the previous chapter. Clearly, masochists get something out of their activities, for they keep coming back for more. What is the nature of that appeal, and what are its roots?

Obviously, one satisfying feature of masochistic activity is sexual pleasure. Although masochists do not always have intercourse with their partners, they do usually have some form of sex. Even professional dominants, who often deny that they are prostitutes because they do not have sex with their clients, typically have the man masturbate himself at the end of the session (Scott, 1983). The relation of masochism to sexuality is explored in detail in Chapter 6. This chapter focuses more generally on the satisfactions and attractions of masochism.

BURDEN OF SELFHOOD

As we saw in the previous chapter, many masochistic practices seem to deny and remove high-level self-awareness. Why would anyone want to escape from self? In particular, modern American society is generally regarded as narcissistic and self-seeking, with endless interest in discovering and fulfilling and cultivating the self (e.g., Baumeister, 1986; Lasch, 1978). It seems especially ironic to suggest that these self-oriented individuals would ever want to escape themselves.

But the modern tyranny of self can become burdensome and oppressive. The pervasive need to cultivate, promote, and assert the self can become too much. People may feel impelled to act as if their selves were marvelous and flawless, but many experiences contradict this view. For example, the man who is always reluctant to admit that he is wrong *must* suspect that occasionally he is in error. At such times, a self-oriented person may become especially uncomfortable, for it is difficult to sustain a positive attitude toward the self when life presents you with evidence of your inadequacy, incompetence, or culpability.

The various factors contributing to the burden of selfhood deserve closer inspection.

Self-Awareness as Unpleasant

There is ample evidence that sometimes people find it unpleasant to be aware of themselves and so desire to escape from self-awareness. When social psychologists first began to study self-awareness, they came to the conclusion that self-awareness is generally unpleasant (Duval & Wicklund, 1972). Later evidence modified and toned down this view, suggesting that self-awareness is sometimes pleasant and sometimes unpleasant (e.g., Carver & Scheier, 1981). There are indeed some circumstances in which people seek out and enjoy self-awareness. Still, it is clear that there are times when being aware of oneself is quite aversive.

One type of occasion that affects self-awareness is receiving an evaluation. After receiving a bad evaluation, people find self-awareness unpleasant and prefer to avoid it or prevent it (Duval & Wicklund, 1972). In one experiment, for example, researchers had people take a test of creativity and intelligence, and then they randomly gave the people either a good evaluation or a bad one. After receiving the evaluation, each person was left alone in a room that had a large mirror directly in front of the person. The researchers secretly timed how long the individual remained in the room. The mirror is a cue that focuses attention on the self, so it is reasonable to infer that people who sit by a mirror for a long time do not mind attending to themselves.

In that experiment, it was found that people exited the room with the mirror more quickly if they had received a bad evaluation rather than a good one. Other people were put through the same procedure except that there was no mirror in the room. These people stayed in the room the same amount of time after getting a bad evaluation as after getting a good one. Thus, it is not simply that getting a bad evaluation makes the person want to leave faster; rather, it makes people want to get away from a mirror faster. The implication is that getting a bad evaluation made people think of themselves in an unpleasant fashion, so they wanted to escape from self-awareness. They did not want to sit in front of a mirror, for the mirror drew their attention to themselves, reminding them of the recent failure.

In another study, people were led to believe that they were inadequate on an important dimension of personality, namely self-expression (Steenbarger & Aderman, 1979). Half of them, selected at random, were led to believe that they could improve and correct this flaw in themselves, whereas the rest were led to think that the flaw was permanent and no improvement was to be expected. Again, these people were left alone in a room lined with mirrors to see how quickly they would leave. The people who thought their personal inadequacy was permanent were the quickest to leave the mirror-lined room. It seems probable that these people felt worse about themselves than people who believed their flaws could be corrected or improved. Thus, again, people wanted to escape from self-awareness when they felt bad about themselves.

In yet another study, people were exposed to an interpersonal rejection or putdown (Gibbons & Wicklund, 1976). Male subjects met an attractive woman who was in fact a confederate working with the researchers. The attractive woman observed the subject and then communicated her "first impression" to him. Half the subjects, chosen at random, received rejecting and unfavorable evaluations. That is, she told the man that he had made a very poor impression on her and that she did not consider him attractive. These men were much more inclined to avoid self-attention than other men (who received a favorable evaluation from the woman).

In this study of putdown and rejection, a different technique was used for measuring avoidance of self-awareness. After being either rejected or flattered by the woman, each man was set to listening to some tapes for 12 minutes. He was able to switch channels on the tape machine. On one channel was a recording (made earlier) of his own voice; on the other channel was a recording of someone else's voice. Listening to your own voice tends to make you self-conscious. The researchers found that the men who were flattered by the woman preferred to listen to their own voices. But the men who had been rejected and mildly insulted by her preferred to listen to a stranger's voice rather than their own.

Performing actions that contradict one's beliefs is another factor that makes people dislike and avoid self-awareness (Greenberg & Musham, 1981). In one experiment, people performed counterattitudinal behavior by reading aloud attitude statements that contradicted their personal beliefs. For example, if the person was opposed to capital punishment, he or she might be asked to read statements saying "The death penalty should be used for serious crimes," and "Stricter punishments, including the death penalty, should be enforced." Other people, in a control condition, read statements that were neutral or consistent with their attitudes.

When subjects finished reading these statements, they were shown (individually) into a room with two chairs arranged back-to-back. One chair faced a mirror, and the other faced away from the mirror. The main measure of interest was which chair the subject chose. The one facing the mirror would presumably make the person self-aware, whereas the other seat would not draw the person's attention to him or herself.

People who had read statements consistent with their beliefs were quite willing to sit facing the mirror. But people who had made statements that contradicted their personal attitudes preferred the chair facing away from the mirrors. The implication is that people wanted to avoid being aware of themselves after performing inconsistent, counterattitudinal acts. People do not want to look at themselves in the mirror after doing things contrary to their attitudes. Contradicting one's basic beliefs makes self-awareness aversive.

All of these experiments have in common the fact that the person experiences a failure to live up to his or her goals and ideals. Indeed, everyday life probably confronts most people with such experiences from time to time. Hardly anyone can live up to his or her highest standards at all times. If most people periodically fail to meet their goals and ideals, then most people probably find self-awareness unpleasant now and then (Wicklund, 1975a).

Masochism is not the only way people have of escaping from self-awareness. Research by Jay Hull and his associates has indicated that alcohol use impairs the mind's capacity to focus on itself. Thus, alcohol seems to function as a viable means of escaping the self. In particular, people seem to drink more alcohol after experiencing failure, after experiencing some forms of stress that "make you feel like two cents," and when undergoing major life changes that reflect unfavorably on the self, than at other times (e.g., Hull, 1981; also Hull & Young, 1983; Hull, Young, & Jouriles, 1986). Other theorists have suggested that smoking cigarettes may function as a way of distracting one's attention away from oneself (Wicklund, 1975b; see also Liebling, Seiler, & Shaver, 1974).

Thus, there is plenty of evidence to show that being aware of yourself can be unpleasant at times, so people sometimes desire to escape from self-awareness.[1] If masochism revolves around the desire to escape from self-awareness, it is not alone. Masochism may be one unusual way of doing what many people do in other ways, namely responding to certain conditions by escaping the self.

Pressures and Responsibilities

Having to make many choices and decisions is stressful. Being required to make many choices or responses causes ulcers, even in rats (Weiss,

---

[1]Most of this research has not kept any distinction between high and low levels of self-awareness, but it is apparent that higher, more meaningful levels are the ones involved. Evaluations of one's personality or global interpersonal attractiveness are important aspects of self, persisting over time and affecting a wide range of concerns and activities.

1971a, 1971b). Although people prefer to have control, a demand for many and frequent decisions, especially under pressure or uncertainty, can cause fatigue and stress.

A recent study explored what people like least about their sex roles (Spence & Sawin, 1984). Men's greatest complaints about being men were the occupational and competitive demands, particularly the pressures to be successful and the weight of responsibility. Thus, many men may well desire occasional relief or escape from these pressures and responsibilities.

A successful self in particular can become the focus of others' high expectations, which can also be burdensome. It is stressful to have to live up to the expectations of others, especially when these expectations are high. When other people expect you to continue to succeed and excel, you may begin to feel stressful pressure, leading to poor performance as well as emotional turmoil and depression (e.g., Baumeister, Hamilton, & Tice, 1985; Baumeister & Steinhilber, 1984; Berglas, 1986; Seta & Hassan, 1980).

Levels of thinking are also involved in responses to pressure. One recent study began by selecting people who typically think at high levels (Pennebaker, in press; Pennebaker, Hughes, & O'Heeron, 1987). These people were then individually exposed to an unpleasant stressor, namely repeated blasts of loud noise. By random assignment, half the people were given some control over how much noise they received, whereas others had no control. Although control has generally been shown to be preferable in reducing stress, this study showed some undesirable side effects of having control. The people who had control ended up reporting more unpleasant feelings than the others. They also continued to think at high levels, unlike the others. The implication is that people tend to escape from unpleasant, stressful experiences by moving to low-level thinking—but having control makes that escape impossible.

This experiment sheds light on masochism, for it suggests that control may often go with bad feelings and high-level awareness. The masochistic solution is to relinquish control, allowing the escape to low levels of awareness. It is not surprising that people with many responsibilities and pressures might desire such an escape, at least temporarily.

There is some evidence that masochistic desires are stimulated by having to maintain a high level of personal esteem and control in the face of daily threats. A research study on powerful, successful male politicians found their daily lives to involve a constant struggle to sustain a terrifically favorable public image of self in front of all others, including many political opponents who may be doing their best to attack and undermine one's good image (Janus et al., 1977). The researchers found that a surprisingly large number of these men go to prostitutes to be dominated. It seems likely that the appeal of masochism to these men is that it provides a powerful, temporary escape from the constant demands for feeding and supporting their personal and professional egotism.

Conclusion

On both theoretical and empirical grounds, there is ample reason to think that people sometimes want to escape from self-awareness. Two categories of people are particularly relevant and may be "at risk" for masochism. First, people who feel bad about themselves may desire relief from self-awareness, for the more they focus on themselves, the worse they are likely to feel.

Second, people with demanding, responsible jobs, and those who frequently must assert their power or defend their esteem, may desire occasional relief from these pressures. The need to sustain high levels of esteem and control (that is, agency or responsibility) probably contributes most heavily to the burden of self. And those with the heaviest burdens may well be inclined toward the strongest modes of escape—including masochism. There is consistent, if never entirely solid, evidence that people with the most demanding jobs and roles (and therefore with the most burdensome selves) furnish a disproportionately high number of masochists (again, Janus et al., 1977; Scott, 1983; Smith & Cox, 1983). Masochism does not reflect their habitual attitude toward life. Rather, it represents a break, a temporary escape. As one woman told me, "I don't care to be dominated anywhere except in bed."

On the other hand, most people feel such pressures occasionally, and nearly everyone feels bad about him or herself once in a while. It is thus plausible that escapes such as masochism (and many others, including alcohol use) would potentially have a wide appeal.

GUILT

Many theorists have made guilt a central feature in their accounts of masochism. Freud thought that "moral masochism" was a desire for punishment that arose from a feeling of guilt. Stekel (1953) believed that guilt feelings were what converted aggressive, sadistic desires into masochistic ones. In contrast, recent treatments of masochism have often made few or no references to guilt; guilt is especially absent from treatments based on empirical data (e.g., Greene & Greene, 1974; Scott, 1983; Weinberg & Kamel, 1983). These studies give the impression that guilt is often a minor or unimportant factor in masochism.

Because the guilt hypothesis can be formulated in a variety of ways and is difficult to evaluate, it comes up repeatedly in our examination of masochism. In the preceding chapter, we considered the hypothesis that masochists use pain as punishment for guilt. It became clear that many masochists do not use pain in this way, but some of them do. The next chapter takes a close look at sex guilt. The question that concerns us in this chapter is whether relief from guilt forms one of the principal forms of satisfaction in masochism.

Pervasiveness of Guilt

How much do people actually feel guilty? This is hard to establish. Probably most people occasionally do things they regret or feel in retrospect were wrong. People may look back on some of their actions and feel these were unjustified, and so some guilt may ensue. Some people clearly suffer more than others from such feelings. For example, some people seem to be experts at rationalization, and others maintain strict control so as not to do anything they might feel guilty about (cf. Weinberger, Schwartz, & Davidson, 1979). Neither of those groups is likely to feel much guilt.

Existentialists have proposed that a certain amount of guilt is an inevitable part of the human condition. Guilt is part of life. This type of guilt, called *ontological guilt,* refers to the dismay one feels for not fulfilling one's potential, for not taking advantage of one's opportunities. Because life is finite, one can only do so many things, and so one must pass up many others. You can only marry one person at a time, you can only have one or two jobs at a time, and you probably cannot cultivate all your talents and abilities to the utmost. So you end up with some guilt over the opportunities and possibilities that you neglected (Heidegger, 1927).

Everyday forms of guilt, like ontological guilt, are widespread. It may well be that powerful, responsible people have the largest share of such guilt, which would be consistent with the relatively high frequency of masochism among such people. Having a great deal of power and influence may well involve making some decisions that will affect other people, for better or worse. Military commanders have to give commands knowing they are sending some soldiers to their deaths. Managers cannot promote everyone, and when money is tight they may have to lay off some workers. Administrators have only limited resources to divide up, and so not everyone can get everything he or she deserves. People in such powerful positions might plausibly feel some guilt and regret about the consequences of their actions.

Effects of Guilt

Social psychology has not learned a great deal about guilt. There is little evidence to suggest that guilt makes people want to be punished. But there is not much evidence in general about the effects of guilt.

One established fact about guilt is that it increases helpful, altruistic motivations. That is, people who feel guilty are more likely to help someone at the next opportunity than are people who do not feel guilty. In various experiments, people who cause harm or inconvenience to someone show significant increases in the amount and frequency of help they give. People who tell a lie, who knock over a carefully sorted box of index cards for another student's thesis, who damage an expensive machine, or who cheat on a test become helpful (Freedman, 1970).

It is important to note that guilt makes people more willing to help anyone, not just the victim of their transgression. After doing something wrong, a person will feel guilty, and he or she will be more likely to help the person who was harmed, or someone who merely knows about the guilt—or even someone who does not know anything about what the person did. Guilt engenders a general attitude of all-purpose helpfulness.

The accepted explanation for these findings is that people commit positive acts of helping in order to make themselves feel better. Doing a good deed apparently relieves feelings of guilt. It is not simply a matter of making amends for what they have done wrong, but rather of making themselves feel better about themselves. Thus, the effects of guilt seem to emphasize the person's inner, emotional state.

Further evidence for this conclusion comes from studies showing that relief of guilt feelings removes the urge to help. In one study, Catholics were asked for charity donations either before or after attending a church ritual designed to remove guilt (confession). People were more generous before confession than afterwards (Harris, Benson, & Hall, 1975; see Rosenhan et al., 1981). Confessing to a researcher likewise eliminated the generosity caused by guilt (Regan, 1971; see also Freedman, 1970). Guilt makes people helpful only as long as they feel guilty.

Some theorists have suggested that masochists submit to punishment so that afterward they can go out and do things that would otherwise promote guilt. In this scheme, masochism involves a kind of punishment in advance, and it holds that punishment makes people more willing to do antisocial or morally wrong acts. This theory seems illogical and contrary to evidence. Punishment does not generally make people feel like doing things that are morally wrong. For example, a sound spanking or other punishment makes children behave better, not worse, for a period afterward. Likewise, most drivers drive more slowly after getting a speeding ticket.

Retaliatory impulses are the closest thing to the idea that punishment makes people behave in antisocial or wrongful ways. After being punished unjustly, a person might feel angry enough to try to get even, even by doing something wrong or objectionable. But this does not appear to apply to masochism. Masochists almost never report getting up and retaliating for the spankings they receive. In fact, they almost never describe them as unjust. In many cases, especially those written by males, justice is simply ignored as if it were totally irrelevant to the masochistic drama. When masochists do mention justice as a consideration, they almost always describe their spankings and chastisements as well deserved. So the idea of retaliation may be dismissed as irrelevant to masochism.

Action identification theory (Vallacher & Wegner, 1985, 1987) provides a possible explanation of what is wrong with the theory that masochism relieves guilt in advance. Pain and other punishments bring awareness down to low levels. These might have some value for escaping from high-level thoughts in which one perceives oneself as wrong, inadequate, or guilty. But the last thing the person would want to do is to return after the punishment to a high-level awareness of his or her actions as wrong. To do something immoral or antisocial after punishment would draw one's attention to the objectionable features of one's actions and probably make one feel bad about oneself. Instead, it seems far more plausible (and more consistent with common observations) to expect that people want to feel good about themselves after punishment, so they will tend to perform actions that are morally good and socially valued.

Thus, the theory of advance punishment is somewhat implausible in principle, and there is little evidence that it is true. Being punished does not seem to make people feel that they are then entitled to go do something wrong.

It is worth noting that people do seem to see value in suffering in advance, unlike advance punishment. People seem to believe that they are going to get a fixed quota of suffering, so if they choose to suffer now they will suffer less in the future. In one experiment, people administered electric shocks to themselves, and this led them to expect more luck and success in the future than a control group (Curtis, Smith, & Moore, 1984). In another study, some people were led to expect an uncertain amount of suffering in the future, and then they were allowed to choose how much they would suffer in the present (by electric shock). These people chose to suffer more in the present than control groups, presumably because they felt that suffering now would reduce future suffering.

Thus, the belief that current suffering may be effective at warding off future suffering is implicit in some human behavior, even though it is of course a fallacy. Historical evidence shows similar patterns. During the Middle Ages, when conditions threatened to become extremely bad, sects of "flagellants" appeared. These people wandered from town to town, whipping themselves and each other. They called on God to be satisfied with their current suffering and ease up on the world, that is, reduce the level of future calamities (Eliade, 1985).

But suffering in advance does not seem to have any necessary or clear relation to guilt. The theory that punishment creates relief in advance from guilt has little to support it.

What about the view that guilt makes people want to be punished? There is little direct evidence behind it. Most criminals clearly try to evade capture and imprisonment. In other words, people who are quite guilty do not show any attraction to be punished. But perhaps they are exceptional.

A few observers have suggested that masochistic males feel guilty about dominating others, especially women, in their daily lives, so they accept symbolic punishment in masochism (e.g., Scott, 1983; Smith & Cox, 1983). It is plausible that some men may feel guilty about dominating and exploiting women, for men have dominated and exploited women for centuries. The reverse is far less plausible, however. Women would not be attracted to masochism as punishment for dominating and exploiting men, for they have not generally had the opportunity to do so.

There are two obvious problems with this theory. First, men have dominated women throughout history, but male masochism is not apparent throughout history (recall the detailed evidence in chapter 3). If anything, modern men enjoy less of a superior status over modern women than men at many other points in history, yet they are more masochistic, so this historical evidence seems contradict the explanation that superior status makes men masochistic. Second, if guilt arises from superior status and exploitation, then one must assume that guilt is a more important factor in male masochism than in female masochism, but the reverse appears to be true. As already noted, there is more overt evidence of guilt in female masochism.

Some masochists do make reference to guilt, but as we have seen, these references do not run very deep. Masochists describe being punished for failing to do housework or for breaking their diets. It is plausible, however, that these are merely disguised versions of underlying, more substantial guilt feelings. It could be that masochists carry around strong feelings of guilt and desire masochistic activities as punishment. Perhaps they do not want the true nature of their guilt mentioned during the session. This idea too seems to fit the escape hypothesis best. The person desires to do something that may address a disguised version of his or her guilt feelings, leaving the underlying issues untouched.

Thus far, we have considered the evidence that would suggest that guilt is an important factor in masochism. The evidence is far from conclusive. Some versions of the guilt theory are clearly wrong, and others are simply hard to evaluate. Indeed, if one takes the Freudian view that it is unconscious guilt that motivates masochism, one must despair of ever drawing definite conclusions. The hypothesis of unconscious guilt seems almost impossible to prove or disprove.

The best one can say is that some (but not all) masochists do include references to guilt in their activities, but these references are generally superficial and casual. Genuine, sincere guilt about one's activities in everyday life rarely seems to intrude into masochistic scenes. Masochists appear to take guilt rather lightly.

Before we can come to any conclusion, however, it is probably necessary to examine the different ways that masochism might involve or relieve guilt.

Expiation, Atonement, or Escape?

There are three ways to relieve guilt, and these must be kept separate in answering the question of whether masochism relieves guilt. These three ways can be described as the expiation hypothesis, the atonement hypothesis, and the escape hypothesis.

Expiation means *removing* the guilt. An example of expiation would be as follows. Suppose you borrow a friend's softball bat and break it, and then you buy a new bat for your friend. There is no further reason for you to feel guilty. You have completely righted the wrong you committed, and in fact your friend is probably even better off than before, for he now has a new bat. Expiation works very well at relieving guilt. It seems very implausible, however, that masochism works by expiation. Enacting sexual fantasies has very little capacity to undo social or personal wrongs.

Atonement means paying for the guilt by one's suffering. The prison system furnishes a good example of atonement. Going to jail does not right the wrong the person committed, but society accepts the suffering of imprisonment as a kind of equivalent payment. The debt of guilt is thus paid, although the guilt is not removed as in expiation. A murderer, for example, may still be considered guilty of murder even after he has atoned for his crime by spending time in jail.

Atonement is a plausible model for masochistic punishment. Presumably, the person might feel guilty about some recent misdeeds, so the person submits to punishment by a dominant partner, and this punishment is symbolic payment (atonement) for the misdeeds. At the superficial level, many masochistic scenes involve atonement, for the masochist is punished for minor infractions. On the other hand, often the infractions are often merely a pretext for the spanking.

The escape hypothesis holds that masochism does not really address the guilt but merely takes the person's mind off of guilty feelings. An example of escape would be a case in which someone does something wrong and feels bad about it, so he or she engages in some distracting activity and forgets about the guilty feelings. The guilt is not changed or corrected, but the person's emotional state is relieved of the guilt.

Earlier, we noted evidence that actual guilt motivates people to do good deeds for anyone, not just their victims, which suggested that the main effect of guilt is the desire to change one's emotional state. This evidence seems most consistent with the escape hypothesis. Whether guilt makes people desire punishment as atonement is in doubt, but it is clear that guilt makes people desire to escape their guilty feelings.

The escape hypothesis might best explain the attraction of masochism to individuals who feel guilty about things they cannot do much about. We have already discussed the fact that powerful, responsible positions are probably accompanied by a certain, inevitable amount of guilt. A supervisor, for example, may have to fire some of his workers because the company is losing money. He probably feels guilty about depriving the workers of their jobs and livelihoods, but there is really nothing he can do about it, nor has he really done anything immoral or unjust. Such a person might desire something to relieve his feelings of guilt. Genuine atonement or expiation would not be necessary—it is only a matter of making him feel better. The person wants something to change his or her emotional state, without necessarily changing the situation. Consuming a liberal dose of alcohol might be one common solution to this sort of problem. Masochistic submission might be another.

Another sort of evidence would be whether the dominant or the submissive makes any mention of the masochist's wrongs during the session. If masochism is to function as atonement, one would expect some clear discussion of the persons's wrongs or misdeeds. In other words, if you are to be punished as a way of atoning for certain acts, these acts would presumably be mentioned and even figure prominently in the punishment session.

But this does not seem to happen. Masochists and their partners make very few references to major, serious, or actual guilt during their activities. Indeed, they seem not to want to be reminded or their true misdeeds, other than breaking their diet or committing some other minor domestic offense. If real or major guilt is involved in masochism, it is kept concealed and disguised. This too fits the escape hypothesis best.

Conclusion

We have considered several plausible ways that masochism could involve relief from guilt. In general, the evidence for the role of guilt in masochism is weak and sometimes it indicates that guilt plays little or no role.

The expiation hypothesis holds that masochism rectifies social or personal wrongs. This seems highly implausible. The atonement hypothesis holds that the masochist feels he or she pays for past misdeeds by suffering punishment. This could in principle be true, but evidence does not support it very strongly. Masochists sometimes submit to punishment for minor offenses, but these are hardly likely to produce substantial feelings of guilt in most cases. Atonement may be a superficial aspect of masochism, but it is not likely to be one of the major forms of masochistic satisfaction.

The escape hypothesis holds that masochism enables the person to forget about his or her past misdeeds and to stop feeling guilty. This hypothesis is quite plausible and it fits some of the evidence about masochism. Still, this version of the guilt theory can be subsumed under the broader heading of escape from self. Masochists want to escape from self-awareness for various reasons, one of which may be feelings of guilt.

Thus, the theory that masochism is motivated by guilt feelings seems most plausible when it overlaps with the theory of escape from self-awareness. Guilt may contribute substantially to the burden of selfhood, which the masochist wants to escape. Apart from that, however, guilt adds little to our understanding of masochism.

ESCAPE AND ECSTASY

We have seen that masochistic activities remove the high-level awareness of self. Why is that appealing or enjoyable? The masochistic satisfaction of losing self-awareness can be interpreted in two ways, either positively or negatively. Negatively, it is a relief to be freed from the burden of self. Positively, it may well be that the loss of self-awareness is a direct, powerful source of pleasure.

First, consider the negative satisfaction of losing self-awareness. At times, people find high-level self-awareness to be unpleasant, burdensome, stressful, or aversive. They may therefore desire to escape or avoid it. Various feelings of anxiety are associated with highly meaningful self-awareness. There is anxiety over being inadequate, as signified by failure or rejection. There is anxiety in guilt, as when one feels bad about past actions or their consequences. There is social anxiety, such as in the endless concern with the opinions of others and the need to present oneself in a highly favorable light.

Masochism effectively removes high-level self-awareness, freeing the person from the various anxieties that accompany the self. This relief alone could account for the appeal of masochistic escape. Masochism is probably among the most powerful techniques for removing high-level self-awareness.

Now consider the positive side. Could it be that losing oneself creates a strongly pleasant subjective state? Some evidence suggests that it does. The usual name for the pleasure created by loss of self-awareness is *ecstasy*. The word "ecstasy" derives from Greek roots meaning roughly "to stand outside of oneself," or outside of one's mind. Ecstatic experiences, strictly defined, are those in which the individual transcends his or her normal limits and ceases to be aware of self in ordinary terms.

The most commonly described form of ecstasy is the one that occurs during peak religious experiences. Eastern, Middle Eastern, and Western mysticisms all refer to various moments of transcendent bliss. These are not easily achieved; years of contemplation and mental training may be required. But they are generally described as powerfully pleasant. At such moments, the fortunate individual comes to regard the normal self as a tiny shell, in contrast with the immediate feeling of expansion and oneness. Western mystics tend to speak of mystical experiences as merging with God or as an infusion of bliss from God. Eastern mystics tend to speak of merging with a universal oneness, of discovering the true nature of mind and consciousness, or of overcoming the illusion that there are separate selves. Whatever the metaphor, the experience itself indicates that loss of self-awareness is directly associated with intense bliss.

Some people describe passionate love as ecstatic. In principle, one merges with one's beloved, ceasing to feel like two separate selves. It is hard to get reliable data on this, but if this description is accurate and valid, then love too provides ecstasy—bliss through escape from self.

Theorists have puzzled over the nature of aesthetic pleasure for centuries. It is hard to say why people enjoy beauty, for there is usually no practical advantage in appreciating beauty. (Indeed, Kant, 1790/1968, used the lack of practical advantage as the defining criterion of aesthetic pleasure.) The perception itself seems to furnish the pleasure. One model for this pleasure is ecstasy. That is, the person appreciating a beautiful work of art is somehow drawn out of his or her self and merges in some way with the art work. Many theorists have commented on how aesthetic pleasure seems to require some form of loss of self-awareness. A detached, objective attitude prevents full appreciation.

In general, then, there is some plausibility to the idea of ecstasy. Removal of self-awareness may be a source of direct, intense pleasure. Whether this is involved in masochism remains unclear. Until the psychology of ecstasy is based on clearer concepts with more reliable ways of measuring and verifying them, it will have to remain a matter for mere speculation.

THERAPEUTIC EFFECTS

Some have argued that masochism is therapeutic or beneficial. It is supposed to have favorable effects on mental health. Perhaps the strongest exposition of this view has been provided by Cowan (1982). She argued that masochism improves self-knowledge, among other benefits. Precisely what sorts of self-knowledge are provided by masochism she did not say. She argued that self-knowledge often hurts, so being hurt may promote self-knowledge (p. 24; obviously a non sequitur). She proposed that masochism teaches the "deeper meaning" of suffering (p. 41), although she failed to specify what that meaning is.

More important, Cowan suggested that masochistic suffering can be beneficial in that it helps the person to let go of "old, worn-out self-images and attitudes" (p. 50). She said masochism helps the person get rid of "old ego-constructs" that are presumably obsolete (p. 50). Apparently she thinks that masochism facilitates a process of personal growth and change.

The idea that masochism is therapeutic has also been used by masochists to explain and justify their activities. For example, one woman claimed that her own participation in masochism enabled her to learn more about herself and to lose her fears of violence (Lucy, 1982, pp. 34–35). The woman also suggested that after she began participating in S&M, her level of anxiety decreased, she began to feel better about sex, and she became able to communicate better in her intimate relationships (pp. 35–37). Another account described masochistic submission as "a healing process" and claimed that "A good scene doesn't end with orgasm—it ends with catharsis" (Califia, 1982, p. 134).

One must remain somewhat skeptical in reading these first-person accounts. Masochism is a deviant, stigmatized activity, and people who like it may feel a need to justify their activities as beneficial. Claiming that masochism is therapeutic may be a powerful way of justifying it (cf. Weeks, 1985), but such justifications might be mere rationalizations. Still, the alleged therapeutic benefits of masochism deserve consideration. Apparently, the two main benefits claimed for masochism are emotional catharsis and improved self-knowledge. Is there any evidence to support these claims? Unfortunately, not much. It is troubling that no one explains precisely what is learned from masochism. In my sample, the only self-knowledge to arise from masochistic experiences was the knowledge that one enjoys masochism. This is an insight of dubious therapeutic value, and even if there is some value it is only learned once, so no claims could be made for ongoing or repeated therapeutic benefits.

It is difficult to imagine how it is that being tied up, spanked, and insulted can cause people to understand themselves better. Again, perhaps people learn that they can enjoy a new form of deviant sex, but there seems to be little beyond that to promise improvements in self-knowledge. Writers in my sample claimed satisfaction, pleasure, and even personal fulfillment, all of which are plausible effects of masochism. But they did not claim to have learned anything about themselves, other than that they enjoyed masochistic sex.

Another objection to this view is that insight and catharsis are not generally considered sufficient for therapeutic improvement. It is doubtful that prolonged participation in masochistic sex games could by itself lead to any long-term improvements in mental health.

Escaping the self is not completely different from healing the self, so there may be some overlap between the escape theory I have proposed and the therapeutic theory. Both theories say that masochism removes some troubling or bothersome features of the self. Both views explain why people might turn to masochism when they feel guilty, overburdened, stressed, or dissatisfied with themselves.

The main difference between the therapy hypothesis and the escape hypothesis is in their aftereffects. A therapeutic effect is a lasting transformation, whereas an escape is a temporary distraction. Therapy heals you, which means that it changes you in some important way. Escape enables you to forget, but basically you remain unchanged. The two theories therefore make different predictions about what follows after the first one or two masochistic episodes.

A useful analogy would contrast medicine with narcotics. The first is therapeutic, the second is an escape. With medicine, you take it, you get better, and then you stop staking it. With a narcotic, you take it, you feel better, and when it wears off you soon feel like taking it again. So if masochism cures and transforms the self, as the therapy hypothesis entails, then one might expect that the individual would soon cease feeling masochistic desires after having a few such experiences. On the other hand, if masochism is merely an escape, it may follow the pattern of narcotic use: Initial or powerful experiences would be likely to lead to the desire for more such experiences, possibly even progressively stronger ones.

Most of the evidence about patterns of masochistic behavior supports the escape theory rather than the therapy theory. There is almost nothing to suggest that masochistic experiences bring about some healing transformation that ends the need for such "therapy." Instead, the usual pattern seems to be that masochists increase their interest and participation in sexual submission. Consider some of the evidence.

One major survey asked masochists how they felt after their first masochistic experience. The most common response, reported by 85% of the respondents, was a desire to do it again (Spengler, 1977).

Accounts and observations of people's encounters with masochism rarely indicate that the person experienced some therapeutic effect that ended the need for masochistic activity. Instead, most report patterns of escalating involvement (e.g., Califia, 1983; Kamel, 1983; Lee, 1983; Scott, 1983). In other words, after a first experience masochists want to do it more and more often, and often they move toward increasingly intense submissive experiences. They seek longer and harder spankings, greater humiliations, stronger and more elaborate bondage. This pattern of escalation resembles narcotic use much more than it resembles the effects of medicine.

In my sample, 89% of the letters indicated that there would be future contacts involving sadomasochistic activities, and many of the others expressed a desire for them. In contrast, only 3% projected a relationship continuing with the same partner but not including S&M. Thus, once people start, they tend to continue and increase their masochistic activities.

This pattern of increasing, escalating involvement in masochism has led some theorists to characterize masochism as an addiction (e.g., Mass, 1983; see also Linden, 1982). Although viewing masochism as an addiction is probably a metaphoric exaggeration, these views do lend further plausibility to the belief that masochism is more like a narcotic than like a medicine.

Thus, the idea that masochism is therapeutic cannot be given much credence at present. There is little evidence to suggest that masochism has lasting, therapeutic effects. There may indeed be positive effects of masochism, but these can be explained in terms of escape as well as in terms of therapy. More importantly, where the escape and the therapy views differ, the evidence favors the escape hypothesis. Patterns of masochistic activity resemble narcotic abuse more than they resemble medicinal healing.

Masochism is not therapy; it is escape. Masochism does not bring about a lasting transformation of the self that cures inner problems. Rather, masochism effects a temporary transformation or concealment of the self that enables the person to forget his or her troubles and feel better. There is little substance to back up the view that masochism improves self-knowledge and insight, and indeed such claims are hardly plausible when considered closely. No doubt many masochists would like to think that masochism is a form of therapy that makes them better people, but there is no basis for such claims.

OPPONENT PROCESS EFFECTS

An important theory of opponent processes was proposed by Solomon and Corbit (1974). Their theory begins with the principle that people (and animals) maintain a general state of stable equilibrium (*homeostasis*). Opponent process theory says that the body is very active in maintaining the equilibrium. In particular, departures from homeostasis set off other processes that restore the state of equilibrium. Thus, ultimately, each major psychological reaction sets off an opposite reaction.

Opponent process theory has been used to explain drug effects. At first, a new drug user achieves remarkably potent, positive experiences by ingesting the drug. The drug takes the body up to a positive peak. But the drug-induced high sets off some opponent processes, by which the body returns itself to its normal state. As a result, the euphoria of the original drug intoxication is followed by a highly unpleasant period of depression and ill-being. The person then starts to want a new dose of the drug to chase away the depression—that is, to overpower the opponent processes. This new dose sets off more opponent processes, and soon a spiraling, vicious-circle pattern develops.

The user's problem is that the opponent processes tend to be stronger or at least longer lasting than the original drug effects. As a result, the person ends up fighting a losing battle to achieve euphoria. Taking another dose of the drug to counteract the aftereffects is not generally a good idea. The positive effects of the drug are likely to be muted by the opponent processes from the previous dose, but they do set off their own opponent processes. Users often try to outsmart their bodies by taking increasingly strong doses. These work for the moment, but they in turn set off increasingly strong opponent processes. This cycle can lead to escalating involvement with the drug, as well as addiction and the dangers of overdose. Similar patterns have been observed for alcohol, heroin, and cocaine use.

Masochism is in some ways the opposite of drug addiction. The drug abuser gets intense positive experiences from the drug, and he or she then suffers through opponent process aftereffects that may be quite negative and unpleasant. The masochist, on the other hand, creates intensely unpleasant experiences, which may set off opponent processes that would create pleasant, desirable aftereffects. One might compare masochism to jogging and similar forms of exercise. Jogging is generally unpleasant, but it leaves the person feeling good for much of the day afterward, presumably due to the opponent processes. The body responds to the physical stress of exercise in ways that enhance the persons's feeling of well-being.

Each of the masochistic practices could conceivably fit the opponent process theory. Thus, pain is a highly aversive state, and it may cause the body to create endorphins and other responses to restore the normal state (homeostatic equilibrium). Because pain is unpleasant, the opponent processes may cause pleasure. As a result, the masochist might feel very good after a spanking or whipping (Money, 1987).

The same logic could be applied to control and esteem. The masochist experiences utter helplessness and vulnerability. The psyche may respond by setting off opponent processes that would generate strong feelings of efficacy, power, and responsibility. In simple terms, the person may leave the masochistic episode feeling ready to be assertive and efficacious. Likewise, the masochist experiences humiliation, embarrassment, degradation, and loss of self-respect during the session. The opponent processes may cause the masochist to come away with a strongly positive view of him or herself.

Some observations of masochists seem quite consistent with the opponent process account, although there are no systematic data on this. Dominant women describe the aftereffects on their submissive males as quite positive. One professional dominatrix phrased it thus: "Men come to see me and I do what they want. Then, after the session, they smile and walk out, ready to conquer their world again" (Smith & Cox, 1983, p. 82). She described these men as "important [men] with heavy responsibilities for making a lot of difficult decisions" (p. 82). If opponent process theory furnishes a correct account of masochism, then these men would probably derive a great psychological lift from submission. When fatigued or stressed from the pressure of their responsibilities, a masochistic session would allow them a temporary escape and would leave them feeling that much more able to meet their daily challenges.

Other evidence indicates that masochists report aftereffects that carry over into their lives in positive ways. They speak of a positive "intensity" that comes to pervade their lives and activities, resulting from their masochistic scenes. They report "a lingering spiritual or psychic fulfillment" (Scott, 1983, p. 4). Clearly, these remarks suggest that masochistic sex makes one feel good even after it is all over.

As already described, many dominants and submissives refer to the masochist's experience of *catharsis*. We have seen that catharsis is usually mentioned in connection with the allegedly therapeutic effects of masochism. But the opponent process view provides a more plausible explanation for these effects than the therapy view. It is doubtful that acting out sex fantasies could have any real therapeutic effect, as noted previously. But enacting sexual fantasies could have a temporarily positive effect, resulting from the opponent processes set in motion by the psyche's attempt to counteract the pain, loss of control, and humiliation.

Thus, when masochists claim that their activities bring catharsis, they might not be simply trying to justify or rationalize their deviant pastimes. Perhaps they are erroneously regarding opponent process effects to be catharsis and therapy. Opponent process theory says that a masochist might well come away feeling good about him or herself: capable, euphoric, self-respecting. These feelings could easily be mistaken for therapeutic effects.

We have also seen that masochism tends to conform to addictive patterns (repeated use, escalating involvement, and so forth). These addictive patterns would fit in well with an opponent process account. The masochist gets a temporary, bad experience, followed by a strong "high" from the opponent processes. When the euphoric aftereffect wears off, the masochist may be inclined to seek another experience of submission to re-create the good after-feeling. In general, this cycle is psychologically quite plausible, as the analogy with exercise shows.

The opponent process theory makes a valuable addition to the escape hypothesis. It augments the idea that masochism provides an escape from high-level self-awareness, for it suggests that after the masochistic escape would follow a period of highly positive, euphoric self-awareness. This would obviously enhance the appeal of the escape.

Still, the evidence for the opponent process theory is not clear or strong. It is hard to disprove a theory in which either a phenomenon or its opposite can be used as the basis for explanation. In short, the opponent process view of masochism is plausible but cannot be clearly evaluated at present.

MASOCHISM AS LIFE-SCHEME

The final theory to be considered holds that masochism satisfies individuals by providing them with some form of meaning in their lives. Masochism can perhaps be considered as more than a mere, occasional form of escape. For some individuals, it may provide a way of structuring their existence and furnishing meaning.

Earlier, I outlined an overview of human needs for meaning. People need their lives to make sense in certain basic ways. These include having a sense of purpose that provides goals and fulfillments to strive for; having a sense of efficacy and control over one's life and environment; being able to justify one's actions as right and proper, without anxiety; and having a basis for believing in one's worth as a person.

If masochism provides individuals with meaning in their lives, it is almost certainly through the relationship to the dominant partner. This relationship deserves to be examined in greater detail.

Relationship Orientation of Masochists

Masochists are strongly oriented toward relationships. Masochistic sex tends to take place in the context of ongoing relationships. Some of these are part-time or occasional relationships, especially when the masochist is unable to practice submission in his or her primary intimate relationship (see Spengler, 1977).

Some indication of the importance of relationships can be obtained by studying prostitutes who cater to masochists. In the first place, it is clear that many men with masochistic inclinations are reluctant to use prostitutes because they desire the context of an ongoing relationship (Scott, 1983). Somehow it is not satisfying to these men to submit to strangers. They want to submit within the context of a committed, loving, intimate relationship.

Men who do resort to prostitutes often seem to end up forming relationships with the prostitute. From the prostitute's point of view, masochists are good business prospects, because they are more likely than other clients to become steady, repeat customers (Janus et al., 1977). Many prostitutes like masochistic clients for that reason.

The importance of the relationship context can also be seen in my sample of letters. Most of the experiences reported in these letters referred to ongoing relationships. More precisely, 70% of these letters indicated some past relationship and 89% projected a relationship continuing into the future. These figures are substantially higher than is usually the case with letters that describe sexual experiences and fantasies. For comparison, one might examine the related magazine *Penthouse*, in which people describe more conventional sexual practices and experiences. In one recent sample of these letters, only 29% described a prior relationship with the partner and 64% projected a relationship continuing after the encounter described in the letter. Thus, letters reporting ordinary, conventional sexual encounters often describe contacts between relative strangers, but masochists are more likely to report a relationship context.

One possible explanation for the masochistic emphasis on relationships concerns safety. For a masochist to allow him or herself to be tied up and beaten by someone, a great deal of trust is needed. In some circles, masochists do seek out strangers to dominate them, but the element of danger becomes an important factor (Lee, 1983). It would make sense for masochists to stick to ongoing relationships simply for practical reasons of personal safety.

If the pragmatic concern for safety were the only reason for the masochistic emphasis on a relationship context, then masochistic *fantasies* would probably not have such a high prevalence of relationships. Fantasies are not constrained by practical concerns; the element of danger is removed. So one might ask whether masochists fantasize about submitting to strangers, even if their actual behavior is typically limited to familiar, trustworthy intimates.

To check this, is was necessary to go through my sample of letters and select all those that explicitly described a fantasy rather than a (supposedly) real experience. Of these, 28 projected clear future relationship contexts, whereas only 5 projected no such future relationship.[2] Thus,

---

[2]Three additional letters were difficult to code. One involved a masochistic experience with a machine robot, and two others described homosexual experiences with unusual features. One woman referred to being spanked by a male and then induced to have intercourse with a woman, leading to an ongoing lesbian relationship with the woman; the other was chiefly a male transvestite fantasy with some submissive embellishments, and the future was left ambiguous. If all three of these are included as not involving a future relationship, the proportion is 78%.

85% of the pure fantasy letters projected a continuing relationship with the partner. It is quite apparent that the relationship orientation is still quite strong even in masochistic fantasy.

Thus, it is reasonable to conclude that masochists desire the relationship context for reasons that extend beyond the merely practical concern for safety. Safety may be a factor, but it is not the only factor.

The degree of devotion expressed by masochists toward their partners suggests that the relationship furnishes them with an important source of meaning and value. Statements such as "I live to serve" and "My only goal is to please my mistress" imply that the dominant partner's desires provide a rationale for the person's actions, and even for the person's life itself.

These observations suggest that the masochistic relationship may serve as a *value base* for the individual. A value base is something that can provide value and justification without itself needing external justification. To a religious person, the will of God provides such a value base. God's will tells the person what is right, but God's will does not need to be justified on the basis of some other authority. For the masochist, the relationship to the dominant partner may function in the same way.

The activities of masochism, from suffering pain to performing oral sex to following arbitrary commands, are fully justified simply because the dominant partner mandates them. Whatever the dominant partner wants or commands is accepted by the masochist as right. Actions that displease the partner or that contradict the partner's wishes are considered wrong. No further justification is required. That is, the dominant partner does not have to furnish justification to the submissive for the various commands. The dominant's mere whim is sufficient. Even inflicting a whipping can be done merely because the dominant wishes it, or in order to prove that the dominant can do whatever he or she wants.

In fact, many sadomasochistic activities are done with no seeming purpose except to prove that the dominant partner is free to impose any commands or rules that he or she wants. Thus, a dominant woman may require her submissive male to wear women's panties to work, simply to remind him of his submission to her (Scott, 1983). It is hard to argue that she derives any benefit or direct pleasure from his wearing panties. Another typical example involves requiring a female masochist to shave her pubic hair or to exhibit her body to others as proof of her submission.

There are ways to test the theory that masochism provides a value base. People in general are most likely to be attracted to a new source of value if they lack other value bases. So one may predict that most masochists would tend to lack strong affiliations to religion or other important sources of value. For masochists, the relationship to the dominant partner may serve quasireligious functions: It gives them a firm basis for knowing right and wrong, and for acting without anxiety or uncertainty.

Probably the most reliable evidence about the religiosity of masochists comes from Scott (1983). She says quite clearly that "in general, [masochists and their partners] are not religious" (p. 7). Likewise, the masochists I have met were uniformly not religious. Although this evidence is not a statistical survey, it will have to suffice. Thus, the evidence does fit the view that masochism may appeal to individuals who might need a good value base.

To the submissive, then, the commands of the dominant partner appear as fully justified in themselves, and the masochist's own actions need no justification other than whether they please the dominant partner or not. The masochist has no anxiety or uncertainty about how to act. By following the commands of the partner, the masochist can be certain of doing the right thing. One's actions have value and meaning by virtue of the relationship to the partner.

The will of the dominant partner thus functions as a value base. It justifies the submissive's actions, but it does not itself need to be justified.

Life-Scheme Analysis

Let us now consider how masochism functions for providing meaning in life. Something that provides meaning in life is called a *life-scheme*. Masochism can be analyzed as a life-scheme. To describe how it works, one uses the framework of the four needs for meaning in life: purpose, efficacy, justification, and self-worth.

Purpose. Purpose can be subdivided into goals and fulfillment states. Masochism removes most long-term goals, for its focus is immediate. The masochist is prevented from working toward most major goals in life. The masochist's only goals are short-term, immediate ones, especially satisfying the dominant partner or carrying out the partner's commands.

Masochists typically report substantial fulfillment from their submission. These claims seem plausible, for masochists must get some sort of strongly positive satisfaction out of their submission. Thus, one may infer that masochism provides some people with intensely fulfilling experiences. The nature of masochistic fulfillment may be either sexual or emotional (or both). Sexually, masochists achieve pleasure and usually orgasm. Emotional fulfillments are harder to verify, but there is some evidence for them. Intimacy is one important form of fulfillment, and masochism probably provides a great deal of it. During masochistic submission, the masochist becomes extremely close to the partner, to the point of taking the partner's wishes and desires as one's own. Thus, the relationship to the partner probably offers the masochist a great deal of fulfillment through intimacy.

It is worth noting that the dominant partner may find the relationship much less satisfying. The masochist denies him or herself to an extreme degree, merging with the dominant partner. To the masochist, this may be an extreme form of intimacy, but to the dominant partner it is like being alone. There is no separate person with whom to share things or interact, for the submissive partner has become merely an extension of the dominant's self. Thus, it may often be the dominant who becomes unfulfilled and dissatisfied in such a relationship (e.g., Scott, 1983; also this was one central point of Reage's 1954/1966 masochistic novel *Story of O*).

The frequent references to "catharsis" through submission indicate at least that a strong and somewhat satisfying emotional experience has occurred. The intensity of masochistic desires (e.g., Scott, 1983; also the present sample) suggests that more than mere sex is involved. In general, then, it seems likely that masochists are deriving powerful emotional fulfillments from their activities.

Efficacy and Control. For the most part, the masochist's control and efficacy are denied. In being bound, blindfolded, and commanded, the masochist undergoes a drastic and systematic loss of control. What is left is minimal: The masochist may derive some feelings of efficacy through pleasing the dominant partner in sex, or through carrying out the dominant's commands.

Justification. If you can justify your actions, then you can feel confident that you are doing the right things, so you can feel free from anxieties, doubts, worries, and guilt. Justification enables the person to regard his or her actions as having positive value and as being correct and proper.

As we have seen, masochism furnishes the individual with a strong value base that enables the masochist to justify his or her actions. The relationship to the dominant partner enables the masochist to know without any doubt what actions are right and what ones are wrong. As long as the masochist is doing what the dominant partner wants, the masochist knows that he or she is doing the right thing. No uncertainty, anxiety, or guilt is possible. And failures to fulfill the dominant's wishes are swiftly atoned through punishment, so there would be no feelings of guilt or anxiety left over from them.

The appeal of such certainty is not surprising. Compared to anxiety, uncertainty, and doubt, getting some physical pain now and then seems minor. The masochist submits to spanking but escapes anxiety. Probably many people would think that this is a good bargain.

Thus, masochism provides the individual with a potent and effective means for knowing what is right and wrong, as well as for justifying actions. The relationship to the dominant partner is a source of value that can endow the masochist's activities with meaning.

Self-Worth. Masochism is characterized by humiliation and embarrassment, often involving substantial loss of self-worth. It appears that the masochist is allowed very little basis for preserving feelings of self-worth. Except for pleasing the dominant partner by being a "good slave," the masochist has no opportunity to receive a favorable evaluation. A slave has no right to have dignity, esteem, or importance. Thus, masochism has a negative impact on self-worth.

Tradeoff

The life-scheme analysis of masochism can be summarized by saying that masochism is a tradeoff. The masochist relinquishes efficacy and self-worth. In exchange, the masochist receives purpose (fulfillment) and justification.

The main attractions of masochism are probably due to the positive aspects of the tradeoff—the benefits the masochist derives. Masochism gives the person fulfillment and justification. Both of these are in short supply in the modern world. Models of fulfillment have been in high demand ever since Western society decided not to live by Christian promises alone and struck out on the Romantic quest for satisfaction in the present life. The Romantics experimented with passionate love, creative art, the work ethic, and personality cultivation as means of achieving fulfillment (see Baumeister, 1986). Even today, people look for fulfillment in life without being certain where to look or how to achieve the various, nebulous versions of it (such as "self-actualization" and "realizing your potential").

Justification has also been a problem since Western society slipped away from its firm Christian roots. People desire clear, strong value bases to give their lives meaning and direction and to tell them what is right and what is wrong. Nothing has worked as effectively as religion.

Thus, the appeal of fulfillment and justification is not surprising. Both are very much in demand in modern life. Masochism can be seen as offering two very rare and important commodities for giving meaning to life.

On the other side of the bargain, masochism involves sacrificing a certain amount of self-worth and efficacy. People today have an abundant supply of these, but they are normally reluctant to part with them.

Based on this tradeoff, it is possible to speculate about the kinds of people who may be attracted to masochism. A tradeoff is a good bargain if you get something you really wanted. This could apply to quite a few modern individuals, given that justification and fulfillment are in short supply. A tradeoff is also a good bargain if in exchange you give up something that you either had an oversupply of or you are not very fond of. Both of these possibilities could lead to masochism.

One type of masochist would therefore be someone who has an abundance of control and self-worth. It may seem like a small sacrifice to submit to restraint and humiliation if the person normally has ample evidence of his or her control and self-worth. The powerful, egotistical, successful people who are often indicated as masochists (e.g., Janus et al., 1977; Smith & Cox, 1983) would presumably fall in this category.

Another type of masochist would be someone who has little regard for control or self-worth. Some people may not find these to be important things, and so they are willing to part with them in order to obtain the precious resources of fulfillment and justification. These individuals may be among the "natural submissives" to whom Scott (1983) referred. According to her, they form only a small category of masochists, but they do exist.

It is also apparent (see chapter 7) that some masochists seek to improve the bargain in various ways. Some of them participate in masochism in ways that minimize their sacrifice of control and self-worth. They avoid humiliating practices, and they retain a certain amount of control. Masochism as a life-scheme may be especially important among these individuals, for they give up relatively little.

Moreover, many masochists do not make the bargain in complete good faith. Masochists desire to relinquish control, but in truth they retain a fair amount of control. They want to submit, but they spell out exactly how they will submit. They specify in advance what types of bondage, what insults, what commands and humiliations they desire. Many retain "safe words," that is, signals that they can use to tell the dominant partner to stop whipping or spanking them.

Indeed, couples with ongoing S&M relationships often tend to have conflicts about who is really in control. Several illustrations of such conflicts were provided by Scott (1983). In one case, the submissive male kept criticizing the ways that his partner dominated him, while the partner felt that he should submit to whatever she wanted. In many cases, the attempt to establish a full-time S&M relationship encounters difficult issues of adjustment. The submissive male may seemingly desire the woman to tie him up and whip him during sex, but the rest of the time he wants to take on the male role and have his partner wash the dishes and clean the house. To the dominant female, however, doing the cooking and cleaning contradicts her dominant role and undermines one of the major attractions of the arrangement.

Viewing masochism as a tradeoff gets around its paradoxical nature. Masochism appears as a rational, plausible way of finding certain kinds of meaning in one's life. To be sure, most of us are far too attached to our self-worth and efficacy to make the trade, even on a short-term basis. But some may envy the intense fulfillments and the clear, anxiety-free justifications that masochists have.

It is fair to ask whether masochists do indeed regard their activities as a tradeoff. After all, the tradeoff notion makes it seem that the masochist parts reluctantly with control and self-worth, but most signs indicate that masochists are quite ready and eager for these things to be taken from them. They desire restraint and humiliation, rather than simply enduring them in order to reap the benefits of fulfillment and justification. In masochism, however, the costs and benefits may well be closely linked. The emotional fulfillments of masochism presumably rest on achieving an intense degree of intimacy with the partner. The denial of one's own self-worth and efficacy is a vital ingredient in that intimacy. If one person preserves his or her own independence and self-importance, the masochistic intimacy does not develop. True, there are other forms of intimacy in which one does not have to sacrifice self-worth. But those forms of intimacy are different and irrelevant; they have their own problems and difficulties. Masochistic intimacy requires giving up one's own self-worth.

Likewise, the justification offered in masochism is powerfully effective as an antidote to uncertainty, guilt, and anxiety. The person is told exactly what to do and what not to do. This form of justification requires the person to give up control and efficacy. If the person retained autonomy and continued to make free decisions, the masochistic justifications would not function. Only by accepting the partner's will as absolute does the masochist manage to achieve the total freedom from anxiety that he or she desires.

Thus, the sacrifices of masochism may be inseparably linked to the benefits. The masochist may desire humiliation and loss of control, but the basis for that desire is that these are prerequisites for the benefits of fulfillment and justification.

CONCLUSION

This chapter has reviewed several possible models of masochistic satisfaction. It has sought to answer the question of what benefits masochists derive from their submission. Let us briefly review the conclusions.

The first model held that high-level awareness of self can become unpleasant and burdensome at times, and so people may wish to escape from it. Masochism seems quite powerful and effective at bringing about an escape from self-awareness.

There are several variations on the escape hypothesis. One is that masochists experience not only relief and escape but ecstasy through transcending their ordinary identities. This is plausible, but at present there is little direct evidence to support it.

Another variation is that people who feel guilty desire to escape from self-awareness through masochism in order to be relieved of guilt feelings. In this view, masochistic submission does not really atone for guilt or remove the guilt, but it simply allows the person to forget it for a while. This seems quite plausible. Guilt is one form of anxiety, and masochism seems well suited to removing various sorts of anxieties, from decision uncertainty to evaluation anxiety. Escape from guilt feelings could thus be an appealing aspect of masochism. Many descriptions of masochism make no reference to guilt, so it seems unlikely that guilt can be a comprehensive explanation, but it may be involved in some cases.

A final variation is based on opponent process theory, which holds that natural psychological balancing mechanisms are set off during masochism and these may produce very positive, desirable aftereffects. The self may respond to loss of control with enhanced feelings of efficacy and determination. It may respond to loss of esteem with increased feelings of self-importance and personal worth. It may respond to pain and discomfort with strong feelings of pleasure and physical well-being. Although further evidence is needed, the opponent process theory makes a very plausible contribution to the theory of masochism.

Taking a broader perspective, it is apparent that masochism offers satisfaction of some of people's most basic needs for a coherent, valued, meaningful life. Masochism offers people two types of meaningful satisfaction that are quite rare in modern Western society. These are fulfillment and justification. The masochist has a workable, proven model of fulfillment, for submissive experiences reliably lead to strong emotional and sexual satisfactions. And the relationship to the dominant partner provides an unquestioned source of value, enabling the masochist to know immediately what is right and what is wrong as well as how to justify various actions and sacrifices. Masochism thus provides fulfillment and freedom from anxiety, both of which may appeal strongly to many individuals.

Several other possible forms of masochistic satisfaction were considered but rejected. The notion that masochism actually expiates or otherwise gets rid of the person's guilt seems very doubtful. Masochism may provide temporary relief of guilt feelings, but it does not have much potential for resolving true guilt. The relief may be quite important, for probably many people feel guilty at times when their actual guilt is minimal, such as when a supervisor has to lay off an employee. Removing the guilt feelings may be all that is needed. But for someone who is struggling with actual, substantial guilt, engaging in unusual forms of sexual play is not likely to be a viable solution.

Last, the argument that masochism is therapeutic must be viewed with considerable skepticism. Masochism does not appear to have any capacity for effecting positive, growth-enhancing or health-enhancing changes in people. Acting our sexual fantasies does not solve psychological problems or cure illnesses. Impressions of *catharsis* in masochism can be explained as opponent process effects (without therapeutic benefits). There is some common ground between the views that masochism is therapy and that masochism is escape. But where the two ideas differ, evidence provides very little support for the therapy view. Masochism is escape, not therapy.

In summary, masochism provides a welcome relief from the burdens of selfhood, and it provides partial solutions to widespread interpretive needs. It enables people to escape from themselves, and it offers them fulfillment and freedom from anxiety and uncertainty. These appear to be the best ways of understanding the attractions and satisfactions of masochism.

Chapter Six
Masochism and Sexual Pleasure

The term *masochism* was first coined to refer to a pattern of sexual activity, and sexual masochism is the clearest and most familiar form. Ironically, however, most past theories of masochism have ignored the connection between masochism and sexual pleasure. Indeed, Coen (1988) has criticized his fellow psychoanalysts for having neglected the sexual aspect of masochism in their theoretical efforts. Some theorists have dodged the issue by talking about nonsexual masochism. But there is no question that many people derive sexual stimulation and pleasure from submission. No theory of masochism is adequate without providing some explanation for its sexual nature.

It is easy to suggest why people might want to submit to authority, why they might want to be relieved of self-awareness or responsibility, why they might desire punishment, and so forth. But why do people do these in their sex lives? If people want to suffer, why do they do so *sexually*? Submission and suffering can occur in many contexts, and there is no immediately obvious reason for choosing sex over these others. Moreover, it is hard to see how suffering and submission could enhance sexual enjoyment.

This chapter begins with a close look at the sexual activities of masochists. Then it considers various theories about the connection between masochism and sex.

SEXUAL ACTIVITIES

Sadomasochistic activity tends to precede the actual intercourse or sexual contact, although this is far from universal. Sometimes the couple will alternate brief periods of sex play with brief periods of dominance and submission. Sometimes the two even occur at the same time, such as when a couple has intercourse while one partner is tied up, or when they spank or strike each other during intercourse. Still, for the most part, S&M functions as a preamble to sex. The orgasm often marks the end of the scene. Nonetheless, the sexual activity is shaped and influenced by the masochistic scene in a variety of ways.

Past theorists have made some rather astonishing claims about masochistic sex. Stekel (1953) said that masochists are generally impotent or frigid. "If sexual intercourse takes place at the end of a sadomasochistic procedure, it is indeed an exception" (p. 42). He even said that "in the [male] masochist, the surface of the penis is anaesthetic" (p. 43). Stekel saw the desire to avoid sexual intercourse as one of the main motives behind masochism. He was not saying that masochism made people impotent; rather, he thought, impotence made people into masochists (p. 140). Reik said much the same thing: Masochists are afraid of sex, so they engage in masochistic activities that postpone intercourse.

More recently, Shainess (1984) made similar arguments: "Sexual impotence in a woman is the ultimate expression of sexual masochism" (p. 87). She said that female masochists have an "almost involuntary need to cry immediately after orgasm," (p. 92), again suggesting sexual insecurity or problems. Another odd comment in her work is the suggestion that wife-swapping could only occur in a sadomasochistic marriage (p. 109).

All of these theorists based their ideas on observing therapy patients, whose sex lives may well be disturbed for a variety of reasons. It is very risky to draw conclusions about the sex lives of normal people from observations of mental patients. Let us therefore take a careful look at the evidence about sex among masochists.

Frequency of Intercourse

How regularly do masochists have intercourse and experience orgasms? This question is unfortunately impossible to answer. It is clear that Stekel and the others were exaggerating wildly when they said masochists are unable to have orgasms, for many do. But precise figures are unavailable.

My sample of letters is probably not a reliable source of information about frequency of orgasms. People probably choose to write to a magazine about their best or favorite experiences, and such experiences are probably most likely to include orgasms. Also, if people embellish their letters with fictional details and exaggerations to spice them up, one must suspect that such embellishments could well include orgasms. That is, if a person did not have an orgasm but desires to make the description special, he or she may well add an orgasm. Thus, although most letters in my sample reported orgasms, it is probably safe to assume that this high frequency overestimates the true figure.

Researchers who have worked and lived with actual masochists can furnish more accurate estimates. Observations of S&M groups on the West Coast suggest that most masochists do have orgasms, although certainly not always (Scott, 1983). Some people do engage in masochistic activities without intercourse. The extreme case was one man who reported that masochistic sessions ended in intercourse only 3% or 4% of the time (Scott, 1983, p. 176).

Of course, intercourse and orgasms are not the same thing. Many people have orgasms without intercourse. In particular, many male masochists seem to feel that penetrating the dominant woman's vagina somehow symbolically contradicted her dominant role (Scott, 1983). As a result, they feel it necessary for the man to have an orgasm by another method.

Many men find prostitutes to be their only opportunity for indulging in masochism. Professional dominatrices are hired to inflict pain, bondage, and humiliation, exactly as the client specifies. In these sessions, the man usually has an orgasm, although often it is achieved by masturbation (Scott, 1983; also Smith & Cox, 1983). Indeed, many professional dominatrices deny that they are prostitutes, on the grounds that they do not have intercourse with their customers. Other dominatrices do have intercourse with the men, or at least assist them at masturbation.

Thus, the evidence from prostitutes suggests that masochists do generally seem to want orgasm although they do not necessarily achieve it through intercourse.

There are some signs that masochists are especially prone to masturbation. Surveys indicate that masochists masturbate often, more often than other people (e.g., Spengler, 1977). Indeed, even among adults who are married or in some similarly committed relationship, the majority of masochists apparently masturbate at least once per week. One explanation for this high frequency is that many masochists find themselves in relationships with partners who do not want to engage in S&M, so the masochist has no way of indulging the masochistic desires except through fantasy and masturbation. Another explanation is simply the fact that masochists are by nature strongly inclined toward sexual fantasy, and masturbation is one common outcome of sexual fantasy.

Types of Intercourse

Apart from masturbation, what sexual acts are popular with masochists? The present sample of letters probably is a reasonable basis for answering this question. Although the letters may be biased so as to exaggerate sexual satisfaction, there is little reason to think that they would be biased so as to report one form of intercourse rather than another. If masochists do bias their reports of sex acts, it is probably because the masochistic imagination prefers certain forms of intercourse. That would be a legitimate way of learning about the masochistic imagination, which is presumably based on what masochists desire.

Oral Sex. Oral sex is very commonly reported in masochism. Indeed, one researcher found that many male-submissive couples preferred cunnilingus over genital intercourse (Scott, 1983).

The results from the present sample of letters confirms this pattern. Oral sex was the most frequently reported type of sex. Submissives performed oral sex in about two-thirds of the letters. We may assume that kissing and sucking the partner to orgasm is a common, modal part of masochistic scripts.

One may ask whether the desire for oral sex (performed by the submissive on the dominant) originates in the dominant or the submissive partner. The answer appears to be both. It is interesting, however, that dominants reported it even more often than submissives. That is, four out of five letters (79%) written by dominants referred to having the submissive partner perform oral sex, in contrast with only 64% of letters by submissives. This is one of very few activities that showed up more often in letters by dominants than in letters by submissives. Letters by female dominants, in particular, nearly always included cunnilingus. We may conclude that one of the reasons people enjoy the dominant role (perhaps especially women) is receiving oral sex.

Still, most masochists report performing oral sex, and it is a standard feature of masochistic fantasies too. Thus, masochists strongly desire oral contact with their partner's genitals, including bringing the partner to orgasm.

Sometimes the dominant partner performed oral sex on the submissive. This was considerably less common than the reverse. Masochists were about three times more likely to perform oral sex than to receive it. When the dominant partner did use his or her mouth on the submissive's genitals, it sometimes was just a manner of teasing the submissive—it did not proceed to orgasm, but simply raised sexual arousal, such as in preparation for spanking or whipping. In other cases, the dominant partner performed oral sex on the masochist after the session was over. This was sometimes described as rewarding the masochist for being a good slave.

Thus, performing oral sex is strongly associated with the submissive role. When dominants perform it, it tends to occur after the game (and hence the dominant and submissive roles) is ended. Sometime the dominant partner will orally bring the submissive to orgasm during a scene, but this is less common. In contrast, performing oral sex seems to be part of the masochistic role in a majority of cases.[1]

Genital Intercourse. Across all the letters, genital intercourse occurred slightly less than half the time (44%). Thus, in reports of peak masochistic experiences, intercourse is common but not universal. It is more common than anal sex but less common than oral sex.

This estimate of the frequency of intercourse conceals some important sex differences. Heterosexual couples with a female masochist usually reported genital intercourse; heterosexual couples with a male masochist usually did not. This may be partly due to the feeling that when a man puts his penis inside a woman he is dominating or possessing her, and this is compatible with female masochism but contradicts female dominance.

These gender differences are examined in greater detail in chapter 7. For the present, it is sufficient to note that genital intercourse is fairly common but far from universal. It is obvious that masochists are not all averse to intercourse, as some past theories have suggested. On the other hand, it is also clear that many masochists are satisfied without genital intercourse.

Anal Sex. Anal intercourse was reported in slightly over one-third of the letters. This figure is based on combining all reports of anal penetration, whether a penis, vibrator, or dildo was used. Obviously, if one restricts the tally to penetration by penis only, the figure would be smaller, for female dominants cannot by definition penetrate their partners.

One might expect some important sex and role differences to emerge with anal sex, but surprisingly there were none. Anal sex was reported at about the same rate in letters by submissives as in letters by dominants. Likewise, it was reported at about the same rate in letters by males as in letters by females. Interest in anal sex is apparently spread about equally through the S&M population.

There was one major difference, however. The *direction* of anal penetration was far from evenly distributed. Nearly all reports of anal sex involved the dominant partner (male or female) penetrating the submissive one. Out of 76 letters that mentioned anal sex, only 3 reported that the

---

[1] Some professional dominatrices say they never allow their clients to perform cunnilingus, although many clients seem to desire this. Probably this reluctance stems from several factors irrelevant to masochism. For one thing, prostitutes in general are reluctant to have orgasms with their clients. For another, as already noted, many professional dominatrices deny that they are prostitutes because they do not have sex with clients, and cunnilingus would undermine this claim.

dominant partner was penetrated. One of those involved a male homosexual orgy, in which roles were somewhat blurred. In another, a female submissive was told to insert a vibrator in her male partner's anus for his pleasure. And in the third, a male masochist was allowed to have any sexual wish fulfilled as a reward for having submitted to domination, and so he chose to have anal sex with one of the women who had dominated him.

For the most part, however, it appears that being on the receiving end of anal sex is strongly associated with sexual submission. Thus, masochists give oral sex but receive anal sex.

Group Sex. Only a small minority of letters in my sample reported sexual activities in groups. These had some important gender differences, which are covered in chapter 7. For the present, it is sufficient to note that masochists do not often write letters reporting group sex experiences, although some do.

Probably the highest amount of group sexual activity would be found in studies of S&M clubs and organizations. Thus, Scott (1983) studied female-domination groups on the West Coast, and such groups would probably tend to attract people who are most interested in engaging in activities with others. The married couple who engages in S&M privately at home would not be likely to show up in such a club.

Scott found that the people she studied often enjoyed S&M *activities* in groups and at parties, but group *sex* was rare. She said that even in S&M clubs there appeared to be norms of sexual fidelity. Although a masochist might be spanked by another person, the masochist would tend not to have sex with anyone except the regular partner. This pattern confirms once again the strong relationship orientation of masochists.

In short, it seems that many masochists tend to limit their sexual activities to one person at a time. Although the usual promiscuous desires are evident, especially perhaps among males, the S&M group scene tends to emphasize the dominance activities rather than group sex.

MASOCHISM AS SEXUALLY THERAPEUTIC?

From the evidence just presented, it is apparent that many people engage in masochistic activities that lead to sexual pleasure and orgasm. The clinical theories associating masochism with sexual impotence or frigidity must be regarded as either entirely wrong or at least as severely overstated.

On the other hand, there is some evidence of sexual insecurity among some masochists. Previously, I quoted a statement by a masochistic lesbian suggesting that submission relieved sex guilt. The fact that masochistic males often seem content to end a session with masturbation or even without orgasm could certainly be interpreted as a sign of ambivalence about sex. Finally, occasional masochistic males report fantasies of castration (Scott, 1983; also Friday, 1980; none in the present sample), which could mean many things—but sexual ambivalence or insecurity is one possible meaning.

The previous chapter discussed the theory that masochism is therapeutic, that is, that masochism enhances human growth, insight, mental health, and functioning. This theory was rejected as lacking any evidence and as being fairly implausible. Masochism is not psychotherapy. But could it be sex therapy? In other words, could it be that masochism enhances sexual response, performance, or pleasure? There is indeed some evidence to support such claims. Many masochists report intense sexual pleasures, unusual levels of potency, high frequencies of orgasms (including multiple orgasms), and so forth. Must these be dismissed as mere exaggerations, or is it possible that masochism has some capacity for strengthening or increasing sexual responses?

In this section, I propose that a variety of masochistic practices resemble important features of sex therapy. That is to say, masochists do things that sex therapists also do in order to enhance sexual response. These techniques have been studied and are often successful. So it is indeed plausible that masochism improves sexual response.

There may be a kernel of truth, therefore, in the clinical observations that masochism attracts people who are insecure about sex, for these people might indeed find masochism a good way of enhancing their sexual responses. This is not to say that all masochists are sexually insecure. People may want to enhance sex for a variety of reasons. Many people simply desire intense sexual experiences.

For example, when interviewing masochists I asked them what the principal appeal of masochism is to them—what they get out of it. The intensity of the experience, particularly the sexual experience, often figured prominently in their replies. As one woman put it, the power of the sexual arousal and orgasm in masochism far surpassed what she had experienced in normal sex. She (like others) showed no sign of ambivalence or insecurity about her sexuality, and she had enjoyed a diverse and varied sex life. But she had recently turned to masochism because it offered her the most intense experiences she had known.

Thus, if masochism can indeed enhance sex, this will appeal to a variety of people. Some people are insecure about their sexuality; these may be drawn to masochism because it boosts their sexual response up to a normal, acceptable level. Others enjoy full normal sexuality, but may desire masochism because it boosts their sexual response up to the highest levels possible. No doubt there are some masochists in each category.

The field of sex therapy was revolutionized by the work of Masters and Johnson (1970), who introduced new techniques that greatly improved therapeutic effectiveness with many sexual problems. Their work has probably influenced most sex therapists working today. Indeed, one could regard much of modern sex therapy as an extension of Masters and Johnson's pioneering work (see LoPiccolo & LoPiccolo, 1978). So it seems worth while to examine Masters and Johnson's techniques and see how they might resemble masochism.

Social Isolation. One important practice that Masters and Johnson used was to isolate the couple from their social world. Even if the couple lives near the sex clinic, they are encouraged to leave their house and live at a motel for at least a brief period during the treatment. This removes them from their everyday world and frees them from the various pressures and concerns that go with it, enabling them to concentrate on the sexual activities.

This artificial isolation from one's social world is reminiscent of the masochist's efforts to obliterate the everyday world from awareness. The masochist uses pain and fantasy to remove the world, whereas the sex therapist uses physical separation, but the purpose and result seem quite similar. Apparently the concerns and pressures of ordinary life are detrimental to sexual enjoyment in some people, so removing these concerns and pressures facilitates sexual response.

Sensate Focus. An important feature of sex therapy involves cultivating what Masters and Johnson call *sensate focus*. Sensate focus means focusing one's mind on sensations. In sex therapy, people are encouraged to direct their attention to how their bodies and skin feel. Sex therapy involves considerable stroking and caressing. The rationale behind the emphasis on sensate focus is simple: Researchers believe that many people have sex problems because they are worried, distracted, or concerned with evaluation during sex. Focusing on mere sensation improves sexual response.

Therapeutic use of sensate focus is obviously parallel to the focus of attention in masochism. As described in chapter 3, many masochistic activities direct the persons's attention to immediate sensations. Indeed, the special power of erotic pain is that it forces the person's attention to sensations. Many letters in my sample referred to the sensations that persisted after the administration of pain. In particular, after a spanking people report that their bottoms felt warm or sore. It is not surprising that people feel that way, of course; what is important, however, is that people's minds are focused on these sensations. It may also be that sexual caresses are felt intensely after pain, but there is no clear evidence of this beyond a few isolated remarks by various writers.

Thus, both masochism and sex therapy direct the individual's attention to immediate bodily sensations. And this appears to strengthen sexual response.

Relationship Focus. One of the fundamental changes that Masters and Johnson made in sex therapy was their insistence on treating the couple rather than the individual. Many previous sex therapists had simply focused their efforts on the individual who had a sexual dysfunction. Masters and Johnson argued that it is the couple's problem, not the individual's. They noted that in many cases the sexual dysfunction is aggravated by the partner's actions. For example, a woman who has difficulty having an orgasm may find her problem intensified if her lover regards her as cold and frigid, or if he fails to take adequate time and care to arouse her, or if he somehow makes her feel guilty whenever she does show signs of sexual pleasure. In Masters and Johnson's (1970) words, "There is no such entity as an uninvolved partner in a marriage contending with any form of sexual inadequacy" (p. 195).

Ever since Masters and Johnson, sex therapists have shown a strong preference for treating couples rather than individuals. A sex problem is considered to be a couple's problem. The couple is treated in therapy together. And it is the couple who resolves the problem and learns to have a satisfying sexual relationship together.

The emphasis on the couple has some resemblance to the relationship orientation of masochists. As has been shown, masochists seem to prefer relatively stable, committed relationships. They want their masochistic activities to take place in the context of an ongoing relationship.

In masochists, the emphasis on the couple may be the other side of the coin of social isolation. Many couples who engage in S&M may keep it a secret from most or all of their acquaintances, so it strengthens the bond between them just as any shared secret tends to do. Moreover, the removal of the world accomplished during masochistic sessions may function to isolate the couple together. A pair of women whom I interviewed described their S&M activity by saying that it enhanced their intimacy, for during these sessions they were aware only of each other. In other words, masochism focuses the mind on the here and now, and this immediate present may well include oneself and one's partner. Restricting consciousness to self and partner may indeed make one feel very close to this other person.

Restriction and Permission. Another important feature of sex therapy is the initial restriction of sexual activities. Patients are told not to engage in any sexual activities without the clear permission of the therapists. In particular, full sexual intercourse is prohibited at first.

The therapists' initial instructions tell the couple only to touch and caress each other's bodies while avoiding the genitals and the woman's breasts. They may stroke and message each other, but there is to be no sex of any sort. Later in the therapy, they are permitted to touch and caress these sexual zones of the body, but intercourse and even orgasm are still prohibited (unless orgasm happens by accident). Masters and Johnson insist that such restrictions will reduce the destructive pressure that often accompanies sexual dysfunction. If the goal of orgasm is removed, people can enjoy bodily pleasure without feeling pressure to perform or achieve.

With impotent males, sexual activity is at first prohibited. Later, various techniques are used to remove responsibility from the male for his sexual response. Therapists insist that the couple work together with their joint sexual problem. The woman is given the responsibility of inserting the penis into her vagina, which relieves the man of this distracting responsibility (Masters & Johnson, 1970, pp. 207–208). When the penis is successfully lodged in the vagina, the woman is given the responsibility for movements, and she is told to use only slow movements to contain the penis inside her rather than rapid thrusting for the sake of orgasm.

With nonorgasmic women, too, intercourse is at first forbidden. Then permission is given for the male to caress the woman sexually. Later yet, the couple experiments with having the penis inside the vagina but not trying to reach orgasm. The couple learns to enjoy "coital connection" without the demanding or thrusting activity (pp. 306–309).

The common thread among these activities is that the sexually insecure individual is relieved of responsibility for sexual performance. The therapist at first prohibits full-fledged sex, so the individual has no anxiety about implicit or possible demands. This enables the individual to focus attention on the immediate physical sensations he or she is receiving, and this focus helps produce normal sexual desire and response. As more and more sexual activity starts to develop, much of the responsibility is subtly transferred to the partner, so the sexually insecure person is relieved of performance demands.

In masochism, there is often a rough approximation of this therapeutic pattern. In the first place, the masochist is given rules or commands restricting sexual activity. Many masochists describe being commanded not to initiate sex, not to touch their own genitals, or not to have orgasms except as directed or permitted by the dominant partner. Some dominant women and submissive men report "training periods" lasting up to several weeks, during which the man is forbidden to achieve any orgasm. The typical result of this, in their descriptions, is an increasingly strong and all-pervasive feeling of strong sexual desire in the man.

In the second place, of course, responsibility for deciding and initiating sexual contact is usually transferred entirely to the dominant partner.

The submissive female is not required or expected by her partner to have an orgasm. She may or may not have one, but he pretends that he does not care at all. The fiction that he does not care about her pleasure enables her to enjoy sex without feeling that he will reject or disapprove of her (or be disappointed with her) if she fails to have an orgasm. It frees the woman from the sort of performance demand for orgasm that reportedly causes many orgasmic difficulties in women.

Likewise, the male masochist is not expected or required to show potency, proper orgasmic facility, or pleasure. These expectations form some of the more daunting pressures that contribute to male sexual insecurity, and so the masochist is freed of them. Sometimes the male masochist's penis is deliberately ignored, and he satisfies his partner exclusively with his mouth. In such cases, the male masochist is completely relieved of any pressures or demands regarding his penis. He does not need to worry about whether he has an erection, for his erection has become irrelevant.

A third contributor is that violations of these rules and restrictions are punished with spankings or humiliations. Because the masochist finds these punishments erotically stimulating, they further reinforce the sexual pleasure of the response. Such a mini-drama would probably be quite encouraging for a sexually insecure individual. It defines him or her as a highly sexed person who has to be chastised for having such uncontrollable desires. Being punished for excessive sexuality thus casts the masochist as a person with strong sexual impulses, which could be beneficial and therapeutic to someone who is insecure about sexual adequacy.

Thus, the use of rules and restrictions to limit sexual activity is a therapeutic ploy to relieve pressure and ultimately facilitate sexual arousal and response. Masochists may achieve the same end by surrounding the masochist's sexuality with similar rules and restrictions.

Enforced Passivity. As Masters and Johnson repeatedly insisted, a man cannot will himself to have an erection. He has to learn to let it happen, for he cannot force it. They built their sex therapy around this insight, using various means of thrusting the man into a passive role. In sex therapy, the man's wife or girlfriend is encouraged to take the lead during the stroking and fondling. When intercourse begins, she takes charge of inserting the penis inside her. The first intercourse during sex therapy normally uses the female-superior position in which the man merely lies on his back while the woman rides him.

All through this period of therapy, the man is repeatedly told by the therapists that he should not try to force an erection or control it. He has to learn to lie back and enjoy the physical contact, letting the sexual response and pleasure happen to him rather than taking charge.

This enforced passivity corresponds quite closely to the masochist's role. Often masochists use somewhat more extreme means of dramatizing their passivity, such as being tied up. Still, the result is the same: They are relieved of responsibility and initiative for sexual activities and cast in the role of passive participants. Like the therapy patients, the masochists must learn simply to lie back and enjoy whatever pleasure comes their way.

Conclusion

It would be wrong to overstate the parallels between masochism and sex therapy. Nonetheless, it is apparent that there are important resemblances between them. Many masochistic practices are quite similar or parallel to things that sex therapists do to enhance sexual response and treat sexual dysfunction.

Given the extent of these similarities, it seems quite reasonable to think that masochism may indeed improve sexual enjoyment and response. Masochists sometimes claim that the intensity of their sexual pleasure surpasses that of ordinary sex. Although further study is needed, at present we must accept these claims as entirely plausible.

The many similarities between masochism and sex therapy lend plausibility to the various suggestions that some masochists are motivated by sexual insecurity (e.g., Shainess, 1984; Stekel, 1953). It may well be that some sexually insecure people are attracted to masochism because masochistic activities strengthen and increase their sexual responses. Although masochism bears little resemblance to psychotherapy, it does resemble sex therapy, and it may well have positive effects on sexual functioning.

Again, however, one should be careful not to assume that all masochists are sexually insecure. Some people may desire these effects simply because they want sex to be as powerful and intense as possible.

Further research is needed to tell us whether sexual insecurity or sensation seeking is the more important causal factor in attraction to masochism. Quite probably both factors operate, so the ranks of masochists probably include the sexually insecure as well as the thrill-seekers. In either case, masochism's capacity for enhancing sexual response is probably an important part of its appeal.

SELF-AWARENESS

If masochism is essentially the removal of high-level self-awareness, what effect might this have on sex? In general, it appears that self-awareness can interfere with sexual pleasure in several ways, so removing it probably improves sex.

The masochists I interviewed said that masochism helps intensify sexual pleasure because it facilitates getting totally immersed in the experience. They pointed out that in normal sex, one sometimes has difficulty "letting go," a difficulty that prevents full pleasure, but masochism helps one to let go. The term *letting go* implies loss of control, which is one of the essential features of masochism. Subjectively, the loss of self-awareness may well seem a matter of letting go.

The Internal Spectator

One connection between high-level self-awareness and sexuality is related to the therapeutic issues discussed in the previous section. People tend to observe and evaluate their sexual performance, and this attitude represents an important obstacle to sex therapy.

Masters and Johnson (1970) emphasized that an important contributor to sexual dysfunction is the feeling of being a spectator to one's activities. That is, while attempting to make love, the individual may devote part of his or her awareness to observing the activities and evaluating them. A major goal of sex therapy is to get the person to stop doing this.

In males, the internal spectator is an important link in the cycle of impotence. When the man gets into bed, he worries whether he will have a suitable erection, whether he will maintain it for a long enough time to satisfy his partner, and so forth. During the sexual preliminaries, he mentally observes and notes each change in his erection. Any momentary sign of being less than rigidly erect causes him anxiety and increases his worries. This emotional reaction diminishes his erection further, which the internal spectator immediately notices again. Soon the man is starting to panic over the condition of his penis. Penis panic is reportedly not very conducive to sexual pleasure.

Other men worry about whether they will ejaculate too soon for their partner. Still others worry that their performance, technique, or even mere physical penis size will prove inadequate. The internal spectator notes each sign of imperfect response, as well as any sign of less than perfect bliss on the partner's part, and the resulting anxieties help undermine sexual pleasure.

In short, many men worry about performing adequately in sex. They are afraid that they are poor lovers, physically or technically, and that they will be rejected and humiliated by their partners. When they commence sexual activity, they become highly self-aware, as they observe themselves for any signs of inadequacy.

Women are likewise subject to performance concerns. Some women tend to be nonorgasmic, and others find intercourse uncomfortable and even painful. Either way, the woman mentally watches herself and worries that she will not respond adequately. She fears that if she is not responding right, she must not be a real or normal woman. She too may fear that her partner will reject her.

Thus, some women have anxiety if they do not have strong sexual feelings. Other women suffer from sex guilt, which gives them anxiety if they do have strong sexual feelings. They may adopt the spectator role during sex in order to observe whether their sexual enjoyment is excessive, which might mean moral weakness and depravity.

Even today, women may feel it is possible to be too sexual. Their partners can reinforce these fears. For example, a man may not want his wife to make very many sexual demands on him, for fear that he will prove inadequate. He may express this by discouraging or criticizing the woman when she expresses sexual desire, except perhaps when he initiates and encourages it. She may take this to mean that he will reject her if her sexual desires are too strong, and so she may begin to watch herself in order to check her passion before it reaches some mysterious, dangerous level.

Thus, in both men and women, the internal spectator is often destructive to sexual pleasure. Mentally observing oneself in an evaluative fashion is the essence of high-level self-awareness, so the internal spectator must be recognized as one kind of high-level self-awareness. Sex therapists work hard to remove the inner spectator. If masochism effectively removes high-level self-awareness, as the previous chapters have argued, then it may furnish a great boost to sexual enjoyment. Loss of self-awareness may reduce anxieties and fears about sexual adequacy, leading to improved sexual response and pleasure.

Sex and Egotism

Some people participate in sex as a way of bolstering their self-esteem. Engaging in sex constitutes physical, palpable proof that someone else finds you attractive. A high number of sexual conquests can bolster a person's sense of being desirable, attractive, charming, and so forth. Men have long sought sexual conquests as proof of their masculine virility. Women have enjoyed the masculine attention of making love as proof of their feminine desirability.

Egotistical approaches to sex may regard sex as a conquest (or as a performance) in which one proves important, meaningful things about oneself. One proves one's important qualities that extend over time, and so on. High-level self-awareness is thus fundamental in egotistical sex.

There is some suggestion that these egotistical approaches to sex detract from pure sexual pleasure and may even impair sexual functioning (LoPiccolo, 1978). If sex is a way of proving yourself, you are likely to feel pressure to perform effectively, and your internal spectator is likely to be very active.

Masochism's attack on high-level self-awareness probably removes this egotistical aspect from sex. The masochist's sacrifice of self-worth and agency (control) makes it unlikely that sexual participation is an ego-boost. A Don Juan may boast of having had intercourse with dozens of women, but it would be absurd to hear a masochist boast of having licked the boots of dozens of mistresses. Similarly, a woman may feel that having many men court her and make love to her is proof that men find her desirable and attractive. But it is doubtful what similar inference she may draw from having many men spank her. Masochistic submission is simply not something that one boasts about, for it has no ego-boosting properties.

Masochism, in short, prevents an egotistical approach to sex. Because the egotistical approach can undermine sexual pleasure, this effect of masochism may enhance sex.

Inhibition

High-level self-awareness is associated with inhibition. It is what keeps people from doing things that they consider wrong. Deconstructing self-awareness should therefore lower people's inhibitions, which in turn could well improve their sexual enjoyment.

Laboratory studies have supported the link between self-awareness and inhibition. For example, one experiment looked at cheating and self-awareness (Diener & Wallbom, 1976). These researchers reasoned that people will normally cheat for personal advantage unless their moral inhibitions and scruples stop them from doing so. They gave college students a test individually. Near the end of the testing period, the researcher explained that he had to leave, and the subject was given instructions to continue working on the test until the signal to stop (a bell would automatically ring). Half the subjects were made self-conscious by facing a mirror and hearing a tape-recording of their own voice. The other subjects, in the control condition, heard a tape of someone else's voice and did not face a mirror.

When the bell rang, the subject was supposed to stop working on the test, but there was nothing to force him or her to stop. Hidden cameras were used to record whether the subject continued to write down answers to the test after the bell rang, which constituted cheating. Over 66% of the control subjects cheated, at least as far as writing down one answer after the time expired. In contrast, hardly any (7%) of the self-aware subjects cheated. Thus, focusing attention on the self successfully inhibited people from cheating.

Most students regard cheating as morally wrong and objectionable. For them to cheat is thus to do something they consider wrong. The results of this experiment show that self-awareness is one major factor that inhibits people from doing things they consider wrong.

In regard to sex, many people have inhibitions and consider some acts wrong and immoral. Self-awareness may be an important factor in keeping them from performing such acts. Loss of self-awareness, accomplished by masochism, may therefore enable people to shed these inhibitions. Disinhibition could enable people to do and enjoy things that they would ordinarily have avoided. In that sense, masochism may enhance sexual pleasure.

There was ample evidence in my sample of letters that masochistic submission can be associated with removal of inhibitions. Many individuals wrote to say that their masochistic experiences have led them to explore a wider range of sexual activities, and I have heard similar suggestions by masochists I have interviewed. Obviously, the submission itself is something most people would not do, so entry into masochism is almost by definition associated with disinhibition.

There are other signs as well. Some letters, particularly by male masochists, describe how a first homosexual experience occurred during a masochistic episode. Usually a dominant woman presides over such an initiation, although in a few reports the man enters into submissive and homosexual activity at the same time.

Masochistic women report submitting to anal sex or other practices that they normally would have refused. Others relate an initiation into lesbian sex occurring during a masochistic episode, again perhaps initiated by a dominant male.

At least some masochistic experiences, then, are associated with removal of inhibitions. Under the spell of masochistic submission, people perform sex acts to which they would previously have objected. These too could contribute to the sexual enjoyment of the masochist.

Conclusion

There is good reason to think that the loss of self-awareness in masochism can often lead to an increase in sexual pleasure. By removing self-awareness, one removes the internal spectator that generates anxiety and distraction by critically evaluating the person's sexual activities and attributes. Masochism also removes the egotistical approaches to sex that may distract and impair sexual pleasure, especially the male orientation toward sex as an arena for proving one's masculinity. Finally, one removes various inhibitions that might normally restrict the scope of sexual activity and sexual pleasure.

RELIEF OF SEX GUILT

Past theories have suggested that masochism leads to sexual pleasure because it relieves the person of sex guilt. Sex guilt was at the core of the Freudian interpretation of sexual masochism, and it continues to be suggested as a vital factor (e.g., Shainess, 1984). There are various versions of this theory, and each of them must be considered carefully.

The previous section suggested that masochism decreases self-awareness, resulting in the removal of inhibitions. Sexual inhibitions can be considered a form of sex guilt, so the sex guilt theory can be made to fit in with what has already been argued. Still, it is plausible that masochism may reduce guilt and inhibition by other means than loss of self-awareness. More important, the emphasis in past theories has not been on using masochism as a means of overcoming guilt about trying wild, new sexual variations, but rather on guilt connected with ordinary sexual activities and desires.

Punishment

One popular version of the sex guilt theory is that masochism reduces guilt by punishing the individual. According to this argument, the masochist feels a great deal of guilt over sexual desires. Submitting to punishment removes this guilt, because in Western society we have accepted the view that punishment removes guilt through atonement. After being punished, the masochist presumably has the right to go ahead and enjoy the crime for which he or she has already atoned, namely enjoyment of sexual pleasure.

This theory is somewhat plausible. Considered carefully, however, it has some serious flaws. Moreover, it does not fit some of the data very well.

It is true that Western society regards punishment as fitting and adequate atonement for misdeeds. Someone who feels guilty about sexual enjoyment might plausibly submit to punishment and then feel better for having "paid one's debt" to society or whomever. For example, many Catholics report feeling cleansed of guilt after attending confession and performing their penance.

According to the usual practice, however, the crime comes first and then the punishment. The sex guilt theory rests on *punishment in ad-*

vance: The masochist submits first to punishment for sexual pleasure, then enjoys sexual pleasure. Consider someone who is wrongfully convicted and imprisoned, such that the mistake is eventually discovered and the person is released. Hardly anyone would argue that this person is entitled to commit several crimes now, because the prior, wrongful punishment has paid for them in advance. For example, in a recently publicized case, a convicted rapist was released after several years in prison when his alleged victim changed her story and exonerated him. No one was suggesting that he was now entitled to go and rape someone, because he had already served his time in prison.

The sex guilt theory thus ignores the important fact that Western society has no tradition of punishment in advance. Relief through punishment is psychologically plausible, but punishment in advance is dubious. It is worth noting that the idea of advance punishment has been tried in our culture, with disastrous results. The medieval Christian Church—probably the most powerful and sacred authority of its time, and perhaps of any time—dabbled in it. The first version was forgiving embarking Crusaders in advance for any sins they committed during the holy war. This led to some abuses, but people accepted it because, after all, it is impossible to fight a war while keeping the Ten Commandments, and (besides) everyone knew that the Crusades were a special case. Later, however, the Church began applying this principle more liberally, selling Indulgences for cash (akin to paying a fine in advance). People came to regard these Indulgences as licenses to sin, for which they had already done appropriate penance (Eliade, 1985). The results were catastrophic for the Church. Indeed, the immediate cause of the Protestant schism was controversy over the sale of indulgences.

The key point is that even as prestigious and legitimate an authority as the medieval Christian Church could not make people accept the principle of punishment in advance. It was not psychologically acceptable, and many people rejected the Church because of this attempt. It is implausible to suggest that masochists accept that punishment relieves sex guilt in advance, for that assumption runs counter to our cultural and psychological inheritance.

Psychologically, the punishment hypothesis suggests that masochists start out feeling guilty, then punishment relieves them of guilt, so they feel fine about doing things they would normally consider wrong. No experimental studies have shown any mechanism of the sort. There are indeed conditions under which people will choose to suffer (e.g., Comer & Laird, 1975; Curtis et al., 1984; see Baumeister & Scher, 1988, for review). But at present there is no support for the idea that punishment makes people feel guiltless about doing something to which they would normally object.

An even more fundamental problem is that there is no evidence for the notion that guilt makes people want to be punished. As some reviews have noted, the desire for self-punishment has proven elusive in research (e.g., Freedman, 1970). If this is the mechanism in masochism, there should be some evidence that it actually occurs.

Probably the strongest objection to the sex guilt theory comes in empirical evidence about sex guilt. According to the theory, submitting to masochistic punishment should reduce sex guilt, but all signs indicate that it is more likely to raise sex guilt. Masochists feel guilty (if at all) about their masochistic activities, not their normal sexual activities. In order for punishment to relieve guilt about sex, the reverse would have to be true: The person would have to feel guilt about sexual intercourse, but little or none about masochistic submission.

For example, observations of therapy patients indicate that many masochists come to therapy in the first place because they feel guilt and anxiety about having masochistic desires (Cowan, 1982). They do not have guilt about normal sex; indeed, what they want from therapy is to be brought to a state of having only normal sexual desires. Their masochistic impulses represent the problem, not the solution.

Other observers report that some masochistic therapy patients feel terrible guilt after a submissive episode, sometimes resolving never to engage in such practices again (Stekel, 1953). They seem to have no qualms about normal sex. Indeed, their resolutions to give up masochism are often accompanied by a determined effort to embark on a fully normal sexual relationship.

The same pattern appeared in the masochists I interviewed for this book. Some of them expressed concerns and reservations about their masochistic activities (although these did not really reach the level of guilt). But they never expressed any reservations about normal sex.

Further, the apparent fact that there are more practicing male masochists than female ones raises a problem for the sex guilt theory. Women tend to have higher levels of sex guilt than men, so if sex guilt causes masochism one would expect most masochists to be women. But the facts contradict that theory. Either there are more male masochists, or there are equal numbers, but there is no vast majority of female masochists.

In our society, the highest levels of sex guilt are probably found among Catholics, for they belong to a religion with a long and active tradition of hostility toward sexual pleasure (e.g., Bullough, 1976a; Tannahill, 1980). Catholicism also believes strongly in atonement that can remove the guilt from sin, so Catholics would be most likely to accept psychologically the view that punishment makes sex acceptable. For both reasons, one would predict that Catholics would form the largest group of masochists. There are very few data on this, but the existing evidence indicates the opposite. Studies of S&M groups have concluded that masochists tend not to be religious. Likewise, the masochists I have interviewed all rejected and dismissed religion.

The sex guilt theory holds that punishment removes such guilt. This sort of removal would most likely be experienced as a relief. Feelings of guilt are associated with an aroused state (e.g., Schachter, 1971), and reduction of guilt by confession has been shown to reduce arousal (e.g., Pennebaker, 1985, in press). Based on the sex guilt theory, therefore, one would expect the result of a spanking to be a reduction in arousal in the masochist. But this would undermine its value for sex, which requires high arousal. In other words, if the main function of the spanking or whipping is to relieve guilt, the masochist would probably end up in a state of low arousal, and readiness for sex would therefore be low. But all signs indicate that the opposite is true. Masochists are sexually aroused by chastisement and seek it out for precisely that purpose.

One last issue is that the sex guilt theory receives utterly no support in the letters in my sample. No author described masochistic submission as a means of relieving sex guilt or making them willing to engage in sex. Some did report a lowering of sexual inhibitions, which is consistent with the lack of self-awareness and with a low level of thinking. But no one mentioned feeling that the spanking entitled him or her to do something wrong, nor did anyone describe it as advance punishment for sexual enjoyment.

Altogether, then, the advance punishment hypothesis must be discarded. It is scarcely plausible on theoretical grounds, it contradicts relevant evidence, and it is conceptually incompatible with current knowledge about human behavior. If sex guilt plays a role in masochism, it is probably not via the advance punishment mechanism.

Responsibility

The masochist abdicates control and as a result escapes all responsibility for his or her actions. This could have some value for removing sex guilt. The person may feel that it is acceptable to have sex and enjoy it, as long as one has no volition.

This view has some of the same problems as the advance punishment theory. It assumes that the individual feels guilt about sex but not about masochism, contrary to most of the evidence. Bondage is a deviant and stigmatized activity, and most people would probably feel more sex guilt about doing that than about having normal sex.

There are a few bits of evidence that render the responsibility loss theory more plausible than the advance punishment theory, however. Earlier, I quoted a remark by a masochistic lesbian to the effect that bondage enabled her to enjoy sexual feelings without responsibility.

There are not many such remarks, but at least that one supports the idea that escaping from responsibility is important.

On the other hand, it may be significant that that isolated remark pertained to homosexual activity. Homosexual acts are probably considered more deviant and stigmatized than heterosexual acts, and it is plausible that some homosexuals feel conflict and even guilt about their desires. For some of them, bondage and the resulting loss of responsibility might indeed enhance sexual pleasure, by removing doubt and guilt. It is also plausible that at least some individuals would feel as much guilt about homosexuality as about S&M. Thus, perhaps the responsibility loss theory applies when masochism is coupled with homosexuality. Still, this is mere speculation. Among heterosexuals, the responsibility loss theory does not seem likely.

Evidence of disinhibition is also consistent with the notion of responsibility loss, although it can be explained on the basis of other factors (such as removal of high-level self-awareness). As already noted, masochists do report reduction of inhibitions, especially including first homosexual experiences and novel heterosexual actions. They also tend to escalate their submissive activities over time. It is hard to say whether they use masochism as an excuse for exploring novel sexual frontiers, or whether the novel actions are done to strengthen and deepen their masochism. Still, being bound and restrained and submitting to the dominant partner's commands is often presented as a factor contributing to the removal of inhibitions.

Conclusion

In principle, anything that would remove sex guilt could enhance sexual response and pleasure. Some have suggested that the contribution of masochism to sex is precisely that: the removal of sex guilt. On close inspection, however, these theories are flawed.

One theory suggests that the pain inflicted on the masochist functions as a punishment for sexual desires and pleasures, thereby relieving the masochist's sex guilt and enabling him or her to enjoy sex. Another suggests that masochists like to be tied up because this relieves them of responsibility for their actions, allowing them to enjoy sex. There is very little direct evidence to support either theory.

These theories are apparently contradicted by evidence that masochists are far more likely to feel guilty about their masochism than about normal sex. Also, the groups that have the highest levels of sex guilt, such as women and Catholics, do not turn out to be the most masochistically inclined—if anything, these groups furnish fewer masochists than others. The punishment theory also runs contrary to some cultural and psychological patterns, and so it must be regarded as inherently implausible.

Possibly, further research may find some way to salvage the sex guilt theory and to show that it does contribute to masochism. Based on current evidence, however, it must be rejected. Relief of sex guilt does not appear to be an important factor in contributing to the masochistic enjoyment of sex.

EXCITATION TRANSFER

Yet another possible theory suggests that masochistic submission causes the person to become aroused and excited, and this arousal is then converted into sexual arousal. This theory can be called the *excitation transfer* theory, because it is based on a transfer of excitement from one source to another. Several past theorists (esp. Reik, 1941/1957, and Stekel, 1953) have made brief remarks suggesting excitation transfer, although none has elaborated it in any detail.

Social psychology has demonstrated that excitation transfer is real and does happen under some conditions. An arousal created by one cause can intensify a subsequent emotional response to something else. In a famous experiment, college students were given mild injections of adrenaline that were disguised as vitamins (Schachter & Singer, 1962). Shortly thereafter, they were presented with emotionally powerful situations, designed to provoke either anger or happy euphoria. The students responded very strongly, either angrily or joyfully. Their emotions were stronger than those of control subjects who had received nonarousing, placebo injections. Thus, an arousal was created artificially, but it blended in to cause an especially intense emotional reaction.

In another study, male subjects were approached by an attractive female confederate and asked several questions (Dutton & Aron, 1974). The researchers cared little about the actual questions; what they wanted to find out was whether the male subject would flirt with the attractive woman or make romantic overtures to her. Half the subjects were approached after they had just crossed a high suspension bridge that swayed in the wind. These men turned out to be much more likely to make advances to the woman than control subjects who had been on safe, solid ground prior to the questioning. The reason for the difference, presumably, is that crossing the suspension bridge generated a certain amount of fear, which includes a bodily state of arousal and excitement. The men conquered their fear, but some of the arousal remained, and when an attractive woman approached them they felt strongly attracted to her. The excitement of the fear converted into romantic, sexual attraction.

The suspension bridge experiment seems directly relevant to masochism. Masochists submit to bondage, humiliation, and pain, all of which could produce a state of arousal. Being tied up and blindfolded would probably cause some fear because of one's extreme vulnerability. Anticipation of pain would probably also cause fear. Indeed, if dominants go just a little bit farther than the submissive's presumed limit, the submissive would probably feel a strong additional rush of fear, from wondering how far the dominant will go. Finally, humiliation may also create strong arousal connected with feelings of shame and embarrassment.

All of these forms of arousal might plausibly carry over into sexual arousal. The suspension bridge study provides the most direct evidence that fear arousal can convert into sexual attraction, but various other studies have confirmed that excitation transfer does occur. It does not always happen, and there are some limits, but it could be a factor in masochistic arousal.

A further variation of the excitation transfer theory was suggested earlier (see also Ellis, 1936). Spanking produces an effect called *reactive hyperemia*, that is, the warmth and reddening of the skin of the buttocks. Several theorists have suggested that this response might become converted into sexual warmth, especially considering how close the buttocks are to the genitals. Various letters in my sample made remarks that support this notion, such as suggesting that the warmth of one's bottom intensified sexual desires. Although clear proof of this idea is lacking, it seems quite reasonable.

Moreover, mild pain is often used as a caress during periods of strong sexual arousal. Cross-cultural studies have shown that in many other cultures partners will scratch or bite each other during sex (see Beach, 1976; Ford & Beach, 1951). Scratching and biting is not really painful to people during intercourse, but it may help elevate arousal levels.

In short, the excitation transfer theory may well shed some light on masochistic processes. The techniques of masochism seem well suited to create arousal and excitement born out of fear, apprehension, and related feelings. Quite possibly this arousal can carry over into intensified sexual arousal. Excitation transfer has been shown to occur in some settings, although there is no direct evidence about whether it is a factor in masochism. Probably excitation transfer is at best a partial explanation of masochistic sexual excitement. After all, if the masochistic practices were nothing more than a way of generating arousal, people might just as well jump rope or do calisthenics to prepare for sex. But excitation transfer may well be a supplementary source of sexual stimulation in masochism.

MASOCHISM AS FOREPLAY

A last theory has been suggested by Lee, who proposed that "S&M sex may be thought of as unusually extended foreplay" (1983, p. 191). In his interviews, most masochists mentioned the fact that their activities prolonged the period of sexual enjoyment and "made the fun last longer" (p. 191). The same pattern emerged in my interviews; indeed, one couple reported that the decision whether to have normal sex or S&M sex was often based on whether they expected to have sufficient time for the latter.

The foreplay theory makes sense, although it is almost certainly just a partial or supplementary factor. Normal sex does not take very long. Possibly sexual arousal fails to reach its maximum level in some cases because inadequate time is taken. In particular, many couples may spend such a short time on foreplay that the woman is not fully aroused when intercourse commences. As a result, she may fail to have a fully satisfactory sexual experience (e.g., Gebhard, 1978).

The difference in perceptions of adequate time for foreplay was recently dramatized in an episode of a television game show that tests how well newlyweds know each other. The game proceeds by asking questions of one spouse while the other is absent; then the partner is brought in and asked to guess the first spouse's answers. One wife was asked to complete the sentence, "The time my husband spends on foreplay would be enough to _____." The husband suggested "bake a cake" as the likely answer, but the wife's response had been "sneeze."

In contrast to conventional sex, masochism apparently occupies a fairly long time. In normal sex, the couple may decide to have sex, undress, have brief foreplay, commence intercourse, and finish the sex act, all within a quarter of an hour or even less. In contrast, most of the scenes described in my sample of letters or in Scott's (1983) observations seem to take closer to an hour, sometimes even substantially longer. During the episode, the masochist is likely to be fully or partially nude, thinking about sex, experiencing brief sexual contacts such as caresses or performing oral sex on the dominant partner, and enjoying other physical contact with the partner periodically. An hour of this might well allow sexual arousal to reach a high level.

It would be foolish to propose that masochism is nothing else but extended foreplay. Obviously the appeal of masochism includes symbolic and psychological aspects that arouse the submissive person in a variety of ways. Still, the duration of masochistic sex games probably helps produce a higher level of sexual arousal than many other, more conventional practices.

CONCLUSION

The basic fact of masochism is that submission causes sexual arousal, and no theory of masochism can be complete without some explanation for this fact. Yet many past theories have had surprisingly little to say on this topic, focusing mainly and briefly on punishment for sex guilt or on excitation transfer, or often simply dodging the problem entirely.

This chapter reviewed several possible theories about how masochistic activities could contribute to sexual arousal and pleasure. Although most of this remains at the level of speculative theory, some of the ideas emerged as far more likely and plausible than others.

First, there are apparently some important resemblances between masochistic practices and some techniques used by sex therapists to enhance sexual responses and pleasure. These include isolating the individual from everyday pressures and concerns, focusing attention on immediate sensations, emphasizing the relationship context, using rules and permissions to restrict sexual activities, and enforcing a passive role on the individual. These practices seem to work effectively for enhancing sexuality among therapy patients, and it is quite plausible that they enhance sexual enjoyment for masochists. In particular, it may be that people with sexual insecurities may be attracted to masochism for its stimulating properties. This is not to suggest that all masochists are sexually insecure. Some may simply desire their sexual experiences to be especially intense.

Second, various sex researchers have argued that self-awareness is often detrimental to sexual response and pleasure. Thinking of sex in selfish, egotistical terms, or viewing it as a test of one's technique and attractiveness, may prevent one from "letting go" and enjoying the sex fully. If masochism does indeed remove self-awareness, as previous chapters have argued, then the results might well include enhanced erotic responses.

Third, several theorists have proposed that masochism removes sex guilt. In this view, the person feels guilty about sexual desire and pleasure, but masochistic punishment and loss of responsibility remove those guilts and allow the person to enjoy sex. This view has severe theoretical shortcomings and it does not fit the evidence very well. Although relief from sex guilt may be an attraction of masochism for a few, it seems unlikely that such relief is a common or important factor.

Fourth, the excitation transfer theory holds that masochists become aroused by fear and embarrassment, and that this arousal is then converted into sexual arousal. This view seems quite plausible and probably contributes to the erotic value of masochism. Excitation transfer is probably not a full explanation, but it seems reasonable as a partial explanation.

Finally, it has been suggested that the prolonged duration of masochistic activities allows sexual arousal to reach high levels. The eventual sex act may therefore offer greater pleasure than many conventional acts, in which intercourse commences after only a few minutes of foreplay. It seems unlikely that the erotic value of masochism can be totally explained by describing it as extended foreplay, but this theory seems quite reasonable and plausible as a partial explanation.

Much of the evidence seems to fit the possibility that masochists have a threshold of sexual arousal that is different from that of other individuals. More precisely, masochists may need more intense or prolonged stimulation to achieve sexual satisfaction. This idea is consistent with clinical impressions that some masochists have weak or insecure sexual responses. It is consistent with the parallels between masochism and sex therapy, for both intensify sexual responses. It is also quite consistent with the excitation transfer hypothesis and with the view of masochism as extended foreplay. Little direct evidence is currently available, but future research should examine the possibility that people with high thresholds for sexual arousal are particularly drawn to masochism. In any case, it does seem at present entirely plausible that masochism intensifies sexual arousal and pleasure beyond normal levels.

Chapter Seven

Femininity, Masculinity, and Masochism

This chapter suggests a radically new approach to the relationship between gender and masochism. This relationship has long been a controversial subject. Early theories regarded the relationship as fairly clear and straightforward, but it must instead be considered subtle and complex. There are some sex differences in masochism, but perhaps not the ones that have been proposed in the past.

To understand my approach, it is first necessary to address the question that has lain at the controversy about masochism and gender: Are women masochistic? It may well be that both sides on this bitter debate had some valid insights, but there have also been some serious misunderstandings. Next, I suggest that men and women do show some systematic differences in their patterns of masochistic activity. These differences can then be considered from the perspective of what is currently known about sex differences.

One word of caution is needed. The psychology of sex differences has progressed a long way during this century. Masculinity and femininity are no longer regarded as opposites but as separate dimensions. Moreover, the psychological differences between men and women are usually not absolute categories but rather overlapping distributions. Physical height makes a good analogy. The average man is taller than the average woman, but there are many women who are taller than many men. Also, the difference between the tallest and shortest men is bigger than the difference between the average man and the average woman. Sex differences should not be overestimated or considered as absolutes. Instead, they should be regarded as slight differences in broad tendencies.

THE GREAT DEBATE

There has been a long and (in my opinion) somewhat misguided debate about the relationship between masochism and gender. It is necessary to begin by reviewing the main arguments.

Are Women Masochistic?

As is often the case with psychological controversies, the debate was sparked by Freud's work. Freud was apparently mystified by masochistic phenomena. He struggled to make sense of this seemingly paradoxical pattern, and he produced a series of speculative theories. As usual, his ideas were intelligent, although not necessarily correct. Indeed, his views on masochism may well be farther off the mark than many of his other insights.

Freud came to believe that there were several overlapping types of masochism, one of which he called "feminine masochism." Freud saw masochists as submissive, passive, and dependent. He then looked at the women of his day, and saw that they too were submissive, passive, and dependent. He concluded that women have those masochistic traits by nature. In other words, he thought that masochism is part of the biological endowment of women.

Freud's followers have generally retained his belief in feminine masochism. Deutsch (1944) emphasized masochism as one of the core principles of the psychology of women. As she put it, "the attraction of suffering is incomparably stronger for women than for men" (p. 274). She regarded the normal activities of sexual intercourse as masochistic for women, for they involve being invaded, conquered, and (at least the first time) injured. Deutsch said women are not consciously masochistic, for she observed that women deny that they enjoy pain or suffering in any context. Unconsciously, however, women do enjoy such things, in Deutsch's view.

Equating masochism with femininity is complex. Why do men do masochistic things if it is mainly women who are masochistic? One theory is that women are naturally masochistic, so masochism is a sexual perversion only in men. Another theory is that men become masochistic out of a desire to escape their masculinity.

Reich (like Deutsch) suggested that women tend to fall in love with men who abuse and humiliate them. She thought that women must derive some form of satisfaction from the abuse, separation, and unhappiness caused by these destructive relationships. This is the version of the Freudian hypothesis that has brought the greatest controversy.

Modern feminist scholarship has sought to free women from the oppressive stereotypes and self-perpetuating stigmas of the past. One of the favorite targets of feminist attacks is this Freudian view that women are masochistic. It is easy to understand the grounds for the feminist anger over this view. Labeling women as masochistic implies that they enjoy abuse and mistreatment, which might easily be converted into a rationalization for further oppression. These arguments are a form of "blaming the victim," in which women's social disadvantages are attributed to women themselves rather than to an exploitative system or to male wickedness.

Some applications of the theory of feminine masochism were especially infuriating to feminists. The suggestion that women enjoy mistreatment by men has been particularly offensive. Therapists who see women put up with abuse and mistreatment, often returning to the same destructive relationships over and over, have often concluded by calling these women masochistic. The women's movement has struggled to find ways to help battered women, and it suspects that these efforts have been made more difficult by prevailing views that these women desire or deliberately perpetuate their own suffering.

Caplan (1984) has carefully studied the empirical evidence for women's masochism. She argued very strongly that all of this evidence is faulty and has been misinterpreted. Women are not masochistic, in Caplan's view. She has examined each pattern of female behavior that has been called masochistic, and each time she concluded that the women's suffering is not due to any masochistic enjoyment of suffering but rather because they are adapting as best they can to a difficult situation. They are making the best of a sorry range of alternatives.

Consider the battered wife who returns to her husband and resumes the relationship after each brutal incident. According to Caplan, it is fallacious to label her masochistic. Most of these women simply have no viable alternative. They tend to fear that if they left the abusive husband, he would track them down and kill them (often he says this explicitly). Or they have no job and no money, so they see no way of supporting themselves apart from the relationship with the abusive spouse: To them, the choice is putting up with him or starving to death. They may think that staying with the husband, despite the costs, is best for the children. Also, many of them tend to regard each brutal incident as an isolated one, for often the man is contrite and affectionate afterwards and he promises that it will never happen again.

Moreover, women tend to blame themselves, and this includes battered wives. Research indicates that men tend to project their negative feelings externally, blaming and attacking others, whereas women tend to focus negative feelings internally (e.g., Brody, 1985). In a couple, this could easily create a pattern where both the man and the woman blame her for conflicts and problems. He tells her she is bad and wrong, and she tends to believe it. If he beats her, she may think it is partly her fault and he is justified in beating her. She hopes that if she can only behave better, the mistreatment will stop.

None of this indicates masochism. There is nothing to suggest that these women are attracted to their suffering or derive any sort of pleasure or satisfaction from it. In fact, it makes them miserable.

Other evidence suggests that wife-battering has little to do with the wife's actions. Several careful research studies have concluded that there are no apparent personality differences between battered wives and nonbattered wives. In contrast, there are substantial and important differences between battering husbands and nonabusive ones (see Walker & Browne, 1985). Apparently spouse abuse is caused by the dominant partner's needs and feelings. This too is contrary to the pattern of masochism, in which the needs and desires of the submissive partner are generally the causal, driving factor.

In short, abused women are not masochists, but ordinary victims. A similar conclusion emerges from considering other female behaviors that have been interpreted as masochistic (Caplan, 1984).

That is not to say the debate is ended. For example, Shainess (1984) considered women to be commonly masochistic, much more commonly than men. (Some theorists have come to the opposite conclusion. Reik, for example, decided that men are more commonly masochistic than women.) Shainess regarded everything from women's grammatical patterns to their menstrual cramps as signs of feminine masochism. Again, however, many of her interpretations are very debatable, and she provided no convincing evidence that women are inherently masochistic or that they are more masochistic than men.

The small amount of empirical evidence we have about masochism provides further dispute for the theory that women are inherently masochistic. Masochistic sexuality is apparently more common among men than among women (e.g., Kinsey et al., 1953). This view does not prove that men are more masochistic than women, for men engage in nearly all forms of deviant sexual activity more than women. Men's greater involvement in masochistic sex probably is just another instance of this general pattern. Still, this fact is hard to reconcile with the view that women are more masochistic than men. Either the two sexes are about equally masochistic, or men are more prone to masochism, but it seems very unlikely that women are more masochistic.

In short, the view that masochism is a feature of the psychology of women is not tenable. It is misleading and possibly dangerous to label women's typical behavior patterns as masochistic. Arguments for feminine masochism rest on debatable interpretations of complex, ambiguous, and nonsexual behavior patterns. As for sexual behavior, which forms the clearest evidence about masochism, women are, if anything, less overtly masochistic than men.

Probably, most generalizations about an entire gender are prone to error. The Freudian view wanted to consider masochism part of the biological endowment of women, but this seems very unlikely. First, as noted in the previous chapter, masochism appears to be a product of cultural and historical trends, which makes any biological theory of masochism implausible. If women were innately masochistic, they would be masochistic in all cultures and at most or all times in history—but the evidence shows otherwise. If women (or men) are masochistic at all, it is probably because of the way they are socialized by a particular culture.

Second, even in modern Western societies where the rates of overt masochism are the highest, most women show no attraction to masochism. Masochism is a minority pattern, and it appears in a minority of men as well as a minority of women.

Is Masochism Feminine?

If it is wrong to think that women are masochistic, why did so many intelligent observers make that mistake? Some readers might suggest that these theorists were just plain stupid, or that they were ideologically motivated (i.e., perhaps they wanted to pin a negative label on women). On the other hand, perhaps they had some valid insight and simply misinterpreted it.

Consider Freud's impressions, which began the whole debate. Freud saw masochists as passive and submissive, and he noticed that women had similar qualities, so he inferred that there was a connection. His observation may have been accurate, especially in his era. Perhaps only his conclusion was wrong.

In my view, there is indeed a resemblance between the way masochists act and the way our culture teaches women to act. But it is only that: a resemblance, not a connection. It is quite wrong to suggest that most women are drawn to masochism. On the other hand, it may well be correct to say that most masochists are drawn to femininity, as defined by certain cultural ideals.

Try this thought experiment. Masochists like to assimilate themselves to slaves. Suppose you were to have a personal slave or servant, and suppose further that you were able to choose the personality traits that this servant would have. What traits would you select? Probably your ideal servant would be someone who would place your needs above his own, would follow your commands immediately and without question, would anticipate your desires and try to fulfill them, would take care of menial tasks for you and provide you with pleasure, would make few demands on you, would be quiet and pleasant, and so forth. This configuration of traits bears some resemblance to some of our cultural ideals of femininity. It also describes what masochists desire to be like. There is a resemblance.

It is easy to suggest a basis for this resemblance. Throughout most of Western history, women have held a position of inferior status to men and have functioned in many ways more as unpaid servants than as equal partners. It is a commonplace argument that Western ideals of feminine personality are adaptations to this inferior status and power. The masochist, who seeks inferior status and power, would likely fit a similar mold.

Thought experiments are not very solid evidence, however. Are there any data about masochism that could shed light on this resemblance between masochism and femininity?

Probably the clearest possible behavioral sign of gender identification is the way the person dresses. Clothing, for example, is highly differentiated by gender. Men do not wear brassieres or dresses, whereas women rarely don jock straps or neckties. Some actions are also associated with one gender, as are certain names. Indeed, for the most part, male and female names form two nonoverlapping sets.

Behavioral signs such as these enable one to look for gender identifications in masochistic behavior. The letters in my sample were coded for evidence of gender switching, that is, evidence that someone dressed or was named in a way clearly consistent with the norms for the opposite sex.

When tallied up, this evidence produced a striking pattern. First, it is clear that gender switching is associated only with submissives. In no case did a dominant partner, whether male or female, dress or act (or take a name) like a member of the opposite sex. Dominants retained their own gender.[1]

Second, and more importantly, it appears that gender switching is exclusively associated with male masochism. Not a single letter depicted a female masochist dressing or acting as a man. In contrast, two out of every five letters by male masochists contained some clear evidence of gender reversal. Usually this took the form of being dressed up in women's underwear. Sometimes the transvestism extended to shaving body hair, plucking eyebrows, applying lipstick and makeup, wearing

---

[1]These data describe mainly heterosexual activities. There is some evidence that dominant lesbians sometimes adopt masculine or "butch" clothing, as shown in the photographs in the book by Samois. Although this pattern would support my argument here, I have chosen not to emphasize it because the evidence is not strong and there is some ambiguity as to whether masculine attire among lesbians signifies sadomasochism or not.

a feminine wig, or wearing a dress. Some of the male masochists were given female names to use when thus attired.

Other, less common forms of gender reversal included having the male masochist do the housework or engage in sexual activities that were explicitly described as appropriate to a female.[2]

Thus, male masochists show clear behavioral signs of being feminized. In contrast, female masochists show no such signs of being masculinized. Indeed, the only references I found anywhere to dressing up among female masochists involved wearing ultra-feminine clothing. Some depictions of lesbian masochism involved women who normally dressed in unisex or male clothing and never wore makeup. As part of a masochistic episode, they were dressed up in high heels, makeup, frilly underwear, dresses, and other stereotypically feminine articles of clothing (Alexander, 1982; Barker, 1982). Thus, ironically, when women masochists do resort to gender symbolism in clothing, they are feminized rather than masculinized (see also Reik, 1941/1957, p. 241).

The implication is that masochism does indeed have some important resemblance to femininity. Both male and female masochists tend to dress and act in a stereotypically feminine fashion.

One explanation is that dominant females prefer to feminize their submissive male partners as a way of signifying that the normal, superior status of the male is reversed. There is some validity to this view. After all, it is clear that males have nearly always held higher social status and power than females, and the masochistic quest for inferior status would be ill-served by becoming more masculine.

On the other hand, it is misleading to suggest that it is the female dominants who especially desire the feminization of the male masochists. The males want it themselves. If it were mainly the female dominants who desired this, one would expect feminization to be mentioned more often in their letters than in the letters by male submissives. But the opposite is true. Whereas 39% of the letters by male masochists refer to cross-dressing, only 27% of letters by female dominants reported feminizing the man. This difference was not quite statistically significant, but it was nearly so, and it suggests that the interest in feminizing the man comes more from the male masochist than from the dominant female.

Indeed, when female dominants do seek to feminize their male partners, they may have specific ulterior motives beyond facilitating the status reversal. Specifically, their main interest in feminizing the man

---

[2]Simply submitting to anal penetration or performing fellatio are not necessarily female, because male homosexuals apparently perform these actions with no connotation of femininity (cf. Blumstein & Schwartz, 1983). These acts were only coded as feminine if they were clearly discussed as such. For example, in a few cases submitting to anal sex was described as a way of making the male experience what it's "really like" to be a woman.

seems to be to have someone else do the housework. Of all the letters by male masochists that reported feminization, only about half of them reported having the man do housework. In contrast, all but one of the comparable letters by female dominants mentioned having the man do the housework. This difference was statistically significant. Thus, female dominants think of feminizing a male slave as a way of having someone to do the laundry and dishes. Male submissive fantasies focus much less on housework.

Other evidence provides some confirmation of these patterns. One published interview with a dominant woman made clear that she had her male slaves do her housework: "a slave, a male in a little apron, who is chained to the refrigerator. It's nice to have a man tied to the kitchen" (Smith & Cox, 1983, p. 85). Couples who experiment with full-time female domination tend to have conflicts over who would do the housework. The dominant woman naturally expects her submissive male partner to take on the cooking and cleaning, but the man is often reluctant (Scott, 1983).

It appears that both male masochists and their dominant female partners have some interest in feminizing the male, but their interests are somewhat different. Male masochists show a substantial interest in feminization, and desire to do housework is at best a minor part of this interest. Female dominants show less interest in feminizing the male, and when they do have such an interest it is often mainly a matter of freeing themselves from the traditionally female burden of housework.

What, then, is the appeal of feminization to the male masochist? To them, apparently, becoming female contains strong associations with masochistic submission. Although changing one's gender is itself an important means of escaping from one's normal identity, this alone is not a sufficient explanation of the pattern, for it would apply equally well to women masochists—but women masochists do not generally switch their gender to male. The implication is that male masochists hold stereotypes of femininity that seem very compatible with the submissive role they desire.

Conclusion

What can we conclude about the possible relationship between gender and masochism?

First, the argument that all women are innately masochistic must be rejected. There is no evidence that masochism is part of the psychology of women or of their biological endowment. Moreover, it seems quite misleading to regard ordinary (nonsexual) female behavior as masochistic. Instead, it appears that masochism is found in a minority of both men and women, and it is the product of cultural and social factors.

Second, there is some suggestion that males engage in sexual masochism more than females. This evidence is not fully conclusive. Women appear to engage in most forms of sexual deviance less than men, so it is not safe to associate masochism with maleness or masculinity. Given the cultural and historical relativity of sexual behavior in general—and of masochism in particular—the only important point is that masochism appears in a significant number of both males and females. *Masochism is compatible with either gender.* Third, there is some association between masochism and femininity. This is shown by the fact that male masochists are often feminized, whereas female masochists are almost never masculinized. Probably this association is a resemblance, not a connection. The submissive desires of the masochist take forms that resemble cultural ideals and stereotypes of femininity, and sometimes this resemblance makes male masochists desire explicit feminization.

When male masochists desire to be feminized, it is probably not because women are somehow masochistic. Rather, it is because the goals of masochism resemble models of femininity, including submissiveness, passivity, and self-sacrifice. The fact that women's status has generally been lower then men's status may provide part of the attraction, for male masochists seek lower status in various ways. Probably the quest for low status is not a full explanation for the male masochistic interest in feminization, however. Even when status has been lowered by other techniques, male masochists sometimes still desire feminization.

The fact that our culture's ideals of femininity resemble the goals of masochism should not be disregarded. It is probably what confused some past theorists and observers. If feminine ideals look like masochistic ideals, then a woman who conforms to feminine ideals will resemble a masochist in some respects. No doubt many women do seek to fulfill such cultural expectations, and that is probably why Freud and others mistook femininity for masochism. But the resemblance between masochistic and feminine models tells us more about our culture than about the essential or innate nature of womanhood.

Thus, masochism occurs in both men and women, and it has some symbolic resemblance to femininity. These conclusions lead one to suspect that masochism will mean slightly different things to men as opposed to women. One should expect some differences between male and female forms of masochism. After all, men and women have somewhat different approaches to many things, from grammar to morality to mathematics to sex. It would be surprising if they participated in masochism in exactly identical ways.

Oddly, past work has largely neglected the issue of gender differences in masochism. One reason for this difference is that past work was so caught up in the debate about whether masochism was to be associated exclusively with one gender. That is, past theorists were preoccupied with the question of whether women are masochistic and men are not, or vice versa. This preoccupation prevented them from thinking that both men and women engage in masochism but do so in slightly different patterns.

One of the few past theorists who did touch on this issue was Reik (1941/1957). He said that clinical observers had failed to find any discrepancies between male and female masochism. He found it hard to believe there was no difference. Reik surmised there must indeed be differences, although he had little idea of what they might be.

In the next section, I suggest what some of those differences might be (see also Baumeister, 1988b).

MASCULINE AND FEMININE MASOCHISM

This section presents a series of findings of differences between masculine and feminine reports of masochistic behavior. These findings are chiefly based on the present sample of letters to *Variations*. They are based on comparisons between the letters about male masochists and the letters about female masochists. Before starting, several qualifying comments need to be made.

First, all these patterns must be considered quite tentative. In previous chapters, I generally used the evidence from these letters as one form of evidence among several. Conclusions based on the letters were checked against other sources of evidence whenever possible. With gender differences, however, this is not possible, for there are almost no other data about gender differences in masochism.

True, in previous chapters the conclusions and patterns based on the letters have mostly agreed with other sources of evidence (except the Freudian case reports). This agreement suggests that these letters may indeed be valid evidence about the desires, fantasies, and even to some extent the behavior of masochists. Still, it is risky to present an entire section in which almost none of the conclusions can be checked against other evidence. This account of gender differences must therefore be regarded as a very preliminary first step.

Second, the results here are only the ones that are statistically reliable. The percentage of male letters reporting any given activity is almost never identical with the percentage of female letters reporting a similar activity. But many such differences are slight and could be due to random, chance variation. All the differences were subjected to statistical evaluation to determine whether they are probably real differences or merely due to chance. The results reported below are significant differences, which means that we can be at least 95% sure that they are not due to chance variation (because chance variation does not give a difference that large more than 5% of the time).

In writing this section, I have tried to use a minimum of statistical information and jargon. Readers who want the specifics and details may consult the tables in the Appendix for full information. These tables list the actual tallies and percentages, as well as the statistical evaluations.

Third, a potential problem for this section is that there is no way to verify whether the author is truly of the gender that he or she claims to be. Letters are signed male or female, but it is possible that some authors misrepresent themselves. Indeed, it seems likely that some letters to some magazines are written by men who pretend to be women, and some letters in this sample (although not many) impressed coders as being in that category. The opposite possibility, that female authors sign themselves as male, is not considered as likely, although in principle it could happen too.

This potential problem can be evaluated in several ways. If a masochistic male were to write a letter in which he pretended to be a dominant female, this would not greatly distort the results here, for in many cases I have grouped the letters by couples: male masochists with female dominants, and female masochists with male dominants. As we see, these groupings appear to be justified, for in most cases there are clear resemblances between the complementary sets of letters. Female masochists report activities similar to what their partners (male dominants) report, whereas the letters of male masochists resemble the reports of their partners. (Only a few letters in this sample involved homosexual S&M.)

On the other hand, if a male masochist were to write a letter pretending to be a female masochist, this would distort the results. His (male) ideas would be taken as evidence about female masochism.

How serious is this problem? Probably it is not very common. Male (heterosexual) masochists are interested in scenes in which women dominate men. They may find it sexually exciting to imagine a scene from the perspective of a dominant female. But they might well not find it very stimulating to imagine a scene in which a man dominated a woman.

One way to check this potential problem would be to examine letters by men who showed explicit interest in being feminized. As noted previously, some male masochists desire to be symbolically converted into women. To them, masochistic satisfaction includes dressing and acting as a woman. Probably these are the most likely ones to write letters in which they pretend to be female masochists. If they have contributed a significant portion of the letters that are signed as female authors, then we would expect the female-signed letters to resemble those of male transvestite masochists.

To evaluate this potential problem, the letters signed by male masochists were sorted into two groups: those involving feminization of the male, and those reporting no feminization. The key question was, do the male transvestite masochists resemble the other male masochists or the female masochists?

The answer appears to be that despite the lingerie and makeup, the male transvestite masochists remained masculine masochists. The groups were compared on three of the dimensions that produced the biggest differences between male and female authors (see later): public display, relationship context of punishment, and oral humiliation. On each measure, the transvestite males scored about the same as the other male masochists and differed from the female masochists. Indeed, on two of the three measures, the transvestite male masochists were farther away from the female masochists than the other male masochists were. In other words, the transvestite male masochists showed more extremely masculine patterns than the other males (although this difference was not significant). In short, male transvestite masochists resemble other male masochists; they do not resemble female masochists. This suggests that the letters signed by females were not written by male transvestite masochists.

Thus, although some authors may have misrepresented their gender, this is probably a minor problem. Indeed, to the extent that authors did misrepresent themselves, one would expect few significant differences to emerge. For example, in the extreme case, if all the letters were written by male masochists, then one would expect almost no differences between male and female masochism. And it is evident that the men who were most explicitly interested in becoming female did not describe experiences that resembled those of the female authors.

Having covered these preliminary concerns and problems, we can now turn to the specific patterns.

Major Masochistic Practices

Pain and Bondage

Letters signed by female masochists were slightly more likely to report pain than letters signed by male masochists. Most letters reported some pain, usually a spanking or whipping. These included 70% of the letters by male masochists and 85% of the letters by female masochists.

The slightly higher percentage of female masochists reporting pain should not be emphasized too much. It is partly by default. There were slightly more letters by male submissives in general, and by simple count there were about an equal number of male masochists as female masochists who reported pain. The deficit in female letters is elsewhere (see later, in the humiliation categories). At any rate, the conclusion is that if women participate in masochism, they generally emphasize pain as a central component. Male masochism is not as exclusively linked to pain, although it is present in the majority of cases.

On the other hand, there may be an important difference in the degree of pain suffered. It was instructive to contrast letters reporting only a simple spanking with those reporting more severe pain, either involving a whipping or involving multiple sources of pain (e.g., a spanking plus nipple clamps). It appears that female masochists prefer lesser amounts of pain than male masochists. Of the letters by males that reported pain, two-thirds reported the more severe forms of pain, compared to only one-third of the female letters involving pain. Thus, female masochists mainly reported being spanked, whereas male masochists reported either whippings or multiple sources of pain.

This difference was confirmed by examining the letters written by the dominant partners. Female dominants reported administering whippings or multiple sources of pain much more often than male dominants did.

Thus, male masochism seems generally to emphasize more substantial levels of pain than does female masochism. This might be part of a general pattern by which males seek more intense sensations in general than females. Still, one should be a bit cautious about this difference. It is plausible that women's pain thresholds in general are lower than men's, or that their skin is more sensitive. It is also plausible that the editors toned down the severity of pain in the female letters, although this explanation seems contradicted by the one-third of female letters that did report more substantial varieties of pain.

Some evidence from other sources suggests that male masochists occasionally take pride in how much pain they can endure (Scott, 1983; Janus et al., 1977). Writings on female masochism have not made similar claims about taking pride in the extent of one's pain. Still, although this evidence is consistent with the present pattern, it is not very strong.

With bondage, there was a hint of a difference. Slightly over half of the letters about female masochism reported bondage, whereas about two-thirds of the letters about male masochism reported bondage. This difference surpassed the 90% certainty criterion but did not reach the 95% one, so it must be regarded with some caution.

If there is indeed a greater tendency for male masochists to use bondage, it might be due (at least in part) to the fact that women are usually physically weaker and smaller than men, so the male submissive may need to be tied up to be fully dominated. On the other hand, it might suggest a greater interest in loss of control among male masochists.

Thus, there is some evidence that female masochists are more likely than male ones to report pain. When male masochists do report pain, however, it is generally of a more intense variety than what female masochists report. Finally, there was a tentative indication that male masochism is more likely to involve bondage.

Guilt and Punishment Context

Past research on guilt has produced conflicting findings. Some researchers believe that women have more guilt than men, especially as adults (e.g., Hoffman, 1975). Others distinguish "shame" from "guilt," associating shame with women and certain types of guilt with men (Lewis, 1985). It also appears that women have more sex guilt than men. A reasonable conclusion is that women have somewhat higher levels of guilt than men, but there are some exceptions and the evidence is not fully convincing.

The role of guilt in masochism can be evaluated by looking at the rationale for punishment in reports of pain. This analysis eliminated the pure fantasy letters, for these often tended to omit information relevant to guilt. Indeed, some fantasy letters referred to being captured by pirates or sold in slave markets, and the whippings in those were often ambiguous as to guilt. Also, this analysis eliminated letters that made no reference to pain, such as letters focusing exclusively on bondage.

The remaining letters were sorted into three categories (this sorting was described in a previous chapter). The first category contained letters portraying the pain as punishment for some actual misdeed. The second category, "trumped-up" guilt, contained letters in which the pain was administered for some offense that was part of the game, such as if the masochist broke some arbitrary rule or failed to perform oral sex to the partner's satisfaction. The third category consisted of letters in which there was no attempt to present a punishment context for the pain.

This distribution of letters among these three categories did not differ greatly. Female submissives had the highest rate of describing the pain as punishment for actual misdeeds: Slightly over half of their letters (of those involving pain) fell in that category. In contrast, female dominants had the lowest rate, with only about one out of every four letters indicating punishment for actual guilt. Thus, female masochists reported guilt contexts, whereas female dominants inflicted pain on an arbitrary or trumped-up basis. Letters by males fell in between. There was a tendency for female-submissive couples to report more guilt contexts than male-submissive couples, but this difference fell between 90% and 95% certainty.

A clearer pattern emerges if one considers the relationship context for the pain. Some letters referred to S&M activities as an integral part of the interpersonal control and power dynamics of an ongoing relationship, in contrast with the majority of letters that described these activities as isolated games or occasional events. Examples of using pain as an integral part of the relationship would include cases in which the masochist reports being spanked by the partner whenever the masochist fails to complete household chores adequately or on time.

Female submissives were most likely to refer to pain as part of a pattern of punishment for misbehavior in an ongoing relationship. Whereas 38% of the letters by female masochists reported such a context, only 14% of the male masochists referred to regular punishments by a relationship partner for misbehavior, and this difference was statistically significant.

Letters by dominants reported a relationship context for pain at about the same rate whether written by a male or a female. Furthermore, this rate was about the same as that of the male masochists. The female masochists stood out as having the highest tendency to report a relationship context for punishment, and indeed their rate was significantly higher than that of all the other groups combined.

Thus, interest in using pain on a fairly regular basis to punish misdeeds is associated mainly with female masochism. Although still a minority pattern, this context apparently appeals much more strongly to female masochists than to any other category of people in S&M. This result is consistent with the greater relationship orientation of females in general and especially in sex (e.g., Blumstein & Schwartz, 1983).

Another way of looking at at this difference is that the pain experienced by male masochists was more strictly divorced from their everyday lives than the pain described by female masochists. The references to masochism as escape from everyday reality appear to describe the suffering of male masochists better than that of female masochists, at least on this dimension.

These activities of masochistic women might suggest to some that abused or battered wives are indeed masochistic. This conclusion would be fallacious. It must be kept in mind that the masochistic women who report these punishments do not suffer injuries or general beatings. Rather, female masochists desire only to be spanked, usually in a mild fashion, by a stern but loving husband, and they generally discuss their consent to these activities and even their enjoyment of them.

Humiliation

Masculine and feminine letters differed substantially with regard to humiliation practices. We proceed through these practices individually, deferring a summary consideration of general humiliation until the end.

Display Humiliation. A first category of humiliation involved being displayed in an embarrassing or humiliating fashion to others. A good example was the prototype reported by Reik (1941/1957) and quoted in chapter 4, in which a woman lies naked on a table with legs spread apart while a man looks at her sex organs.

In the present sample of letters, there was a clear gender difference in display humiliation. Display was a much more common feature of feminine masochism than of masculine masochism. Indeed, nearly half the letters by female masochists reported display of some sort. Male masochists reported it significantly less often.

Male dominants likewise reported displaying their partners more often than female dominants reported it, although this difference did not reach significance. The female masochists reported it more than any other group. Thus, interest in display is mainly associated with female masochism.

It is worth adding that males and females submitted to display differently. For males, being displayed was a means of accentuating other degradations. They were displayed while tied up or dressed in women's clothing or performing embarrassing actions. Female masochists tended instead to describe simply being displayed naked, as in Reik's patient's fantasy.

To understand this difference, one must consider norms of sexual modesty. Women are taught to be modest, to hide their genitals and underwear from public view. Males receive much less pressure about sexual modesty. Indeed, a male who fears to be seen naked may be regarded as effeminate. Thus, being displayed naked would be much more of an emotionally powerful experience for a woman than for a man.

In contrast, women are accustomed to being seen in dependent roles, and they are not taught shame about wearing male clothing. Males are taught to impress others with their autonomy and independence, and they must never wear women's clothes. So males might find it more humiliating than females would to be seen in some demeaning attitude or dressed in the clothing of the opposite sex.

Still, overall, it appears that display is a much more central feature of feminine masochism than of masculine masochism. Display is often the principal form of humiliation in a woman's masochistic episode, whereas for males display (if it occurs at all) tends to be just a supplement, a way of accentuating some other practice.

Degradation (Status Loss). Being displayed nude in front of others is no doubt quite embarrassing, but it does not entail any sort of loss of status. A woman does not become less than a woman simply because she is seen naked. In contrast, there are other forms of humiliation that clearly involve loss of status. In them, the masochist is reduced to some level of being below his or her normal level.

One type of humiliation that entails status loss is being treated like an animal. The most common animal schema in masochism is the dog. Masochists who submit to such treatment typically wear a collar around the neck, and a leash is attached to the collar. Sometimes they are required to walk on all fours, to eat and drink from bowls on the floor, to fetch things with their mouths, and so forth. In the present sample, only a small minority of letters reported such practices, and these involved predominantly male masochists. Males appear to desire "animal" humiliation more than females. The corresponding pattern was found in letters by dominant partners. Indeed, not one letter by a male dominant described treating his female partner as a dog or other animal, whereas about 15% of letters by female dominants treated their male partners in that way.

A second category of status degradation involves being treated like an infant. These masochists reported being dressed up in diapers, which they would often wet (sometimes serving as the pretext for a spanking). They described being bathed, having their diapers or other baby clothes changed, being kept in playpens, and so forth. This pattern was rather rare.[3] Still, it was exclusively associated with male masochism. No female masochists reported being reduced to the status of a baby, nor did any dominant writer (male or female) mention such a practice.

Thus, whereas feminine masochism favors display humiliation, male masochism appears to favor status degradation. Male masochists seem to like to be reduced to beings of lesser status, such as dogs or babies. It is also noteworthy that many males reported being feminized, which also entails loss of status insofar as men generally have higher status than women. Taken together, these various patterns of degradation appeared in over half the letters by male masochists but only in a very small minority of letters by female masochists. Presumably, status is a central issue in male identity, and the desire for loss of status is a central feature of male masochism.

Verbal Humliation. Verbal humiliation encompasses being insulted, being discussed in embarrassing or degrading terms, or being required to beg (whether for pain or pleasure). No significant differences emerged on this measure. It was most commonly reported by male submissives and least often by male dominants, but even that difference was not reliable.

Urination. An extreme form of humiliation involves receiving the dominant partner's urine on the masochist's body. This practice,

---

[3]It must be noted that *Variations* contained other sections devoted entirely to adult baby activities. These were not included in my analyses because they made no clear reference to S&M activities.

sometimes called "golden showers," is described by Scott (1983) as "the ultimate insult." In the present sample, it was fairly rare, and it was associated about equally with male and female masochism.

Other researchers have reported that occasional masochists like to have their partners defecate on them (e.g., Smith & Cox, 1983; Weinberg et al., 1984). Many people object to this practice on hygienic grounds, for it is reportedly quite unsafe. It was not mentioned in my sample, quite possibly because the editors of *Variations* delete any activities that are nonhygienic or dangerous.

One may speculate that male masochists would be more inclined to desire defecation than female ones. This would fit two of the patterns that have been suggested so far: First, male masochists seem inclined toward more extreme and intense practices, and second, male masochists seem more inclined toward the heavily degrading activities. If future research can verify this prediction, it would provide valuable confirmation of these speculations. For the present, however, there is no information about possible sex differences in this activity.

Oral Humiliations. Several masochistic practices used the mouth for purposes of humiliation. Four main types of oral humiliation appeared in the present sample. In one, the masochist kisses the feet of the dominant partner, which is an age-old gesture of submission. A rather novel variation on this theme had the masochist kiss the buttocks or anus of the dominant partner. A third type involved having women's panties stuffed in the masochist's mouth, often as an impromptu gag. Although it was clear that the panties were women's apparel, it was not necessarily the dominant woman who had worn them. Sometimes the male submissive had worn the panties himself. Other times, a female masochist had her own panties stuffed in her mouth, although this was less common.

The fourth category involved being required to lick up sexual fluids. Most commonly this involved male semen, although sometimes it was a combination of male and female secretions that had mingled during sexual intercourse. Male masochists sometimes reported licking up their own semen, whether off the floor, off the feet of their dominant partner, or from her vagina. Some masochists were humiliated by seeing their partners have intercourse with another person, after which the masochist was required to lick both partners' genitals until clean. And both male and female masochists reported licking their partner's genitals after sexual intercourse.

Oral humiliations were strongly associated with masculine masochism. Male masochists were nearly six times more likely than female masochists to report oral humiliations. This was one of the biggest differences obtained in this research. It appears that male masochists desire to be humiliated through their mouths much more than female masochists.

Cuckolding. A last form of humiliation involved having one's partner have sex with someone else. This expresses a symbolic defeat in sexual competition, implying that your partner wants someone else rather than you. This was a difficult category to code, for it is not necessarily humiliating to have one's partner have sex with another person. If one restricts the analysis to letters in which this was clearly presented as a form of humiliation, one finds that it is associated with masculine masochism. In fact, female masochists never reported it.

As noted, this difference is somewhat problematic because it requires some subjective judgment as to whether the partner's infidelity was humiliating or not. Perhaps female masochists simply did not mention that it was humiliating when their partner had sex with someone else. One way to get around this problem is to count all cases of partner infidelity, regardless of whether humiliation was explicitly mentioned or not. For this analysis, it is best to delete the one or two cases in which the dominant partner engaged in homosexual intercourse with another. Most heterosexual people do not feel sexually competitive toward members of the opposite sex, so a partner's homosexual intercourse may be much less threatening and humiliating than a partner's heterosexual intercourse with someone else.

Among these data, partner infidelity was again associated almost exclusively with male masochism. Whereas 11% of letters by male masochists referred to the dominant partner having sex with another man, only one letter (1.4%) by a female masochist described her male partner having sex with another woman.

It is also noteworthy that letters by dominants almost never referred to having sex with others. One would at least expect that fantasies of multiple sexual partners would appeal to male dominants. After all, one reason men desire power is for sexual access to multiple women. But it was not the pattern found in this sample. Male dominants generally described having sex only with their submissive partner. Indeed, ironically, male submissives were significantly more likely than male dominants to report sexual contact with someone other than the partner!

The implication is that the female masochist enjoys the sexual fidelity of her partner much more than the male masochist enjoys the fidelity of his partner. Although most male masochists do not report having their female partners have sex with others, such activities are a vital part of male masochism in at least an important minority of cases. In contrast, partner infidelity is almost completely absent from female masochism.

There is some other evidence supporting this view. Leopold von Sacher-Masoch, for whom masochism is named, apparently was quite attracted to the humiliation of being cuckolded. His efforts to convince his reluctant wife to have sex with other men led to marital conflicts (Cleugh, 1951). Regarding female masochists, Shainess (1984) suggested that a central feature is being exceptionally, exclusively attractive to their partners, so partner infidelity may be avoided because it would threaten and undermine this feeling of attractiveness.

Humiliation Overall. Combining all categories of humiliation together makes it possible to compare the relative importance of humiliation in male versus female masochism. In general, humiliation seems to be featured more in male masochism than in female masochism.

One index of the importance of humiliation can be computed by counting the letters that contain no reference to any humiliating practices. One out of every four letters by female masochists was completely devoid of humiliation, compared to only one out of every ten letters by male masochists. A corresponding difference was found in letters written by dominants. Half the letters by male dominants reported no humiliation at all, compared to only 15% of letters by female dominants. Thus, female submissives were much more likely to escape humiliation altogether than male masochists were.

If one omits the "display" category of humiliation, the difference becomes dramatically large, because most of the humiliation in the female letters involved display. Indeed, if one drops both display and the somewhat amorphous category of verbal humiliation, one finds that the great majority of letters by female masochists had no humiliation. The remaining categories of humiliation appeared in less than one-fourth of the letters by female masochists. In contrast, they appeared in 87% of the letters by male masochists.

Letters by dominant partners replicated this difference. Only one out of every five letters by a male dominant reported humiliating the submissive partner in some way other than displaying her. Four out of every five letters by female dominants reported some humiliation other than display.

Thus, humiliation in general is more strongly associated with masculine masochism than with feminine masochism. When female masochists do undergo humiliation, it is usually a matter of being displayed naked, or possibly verbal humiliation (such as being required to beg or to count each spank aloud). Apart from verbal humiliation and display, humiliating practices appear to be a minor part of feminine masochism, whereas they are a major and pervasive aspect of masculine masochism.

Sexual Activities

Genital Intercourse

Having covered the major masochistic practices, we turn now to examine the sexual activities reported in the letters. It seems reasonable to begin with genital intercourse. How commonly do masochists report having full genital sex?

It appears that genital intercourse is far more common for female than for male masochists. Only 27% of the letters by male masochists said they had genital sex, whereas 61% of the letters by female masochists did. The corresponding pattern is seen in letters by dominant partners: Male dominants usually reported having genital sex, whereas female dominants generally did not.

Past theories about masochism have suggested two theories that could explain this large difference in genital sex. First, as some psychodynamic observers have proposed, it could be that males who fear genital intercourse are drawn to masochism. The strong form of this theory, that male masochists are impotent, cannot be confirmed in these data, for the majority of male masochists had orgasms one way or another. But perhaps many male masochists are somewhat insecure about intercourse and so prefer not to have genital sex with their female partners.

The second view is based on the notion that sexual penetration carries a symbolic message of dominance or conquest (cf. Brownmiller, 1975; also Bullough, 1976b; Deutsch, 1944). For a male dominant to penetrate the vagina of a female masochist would thus uphold and confirm their respective roles, but it might contradict a female's dominance to allow her masochistic male partner to enter her. In interviews, some male masochists and female dominants have expressed this view (e.g., Scott, 1983). They say it would not seem right or appropriate for a submissive male's penis to penetrate his mistress.

This second theory is consistent with other evidence. In these letters, many of the female-dominant couples who did have genital sex employed some symbolic device to maintain the woman's symbolic superiority. Some of them had the woman sit on top of the man during intercourse, thus symbolizing her control and supremacy. (Indeed, this position is sometimes called the woman-superior position.) Others kept the man tied up during the intercourse. Others required him to perform cunnilingus before or after intercourse. Others deferred intercourse until after the S&M session was over, presenting it to the male as a "reward" for his submission. Deferred intercourse is presumably based on the premise that the S&M roles have ceased.

Still, it seems possible to view sexual intercourse as occurring between equals rather than necessarily symbolizing male conquest and supremacy. In such a case, genital sex would constitute a mutual expression of love, affection, and desire, rather than expressing the man's dominance. If nothing else, genital intercourse expresses that the partner who initiated it finds the other sexually attractive and desirable. In this view, the greater rate of genital sex reported in female masochism suggests that the partner's love and attraction are more centrally important to female masochists than to male ones.

Anal Sex

Anal penetration can be performed using a dildo or vibrator, so it is possible for female dominants to perform it as well as male ones. Combining all these forms of penetration, anal sex appears to be about equally common in all categories of letters. Between 30% and 40% of the letters in each category reported anal intercourse. Thus, anal sex was not associated with either masculine or feminine masochism.

As noted earlier, there was an important role difference. The direction of anal penetration nearly always involved having the dominant partner penetrate the submissive. Anal sex apparently does carry a strong symbolic message of dominance. Receiving a penis (whether genuine or artificial) in one's anus is associated with a submissive role. But it is associated equally with masculine and feminine submission.

Oral Sex

Most letters in all categories reported having the submissive partner perform oral sex on the dominant partner. The reverse, in which the dominant performs oral sex on the submissive, was much less common, although it was reported in a substantial minority of cases.

The lowest frequency of oral sex was reported by female masochists: Slightly over half of them reported performing oral sex on their partners. This rate was significantly lower than the rates in all other categories combined.

Oral sex (performed by the submissive) was one of the few activities that was reported more frequently in letters by dominants than in letters by submissives. The highest rate was in letters by female dominants: 84% of them mentioned receiving cunnilingus. Apparently, one of the main attractions of the dominant role is receiving oral sex.

The lesser rate of oral sex among female masochists could be due to their emphasis on genital sex instead, although oral and genital sex are not mutually exclusive, for many letters reported both. This low rate also fits the evidence that female masochists have a lower rate of oral humiliation than male masochists. The mouth appears to be a much more important focus of male masochism than of female masochism.

Still, it must be kept in mind that the majority of female masochists did perform oral sex, and the difference between their rate of oral sex and the rate of male masochists was not quite large enough to be statistically significant.

One might suggest that male masochists tend to be more likely to perform oral sex because it is somehow humiliating or degrading to them, for as we have seen male masochists seek degrading forms of humiliation. In genital sex, the two people are in a sense equal partners, from a purely biological standpoint. Both are receiving genital stimulation and may have orgasms, and so forth. In contrast, oral sex is the use of one person's mouth as a pleasure device for the other, so inequality is implied.

The theory that male masochists emphasize oral sex because it signifies degradation is supported by some comments by male masochists on their performance of oral sex. They spoke of being "used" or of "servicing" their partners, as if they were reduced to mere masturbation devices for their partner—thus reduced to something less than fully human. Indeed, one male masochist related that his mistress had him hold the end of a vibrator in his mouth and then insert the other end into her vagina. This practice reduced him in an important sense to a mere extension of a mechanical device, and he described it as extremely humiliating.

Another possible suggestion would hold that women are somehow less oral in general than men or are less inclined to use their mouths in sex. This view is contradicted by other evidence. One may consider mouth-to-mouth kissing as the purest form of using the mouth for sexual pleasure. Kissing is more frequent in all-female (lesbian) couples than in heterosexual couples, and it is less common in male homosexual couples (Blumstein & Schwartz, 1983). Thus, women do appear quite capable of an oral orientation toward sex.

Summary

The sexual practices may be summed up as follows: Genital sex is associated with feminine masochism. Oral sex (using the submissive's mouth) is associated with both, but slightly more with masculine masochism. Anal sex (using the submissive's anus) is associated with both genders equally.

Audience Involvement

A substantial minority of letters reported having someone present in addition to the dominant and submissive. It appears that masochists desire audiences more than dominants do, although masochists desire these other people to be strangers who have been brought by the dominant partner. The audience or third party was significantly more likely to be an acquaintance of the dominant than an acquaintance of the submissive.

Male and female masochists refer about equally to the presence of other people for their submissive sex scenes. But the role of these third parties is different in male versus female masochism.

Third persons can have either of two roles. They can be a mere audience and witness to the spectacle, or they can actively take part in the activities. In letters by male masochists, if there is someone else present other than the dominant partner, this third person nearly always (84%) gets actively involved in the scene. Male masochists thus strongly favor participant audiences. In contrast, letters by female masochists report participant audiences and nonparticipating spectators about equally often.

Apparently, male masochists desire the presence of others in order to furnish more partners for sex or for sadomasochistic activities. Having a passive spectator who does nothing more than provide a witness seems to have little appeal for the masculine masochist. In contrast, the passive spectator does appear to have substantial appeal for the feminine masochist.

These patterns of audience involvement are consistent with differences that emerged in previous sections. Male masochists desire additional partners to intensify the sexual satisfactions or the humiliations, consistent with the masculine orientation toward intense experiences. Female masochists desire to be observed, inspected, and desired. They are content to have attention focused on them, without necessarily requiring further activities.

SUMMARY AND INTERPRETATION

We have seen a variety of differences between the activities reported by male as opposed to female masochists. These differences may be summarized to give respective profiles of the two versions of masochism. They suggest that the attractions of masochism to men are somewhat different from its attractions for women.

Masculine masochism exceeded feminine masochism in severity of pain, in overall humiliation, in status loss and degrading humiliations, in oral humiliations, in partner infidelity, in active participation by audiences and third parties, and in gender switching (transvestism). There were also trends suggesting that masculine masochism has more bondage and more performance of oral sex than feminine masochism.

Feminine masochism surpassed masculine masochism in the frequency of pain (instead of other practices), in presenting pain as punishment for actual misdeeds in the context of an ongoing relationship, in display humiliation, in genital sex, and in the presence of nonparticipant spectators.

One basic difference concerns power and status. Males have generally higher power and status than females in Western society (as in most societies). Male masochism appears to be centrally concerned with escaping this superior status. Men describe being degraded, which removes their freedom and dignity, and they emphasize being tied up, which prevents them from exerting the power and control that normally accompany high (and male) status.

Female masochists, in contrast, generally start our already lower in status and power than their male partners. There would perhaps be little attraction to them of being degraded and constrained, for society has already done that to them for centuries. For many women, adopting an inferior role would hardly be a departure from their normal lives.

One of the benefits of women's liberation is that modern women are sometimes able to achieve high levels of power and status. As a result, they sometimes end up earning more money and having more prestigious occupations than their spouses and boyfriends. Such cases may tend to breed marital discord and conflict (Blumstein & Schwartz, 1983). What happens to such couples in masochism?

Only a few letters in this sample reported such situations, but in these it was generally the female who showed interest in being made to submit. Moreover, her submission tended toward the patterns of masculine masochism more than toward feminine masochism. For example, one man wrote that his wife was a manager of a large office, whereas he was a lowly clerk whose salary was far less than hers. On weekends, however, she became his sexual slave and he would tie her up, whip her, and humiliate her in various ways. In another example, a woman who described herself as a successful and liberated woman fantasized about being bound, being forced to perform oral sex, and being treated like an animal. These practices—bondage, whipping, degrading humiliation, and oral sex—were all associated more strongly with masculine masochism than with feminine masochism. Although there are not enough cases to furnish any clear-cut proof or test, there is at least a suggestion that when women take on the prestige and power that normally accompany the masculine role, they move toward the masculine forms of masochism.

Thus, masochism can involve escape from high status, but this applies mainly to males. Females are drawn to masochism for something apparently quite different, except perhaps when they have reached the superior status that males normally enjoy.

The major themes associated with masculine masochism are degradation, deprivation of control, and intense sensations. The first two of these indicate a removal of the male ego. The man's prestige and power are nullified, and he is treated as something less than a man. He is treated like an animal or infant or woman (or even a mechanical device), he is rendered helpless and passive by bondage, and he is multiply humiliated. His male organs are ignored, and in sex he is reduced to a mere mouth. Indeed, his mouth, which ordinarily may be accustomed to the male prerogatives of boasting and commanding, is the focus of various humiliating practices. It becomes used to lick a woman's vagina or feet or anus, to consume his own sexual juices, and so on. His female partner may have sex with other men, thus expressing his symbolic defeat in male competition.

The orality of male masochism is probably associated with the third theme, namely the quest for intense sensations. Male masochism is heavily focused on the mouth, both in sex and in humiliation. The mouth is one of the most sensitive parts of the body in strictly physiological terms, but it is less loaded with emotional symbolism than the genitals. Female masochism, in contrast, focuses more on the genitals and less on the mouth, suggesting emphasis on emotion rather than sensation.

Male masochism's emphasis on intense sensation can be seen in the fact that male masochists report more severe pain than female masochists. Furthermore, when other people are present during masculine masochism, they join in the activities. Thus, the function of other people is to intensify the experience for the male masochist. The quest for intense sensations is a familiar feature of masculinity, so this aspect of male masochism is consistent with normal male psychology rather than contradicting it.

The theory of masochism as escape from high to low levels of selfhood appears best able to integrate these diverse patterns of male masochism. The symbolic aspects of the male ego (including responsibility, control, and pride) are systematically denied in masochism, thus removing the high-level aspects of the self. But the focus on sensations, which involves the lowest and most immediate levels of self, is retained and emphasized.

The main themes of feminine masochism appear to be minor pain in symbolic punishment for misdeeds, especially in a relationship context; desirability to the male partner and possibly others; and emphasis on emotion and symbolism rather than on sensation.

The most important contrast between masculine and feminine masochism is perhaps the relationship to the dominant partner. The masculine masochist is reduced to something less than human, leaving the dominant partner alone in a sense. But the female masochist remains a partner in a relationship, and many masochistic practices even seem designed to accentuate her partner's attraction and attachment to her. Unlike her male counterpart, she does not undergo reduction to an animal or baby; she remains an adult. Indeed, her sexual appeal as an adult woman is emphasized. She is displayed naked, making her acutely aware of being desired sexually by her partner (and possibly others too). Whereas the male masochist's dominant partner may have sexual intercourse with other men, the female masochist enjoys the sexual fidelity of her partner: His sexual desires are directed exclusively toward her. Third persons are often introduced as merely passive spectators, making her again the center of attention and sexual desire. The female masochist retains her adult identity, in contrast to the male masochist who is often reduced to something emphatically less than a man. In female masochism, the forms of humiliation serve to emphasize her sexual attractiveness to her partner, rather than to contradict it.

The sexual activities also reflect this difference. Genital sexual intercourse is a vital aspect to feminine sexual satisfaction in general, perhaps because it symbolizes intimacy and sharing and love (Blumstein & Schwartz, 1983). The female masochist commonly has genital intercourse with her partner. Although she may be tied up at the time, this intercourse is still palpable proof that he finds her desirable as a woman, in stark contrast to the relations between the male masochist and his partner. The male masochist often seems reduced to merely a masturbation device for his partner, but the female masochist remains a woman.

Feminine masochism emphasizes the relationship to the dominant partner in other ways too. Women were far more likely than men (nearly three times) to describe the punishment as a regular feature of an ongoing relationship. Thus, typically, the woman would write that she is punished by a spanking for normal, everyday misdeeds. These spankings are then followed by sexual activity.

This pattern fits well with several features of the psychology of women. First, women are strongly oriented toward relationships. To a woman, a relationship does not entail the burdensome role of provider that it does for a man. Instead, it tends to signify a nexus of intimacy and fulfillment (Blumstein & Schwartz, 1983). There is some evidence that women are more insecure in their relationships than men, signified by a greater fear of abandonment and of partner infidelity (Blumstein & Schwartz, 1983). Moreover, adult women may tend to have a stronger sense of guilt than men (e.g., Hoffman, 1975; also Brody, 1985). Females are socialized to inhibit the expression of bad feelings, causing them often to direct these feelings inward toward themselves (e.g., Brody, 1985). Finally, women associate virtue with self-sacrifice, and they may confuse self-sacrifice with caring for others, so that self-sacrifice becomes an end in itself (Gilligan, 1982).

Putting these facts together, one may suggest the following picture. Many adult women may desire to participate in a long-term, ongoing relationship, but once in it they may feel periods of guilt and doubt and may blame themselves when things go wrong. The tendencies toward self-blame and self-sacrifice may produce episodes of unhappiness and depression (indeed, women are far more prone to depression than men, e.g., Lewis, 1985). Self-doubt and self-blame may intensify the woman's fears that her partner will leave her for another.

If this picture is reasonably accurate, it indicates some possible sources of the appeal of masochism. First, although punishment might seem to acknowledge and confirm the guilt, when the punishment is ended the woman may feel relieved of the burden of guilt. Of course, if the woman has really done something seriously wrong or immoral, acting out a spanking game would not change anything or help deal with the guilt. But if the problem is merely a vague set of guilt feelings based on a general tendency to blame oneself, a masochistic episode may be an effective solution. To put it another way: If the woman is really, seriously guilty, then a masochistic spanking will be useless, but if she merely tends to feel guilty, masochism may help relieve these feelings.

Moreover, if the spankings are supposedly a regular feature of the relationship, then the woman need feel no accumulating sense of guilt. She can feel that she has been suitably punished for anything she has done wrong. If no spankings occur for a time, she can take this as a sign that she has done nothing wrong. Thus, women may be especially attracted to the idea that spanking punishments are a regular feature of the relationship. It may mean to her that she has been amply punished for past misdeeds and that she need not worry or brood or feel guilty.

Indeed, it is hard to take these reports any other way. One seriously doubts that very many modern couples really have an ongoing arrangement by which the husband regularly spanks his wife for any minor misbehavior. Such arrangements probably reflect the fantasy embellishments of female masochists. They believe they would be happy in such an arrangement, presumably because they imagine it would free them from guilt feelings and insecurity.

Furthermore, as we have seen, feminine masochism tends to dramatize the male partner's attraction to her (including his exclusive attraction to her). Such demonstrations may begin with displaying her naked so he can view and desire her, and it often culminates in full genital intercourse. Probably this emphasis on partner attraction would also appeal strongly to the woman because it would allay any doubts about her attractiveness. If she is insecure about whether she pleases her partner, she may enjoy the palpable proof of this love and desire that she gets in masochism.

In short, feminine masochism has some features that may seem to represent a very attractive relationship to the woman. Her partner's love and desire for her are confirmed. She is freed from any need to feel guilty or insecure. Indeed, many women associate self-sacrifice with virtue (cf. Gilligan, 1982), and masochism involves simple and direct forms of self-sacrifice, such as in submitting to mild physical pain. Women are willing to sacrifice themselves and suffer for the sake of others, and masochism features this by having the woman accept suffering for the sake of love. Thus, masochism may not only relieve feelings of guilt but may actually foster positive feelings of virtue. Finally, the masochistic episode ends with her pleasing her partner sexually in a way that is likely to bring mutual satisfaction and enhanced intimacy.

A last feature of female masochism is its emphasis on emotion, in contrast to the focus of male masochism on sensation. In general, women report feeling and expressing more emotions than men, which is consistent with the emphasis on emotion in masochism. The use of display humiliation probably produces intense feelings of embarrassment, causing emotional arousal rather than degradation. The emphasis on relationship context and on genital intimacy may cultivate the feelings of love and passion. The reduced level of pain in female masochism may indicate a greater emphasis on symbolism and anticipation, which again would tend to produce emotional arousal rather than maximum direct physical sensation. And the emphasis on the genitals (in both humiliation and sex) rather than the mouth may also promote emotion more than sensation, for the genitals are associated with stronger emotions than the mouth.

In an important sense, then, female masochism is simply an exaggeration of normal stereotypes of femininity. One could even call it a caricature. This is quite different from masculine masochism, which appears to contradict and repudiate many features of normal stereotypes of masculinity. Feminine masochism preserves and even enhances many normal features of our culture's ideas about women, including relationship focus, guilt feelings, openness to emotion, and self-sacrifice. In addition, women in general appear to be somewhat more sexually possessive of their relationship partners (Blumstein & Schwartz, 1983), and this too is preserved and amplified in masochism.

To conclude, let us consider how the two forms of masochism fit the main theories presented in this book.

Escape from Self

This book has described masochism as a means of escaping the self, that is, of deconstructing self-awareness.

Masculine masochism fits clearly and easily into this pattern. The masculine self is independent, autonomous, proud and dignified, powerful, competitive, and respected. Masochism systematically removes this self. The man is transformed into something less than a man, through symbolic treatment as a baby, woman, or animal. His autonomy and independence are denied by tying him up, giving him commands and rules, and so forth. His maleness is abused and contradicted by ignoring his penis, by having his partner look elsewhere (even to other men) for sexual satisfaction, and by feminizing him. The superior status that normally accompanies the male role is systematically and dramatically taken from him.

All that is left is the low-level focus on intense sensations. Masculine masochism emphasizes especially intense sensations, ranging from focusing humiliations on the mouth to providing severe pain. Indeed, if the male masochist is left with any source of pride, it is for enduring impressive amounts of pain. Thus, the masculine self is contradicted at the high levels of meaning and promoted only at the lowest, most immediate and superficial level (i.e., bodily sensation).

Feminine masochism does not fit quite so easily into the theory of escape from self. The break with normal, everyday life is less complete in female than in male masochism, as can be seen in the emphasis (at least in fantasy) on integrating the masochism into the relationship context. There is less emphasis on denying the self in all respects, and indeed many features of the stereotyped feminine self are retained and emphasized in masochism.

Self-control may be one aspect of self that is removed in female masochism. Women are normally required to develop remarkable capacities for self-control. They are taught to maintain modesty at all times, to control their impulses and their sexuality. Proper ladylike behavior entails concealing one's sex organs and sexual desires, stifling all negative emotions, and maintaining constant poise. Further evidence suggests that women tend to measure their achievements by internal standards more than men do (Gaeddert, 1985), again suggesting strong internal control. When things go wrong, women blame themselves, and they focus negative affect inward. Together, these factors suggest that the burden of selfhood can become heavy for women at times too, for they are required to be quite strong in controlling themselves.

Masochism may provide a temporary escape from these burdens. Sexual modesty is deliberately flouted by display humiliation. Part of the female masochist's pleasure in being displayed naked may well be the freedom from the familiar burden of feminine modesty. Any shame or ambivalence (the emotional mechanisms of internal control) she feels about her sex organs is set aside as she is compelled to let others see them without inhibition.

The woman's need to control herself in multiple ways is removed in masochism, for she falls under the complete control of an external agent. She is free to be wanton, impulsive, and so on, except as her partner restrains her. Freed from responsibility and explicitly punished for misdeeds, she escapes the need to doubt and blame herself for possible faults.

Part of the normal pattern of female self-control involves suppressing one's own wants. Women learn not to seek their own pleasure or to ask for things. Indeed, one reason for the low frequency of sexual intercourse among lesbians is the fact that neither woman wants to ask for sex or otherwise initiate it (Blumstein & Schwartz, 1983). Some masochistic practices deliberately contradict this inhibition of desire. The female masochist may be required to beg for sex, which probably runs contrary to the way women are brought up.

Still, apart from the issue of self-control, the escape from self does not fit the distinctive features of feminine masochism as well as it fits masculine masochism. This is not to say that women do not enjoy the escape from self. Most people have both masculine and feminine aspects to their personalities. Many women appear to practice the masculine forms of masochism. Indeed, some anecdotal evidence suggests that as women become liberated from their inferior, restricted status and take on responsible, demanding jobs, they may become increasingly attracted to masculine forms of masochism (e.g., Cowan, 1982; Shainess, 1984). The distinction between masculine and feminine masochism is probably not based on the biological categories but rather on the *social* categories of male and female, that is, on the way society teaches people to be male and female. There is probably considerable overlap. Although the special features of feminine masochism do not fit neatly into the escape from self theory, many women are probably drawn to masochism precisely by the escape it offers.

Tradeoff in Meaning

The second main theory has presented masochism as a means of getting fulfillment and justification in life. In exchange for these benefits, the masochist accepts certain costs, particularly relinquishing control and self-worth. This view seems to fit feminine masochism better than masculine masochism.

Most important, feminine masochism emphasizes the positive benefits of the tradeoff, downplaying the costs. First, consider fulfillment. In masochism, the two main forms of fulfillment are relationship intimacy and sexual pleasure. The female masochist apparently derives richer fulfillment than the male one, to the extent that her submission promotes greater intimacy and mutuality. She is made to feel the love and desire of her partner, unlike the male masochist. Feminine masochism may even offer greater sexual fulfillment than masculine masochism.

The male masochist must often be content with masturbation, but the female masochist usually has genital sex with her partner. The rules restricting orgasms appear to be more common among male masochists than female ones, which suggests that female masochists are more at liberty to enjoy multiple orgasms at will. This again would suggest greater fulfillment in feminine masochism.[4]

The second benefit of masochism, the gain in justification, is also featured in feminine masochism. In general, people desire to have a secure value base so they can know clearly what is right versus wrong and can be free from anxiety and doubt. Feminine masochism features issues of punishment and misdeeds, and it emphasized the relationship that forms the masochistic value base. These features are present in masculine masochism, but they receive greater emphasis in feminine masochism, so it is reasonable to say that feminine masochism maximizes these benefits of the tradeoff.

The negative sides of the masochistic tradeoff involve giving up self-worth (by submitting to humiliation) and control (by being bound, restrained, given rules, and commanded). Both of these are more pronounced in masculine masochism. As we have seen, feminine masochism has less humiliation than masculine masochism in general. In the most relevant categories—humiliation based on status degradation, which clearly lowers self-worth—female masochists reported far less activity than male masochists. Moreover, there was some evidence that bondage and other forms of control deprivation was more common among male masochists.

Thus, feminine masochism is a better bargain than masculine masochism, from the perspective of a tradeoff in meaning. Feminine masochism downplays the loss of self-worth and of control, whereas it emphasizes the gain in justification and in fulfillment. All the features of the tradeoff are apparent in masculine masochism, but their relative emphasis makes a more attractive deal in the feminine pattern.

The tradeoff theory may thus apply better to feminine masochism than to masculine masochism. Again, this is not to say that males are unaffected by this aspect of masochism. Many letters by male masochists made it clear that they regarded these activities as extremely fulfilling and that they loved the certainty and freedom from anxiety that came from accepting their partner's wishes as the ultimate source of value

---

[4]These comments must be regarded as speculative, for they measure fulfillment by normal and outward standards, which may be inappropriate. For all we know, the male masochist derives greater sexual pleasure and fulfillment from masturbating than a normal person does through intercourse. There is simply no easy way to compare subjective feelings of fulfillment across quite different people. All that can be said is that by normal standards, it seems that more fulfillment is available to the feminine masochist than to the masculine one.

and rightness. Still, the tradeoff theory seems to have the best fit to the feminine version of masochism.

Conclusion

This chapter has suggested a variety of differences between the masculine and feminine approaches to masochism. These should not be overemphasized. Most of the evidence comes from one source, and it is possible that biases in this source could account for some of the differences. Until further research confirms these patterns, they should be considered only a preliminary sketch. Furthermore, masculinity and femininity are not radically separate categories of psychology but blurred constellations of traits. Every individual has masculine and feminine tendencies to various degrees. The attractions of masculine masochism probably appeal to many women, and the features of feminine masochism probably apply to many men. Sex differences are a matter of slight differences in average tendencies, or a matter of slight differences in emphases. It would be quite wrong to take these findings and expect every male masochist to fit the masculine pattern and every female masochist to fit the feminine pattern.

Despite the need for caution, these findings are important. They indicate that there are different approaches to masochism. All masochists do not feel the same attractions or derive the same benefits.

The relation of masochism to gender has been debated ever since the earliest theories about the appeal of masochism. The relationship was at first mistaken and overstated. Recently, in reaction against these early overstatements, theorists have taken to denying that there is any relation at all between gender and masochism. These denials may also be mistaken and overstated. If there are indeed gender differences in masochism, as this chapter has suggested, then gender is not a neutral issue with respect to masochism.

But it is not anything as simple as suggesting that women are masochistic. Rather, masochism exerts a wide range of appeal. Both men and women are drawn to masochism, although it is a minority pattern in both. Participation in masochism, and the benefits people derive from it, may be affected by broader psychological differences between the sexes.

The most general conclusion appears to be that masculine masochism rests on a direct contradiction of male stereotypes, whereas female masochism does not contradict female stereotypes—if anything, it exaggerates or caricatures them. Masculine masochism appears to emphasize the *deconstructive* aspects of masochism, by focusing on the negation of one's normal identity. Feminine masochism, in contrast, emphasizes the *constructive* aspects of masochism, by placing punishment in broader contexts and by relying on symbolic meanings of partners and spectators. Because escape from self is deconstructive whereas search for meaning is constructive, there is some basis for viewing the escapist aspect of masochism as closer to its masculine patterns, whereas the meaning-elaborating aspect of masochism seems to fit feminine patterns best.

Chapter Eight

Sadism

Thus far, we have examined masochism in considerable detail. Sadism has been neglected, and even its links to masochism have been questioned. This chapter considers the issue of sadism. It offers several general observations about sadism and then offers some speculative implications of our theories of masochism.

WHAT IS SADISM?

Sadism is elusive because there are several quite different phenomena that resemble each other superficially. These can be easily mistaken for each other.

A simple definition of *sadism* would be the enjoyment of cruelty and of inflicting pain. This definition does not have a sexual component, implying that sadism may arise in nonsexual contexts. Certainly the infliction of pain, apparently with enjoyment, has occurred in innumerable different cultural and historical contexts. If one includes the enjoyment of watching others suffer as sadism, then one must conclude that sadism is nearly culturally universal. From primitive practices of torturing captives, to public hangings and executions, to gladiatorial entertainments, to violent movies, people seem to enjoy watching others undergo pain and harm.

This apparent universality contrasts sharply with the apparently extreme cultural relativity of masochism. If we define *sadism* broadly enough to include everyone who has ever enjoyed watching a violent movie, TV show, or a boxing match, most of the population probably consists of sadists (at least most of the male population). Sadism in this regard is far more widespread than masochism.

On the other hand, if we restrict the definition to sexual sadism, then suddenly there are very few who qualify. Indeed, even in the S&M subculture, there appear to be relatively few sadists, to judge by the frequent observations and comments of participants.

The individuals who do take the dominant role in sex apparently do so for a variety of reasons. Many people may take the dominant role because their lovers ask them to do so (see Scott, 1983). They may have no particular desire of their own to play that role, and in fact they may often be reluctant or inhibited about doing so, but a submissively inclined partner asks them to help enact the partner's masochistic fantasies. Although these people inflict pain, bondage, and humiliation, thereby dominating others in a sexual context, it seems misleading to call them sadists.

Many of the interviews and other firsthand accounts of dominant sexuality come from prostitutes (e.g., Juliette, 1983; Smith & Cox, 1983). These women also inflict pain, bondage, and humiliation in an explicitly sexual context, but it seems inappropriate to regard them as sadists. Apparently their motives are primarily economic, even if they do come to enjoy their work to some degree. After all, prostitutes are not generally regarded as motivated by sexual desire and pleasure. Interviews with professional dominatrices are probably not therefore a reliable way to learn about sadism.

Thus, there are people who engage in sexual dominance for reasons other than their own sexual desires, and it seems misleading to call them sadistic, especially if they do not derive much sexual pleasure from the activity. Sadism as a behavioral category is probably far more heterogeneous than masochism. It seems likely that most people who engage in sexual submission do so for the sake of their own desires and pleasures, but the same cannot be said about people who engage in sexual dominance.

If the definition of sadism is restricted to people who clearly derive sexual pleasure from dominating others, then there appear to be at least three distinct categories of sadists. First, there are people who started out as masochists and gradually moved into taking the dominant role. These converted masochists seem to constitute the largest category of sadists and dominants (e.g., Kamel, 1983; Lee, 1983). Second, there are the people who have no initial interest in S&M but who begin to take the dominant role at the request of a masochistic partner—and who learn to enjoy that role. They may have little or no masochistic experience or desire, and their pleasure in dominance may derive heavily from the satisfaction of pleasing a loved one. Third, there may be some individuals who explicitly desire to inflict pain, bondage, and humiliation on others in a sexual context. They too may have little or no background or interest in masochism. These are perhaps the purest sadists of them all, and it is plausible that they may contain the highest portion of mentally ill individuals.

SADISM AND THE SELF

We have examined masochism as a way of breaking down and escaping the self. If that is correct, then sadism may appeal to some as a means of building up the self. The core of sadism, at least in its pure form, may be the assertion of self and the strengthening of self-awareness.

Taking the dominant role involves play-acting an exalted, glorified self. Within the immediate situation and context, one has unlimited control and power. (Of course, that is an illusion, for the submissive often retains considerable influence. But the focus here is precisely on the illusion that S&M scenes revolve around.) One's partner treats one as a superior being, a higher form of life. One is free to receive any form of sexual service or pleasure that one wishes. In many cases, the dominant can also require the submissive to perform nonsexual services also, such as housework. It may be necessary for the dominant to sexualize these other activities, that is, to cause the submissive to view doing the dominant's housework as an act of sexual submission; but that is still better than doing one's own housework.

We have also seen that many masochists may be attracted because the relationship to the dominant can serve as a source of value. For that to work, the dominant partner's self becomes almost godlike in the sense of being an ultimate basis for deciding what is right and good. Any desires, impulses, or inclinations of the dominant partner are treated as if they were divinely sanctioned, and the submissive accepts them without question and tries to fulfill them immediately. (Again, this is the illusion, not the underlying reality, of S&M scenes.)

In short, the dominant's esteem and control are magnified and artificially inflated by S&M scenes. Esteem and control are two major features of the self, so it is quite apparent that taking the dominant role bolsters one's sense of self. The scene creates the fantasy that the dominant's self is sacred and omnipotent.

The appeal of enacting such a fantasy is not difficult to ascertain. The self constantly strives for esteem and control. Playing the dominant role in an S&M scene is a way of fulfilling these strivings, at least in a temporary game.

Thus, sadism may appeal to people who desire to have their sense of self bolstered. Sadism magnifies the self, rendering it somewhat larger than life. It offers the individual an exaggeration of self, according to which one has supreme worth, dignity, and esteem; enjoys unlimited power and control; and can treat any whims or desires as sacred, legitimate obligations for the submissive partner.

This glorification of self may appeal especially to people who privately feel very positively about themselves but feel that they have not received the recognition and rewards in life that they deserve. Individuals from lower class backgrounds, which we rarely found among masochists, may be drawn more to the sadistic or dominant role-playing. There is some limited evidence that dominants tend to have such backgrounds (e.g., Samois, 1982; Juliette, 1983), but it is far from conclusive. If that is correct, there would be a certain elegant symmetry between sadism and masochism. Masochism would appeal to individuals who have high external power and status but perhaps privately feel insecure or uncertain about themselves. Sadism would appeal to individuals who have low external power and status but perhaps privately feel that they deserved much better. This would fit the view that people seek consistency regarding their selves (Swann, 1985).

As we have seen, the weight of research evidence indicates that the main initial attraction to S&M is that of the masochistic role. This implies that only a few individuals are drawn into S&M because they wish to enact the fantasy of a glorified self through taking the dominant role. One exception to this unanimity, however, is the observation of some clinicians that their patients seem more fundamentally attracted to the sadistic role. If more systematic observations could verify that the majority of mentally ill people who engage in S&M prefer the sadistic, dominant role, this would lend further support to the view that the attractions of S&M differ dramatically for the normal and healthy individual as opposed to the clinically abnormal. The pure sadists may thus often be people who suffer from a clinically impaired sense of self, and who are drawn to sadism as a way of building up the self through fantasy-based activities.

MASOCHIST AND SADIST: AN IDEAL COUPLE?

We have seen that not everyone who takes the dominant role in sex is a genuine sadist. Indeed, many apparently take that role at the urging of a masochistically inclined partner. We have also seen that such dominants are sometimes reluctant, uncertain, inhibited, and so forth. As a result, they may make less than fully satisfactory partners for masochists. It is reasonable to ask, therefore, whether a true, genuine sadist would be preferable, from the masochist's perspective.

There is reason to doubt that the true sadist would be the ideal partner for the true masochist. The true sadist is someone who enjoys dominating others, imposing his or her will on others. That, of course, is what masochists think they want, but in fact they typically want to be dominated in a very specific, carefully prescribed fashion. Many masochists reportedly become upset and recalcitrant if they are not dominated in precisely the manner they desire (e.g., Juliette, 1983). The true sadist wants to dominate according to his or her own wishes, not according to those of the submissive partner.

Occasionally, of course, there may be a perfect match by coincidence. The sadist and the masochist may enjoy precisely the same form of domination. But to the extent that their preferences differ, they may be dissatisfied. The true sadist does not want to give the masochist what the masochist wants; indeed, the sadist may take pleasure in denying the masochist what the masochist wants. The truly sadistic desire is to inflict something on the masochist that the masochist does not want, in order to make it real domination. If the victim is too willing, the sadistic pleasure may be diminished.

There is a further reason for doubting that a true sadist plus a true masochist constitute an ideal match. As we have already seen, there is some reason to suspect that true sadists may involve a disproportionately high number of mentally ill people. If one assumes that such mentally ill people may suffer some impairments in their capacity for rational judgment, in their common sense, and in their self-control, then it may be risky for a masochist to entrust him or herself to such a person's power. The true sadist may be prone to getting carried away, if nothing else, which could lead to some harm or suffering for the masochist. Knowing when to stop is a vital part of the dominant's role, and the masochist probably wants that decision made by someone in full possession of his or her faculties.

Thus, there is good reason to doubt that a true sadist would make the best partner for a masochist. Lee (1983), who has studied the element of risk in S&M encounters, found quite clearly that "a man setting out to play the slave role does not look for a 'real sadist'" (p. 188). A real sadist would be considered a dangerous and inconsiderate partner. Although the masochist may desire someone to pretend to be dangerous, self-centered, and inconsiderate, the masochist does not want someone who is actually thus.

Perhaps the ideal partner for a masochist would be someone who feels strong interest and empathy for the submissive role. We have seen that many sadists seem to have started out as masochists; such converted masochists might be satisfying as dominant partners, because they understand the submissive role and identify with it. If the sadist is not strongly devoted to making the masochist live out exactly the sadist's own submissive fantasy, he or she can enjoy putting the masochist through some exercises that fit both the sadist's and the masochist's respective desires.

To put it another way: The ideal partner for the masochist would be someone who derives pleasure from causing the masochist to submit in precisely the way the masochist secretly desires. Thus, the ideal dominant partner's pleasure would derive from identifying and empathizing with the submissive partner. A true sadist would not fit that description, but someone with only a casual interest in S&M, or a converted masochist, might.

ON GRADUATING FROM MASOCHISM TO SADISM

Researchers have repeatedly found that the vast majority of sadists (that is, people who enjoy taking the dominant role in sadomasochistic sex games) began as masochists (e.g., Kamel, 1983; Weinberg & Kamel, 1983). We have seen that the reverse does not hold—that is, there is no evidence that most masochists were previously sadists. The implication is that the majority of people who participate in S&M begin as masochists. Some of them eventually begin to enjoy and possibly prefer the dominant role, but others do not.

To explain sadism, therefore, is to understand what causes some masochists to convert to enjoying the dominant role. At present, there is almost no evidence to rely upon, but some speculative suggestions may be made.

One plausible way for an individual to progress from masochism to sadism would involve imaginative identification with one's partner. Initially, the person desires to submit as a masochist. If nothing else, this ensures that the person is quite capable of understanding the pleasures of masochism. Such an individual might enjoy the dominant role because it enables him or her to imagine what the submissive partner is experiencing. The person ceases to submit directly, and instead he or she derives masochistic pleasure from imagining the submissive experiences of others. Being the dominant enables the person to structure and control the experience. In this way, the ex-masochist can ensure that the scene is stimulating to him or herself. The ex-masochist can also be careful to give the submissive partner a fully satisfying experience.

The conversion to sadism may appeal especially to certain groups of masochists. Some individuals were perhaps not strongly drawn to masochism, but they became involved and found the experiences enjoyable; switching roles might be a further, enjoyable novelty to them. Other masochists might be unable to find satisfactory experiences, perhaps because they are unfortunate at finding a partner who will dominate them according to their own wishes. By switching to the dominant role, they can finally experience scenes that will be more satisfactory to them, although of course their experience is partly vicarious.

If the sadist's pleasure derives in large part from identifying with the masochist and imagining what the masochist is experiencing, then a major prerequisite for conversion to sadism is a high degree of empathy and imagination. Past researchers have frequently suggested that most masochists have an active, fertile imagination (e.g., Reik, 1941/1957), so there should be plenty of suitable candidates for conversion to sadism.

Indeed, this form of sadistic pleasure is analogous to the enjoyment of pornography in some respects. One sees the sexual activities and pleasures of others, and one's own pleasure derives in part from imagining oneself in their place. Scott (1983) observed repeatedly that masochists show a lively interest in pornographic materials, especially pertaining to S&M. Becoming a dominant many in may cases be simply a step beyond enjoying pornography. One simply identifies with a living partner rather than a fictional character.

Participating as a dominant would have two potentially important advantages over enjoying pornography. First, one can help write the script and control the action, including pacing it to one's own desires and pleasures. Second, the dominant has an eager slave ready to provide for his or her sexual satisfaction, unlike the solitary consumer of pornography.

Whether the conversion from masochism to sadism proceeds along the route of imaginary identification, or along some other route, remains for further studies to determine. This route does at least make the transition plausible, as well as explaining the close link between sadism and masochism that may researchers have claimed. The pleasure of sadism may often be simply an elaborate or disguised form of masochistic pleasure.

INTIMACY AND SADISM

One serious drawback of sadism is that it seems to offer less chance for intimate fulfillment than masochism does.

Masochism can offer fulfillment by enabling the submissive to feel merged with another human being. The masochist takes another person's will into his or her own mind. Masochistic actions are guided by concern with the dominant partner's wishes, pleasures, and expectations. Moreover, we have seen that some patterns of masochism (especially feminine masochism) offer the masochist ample proof of intimacy, by affirming that the masochist is loved and desired by the dominant partner to the exclusion of all others. The masochist presumably finds this merger with the dominant partner especially satisfying because the dominant partner is made out to be a particularly wonderful and important person.

In contrast, the sadist's partner is almost a nonentity. As we have seen, the prototype for the masochist's identity is that of a slave, that is, a socially dead or nonexistent person. Is the sadist supposed to enjoy merging with a nonperson? In a sense, a sadomasochistic relationship consists of two people becoming one. That one "is" the sadist or dominant partner. For the masochist, this is a satisfying escape from self into another human being. For the sadist, it is simply being oneself, almost like being alone.

The unsatisfying nature of some such relationships is discussed by Scott (1983, pp. 73–75). She recorded that dominant women complain about the "whatever-you-say-mistress syndrome," that is, the tendency for extremely submissive males to respond to all questions or opinions with "Whatever you say, mistress." In the example Scott furnished to illustrate this problem, the male masochist refused to express any preferences, opinions, or decisions, even when his dominant girlfriend genuinely wanted a response from him. The relationship was extremely one-sided, and she came to find it tiresome and boring. He offered her no personality, no stimulation, and no challenge—nothing except the complete willingness to go along with whatever she said or thought.

A famous novel about masochism contains the same message. Reage's (1954/1966) *Story of O* is, to be sure, a highly exaggerated and stylized depiction of masochism. Its popularity derives not from its realistic portrayal of masochism (for it is not very good at that; indeed, the whippings in the book would probably cause medical harm) but because it artfully expresses a major set of masochistic fantasies. Still, the author was careful to depict the interpersonal relationships in a sensitive and realistic manner. The book ends by having the two dominant men abandon the woman just as she reaches extremes of submission. As she becomes a nonperson, she has less and less to offer her dominant partners, and they lose interest.

These problems apply to ongoing, full-time sadomasochistic relationships, and perhaps they are irrelevant to couples who enact S&M fantasies on an occasional basis. Still, it is apparent that sadism is probably not a viable means to achieving intimacy with another, even if masochism is.

SADISM AND SEX

Chapter 5 noted that masochists claim to achieve unusually strong levels of sexual arousal and satisfaction, and there was some theoretical plausibility to those claims. Masochism may indeed intensify sexual arousal and pleasure. If it does, however, then sadism may well be detrimental to sexual pleasure.

Some features of sadism resemble those of masochism directly, and both may be conducive to sexual pleasure. The sense of isolation, the focus on immediate sensations, and similar patterns may promote sensual pleasure in sadists as well as masochists. But there is good reason to regard self-awareness as an obstacle to sexual pleasure, as we saw in chapter 5. Sadism appears designed to strengthen and assert the person's sense of self in many different ways. In the midst of such an episode, the sadist may find it difficult to achieve the loss of self that seems a prerequisite for intense sexual pleasure.

Does sadism weaken or impair sexual responsiveness? It is at least plausible that it does. There is very little direct evidence about this. One journalist who interviewed a series of masochistic women reported that many of them complained bitterly about widespread impotence among dominant males. Indeed, one respondent claimed to have gone to an S&M club in which there were fifty dominant men, all but one of whom were impotent (Santini, 1976, p. 51).

We saw earlier that clinical observers have claimed that many sadomasochistic patients have sexual dysfunctions (e.g., Reik, 1941/1957; Stekel, 1953). These observers have also asserted that sadism was the fundamental dynamic in their patients, with masochism being a secondary or derivative form. It is conceivable that these clinicians had a series of patients who were both sadistically inclined and sexually unresponsive or impotent.

Still, this evidence is far from conclusive. There is at best suggestive evidence that sadism may undermine sexual responsivity, but much clearer and stronger evidence is needed before any general conclusions can be drawn.

Several features of sadomasochism could possibly be explained as arising from a negative effect of sadism on sexual arousal. We have seen that people who engage in S&M prefer to do so in the context of ongoing, long-term relationships. Such relationships might offer the sadist the best chance for sexual pleasure. In the first place, the submissive presumably knows the best techniques to stimulate and please the dominant partner. Moreover, the dominant may feel comfortable about relinquishing control long enough to experience sexual pleasure (especially orgasm) because he or she can be sure of resuming control immediately, because the relationship is already negotiated and stable.

We have also seen that S&M scripts involved a very high frequency of oral sex, usually with the submissive performing oral sex for the pleasure of the dominant partner. The act of oral sex can be considered a means of maximizing the sexual stimulation of the dominant partner.

Perhaps one reason for its popularity in S&M is that it is a strong or effective way of overcoming the obstacles and producing sexual pleasure in the dominant partner.

CONCLUSION

This chapter offered several speculations about sadism, based on the implications of our study of masochism. Sadism is elusive to study because it appears to be far more heterogeneous than masochism; many people may take the dominant role in sex for reasons other than pure sadistic pleasure. If sadism is the theoretical counterpart to masochism, then sadism may revolve around glorifying and asserting the self. The resultant strengthening of the sadist's sense of self might prove an obstacle to sexual pleasure and response.

There may be good reason to doubt that a true sadist would make an ideal partner for a masochist. Although masochists believe they want to be thoroughly subjected to another's will, in practice they often have very specific ideas about how they wish to be dominated. A masochist may find a true sadist unwilling to dominate him or her in the manner that the masochist desires. Likewise, the sadist's pleasure may be diminished if the submissive partner is too willing and enjoys the scene too much.

The study of sadism should begin with the empirical observation that most sadists are apparently ex-masochists. To understand how people become sadists, one should emphasize learning about how masochists convert to sadism, and why other masochists never make that transition. One possible mechanism involves vicarious pleasure: A masochist learns to take the dominant role and enjoys the masochistic partner's submission by imagining what the partner is feeling.

The irony of sadism is that it may be less satisfying than masochism, even though the S&M scene seems thoroughly oriented toward the feelings and desires of the dominant. The sadist's opportunities for emotional intimacy are greatly diminished by the masochist's loss of self, for the sadist ends up with the only self in the room, almost alone. And even sexual pleasure may elude the sadist in many cases. The masochist, in contrast, may well experience intense fulfillments of intimacy and sexual pleasure. Thus, despite the apparent superiority and advantages of the dominant role, the sadist may really derive less fulfillment from the scene than the masochist.

Chapter Nine
Clinical Implications

Masochism has long been considered from the perspective of clinical psychology. This book has sought to provide an alternative view of masochism, understanding it from what is known about normal behavior. Still, it is worth giving some consideration to the clinical views and issues.

In particular, clinical psychologists sometimes find masochists among their patients, and they need to have some basis for treating them. Past treatment approaches have been based on the view that masochism indicates a serious disturbance. If the present view is correct, masochism is not itself a sign of psychopathology, although the mentally ill may be drawn to engage in unusual sexual activities. But the clinicians still need some basis for dealing with masochistic patients. This chapter sketches some outlines for an approach based on this book's views.

Additionally, several clinicians have recently put forward a view of masochism that seems to them to make sense of the masochism they have observed in their patients. Their view seems on the surface to be diametrically opposed to the view that masochism is an escape from self, for it views masochism as a way of strengthening one's sense of self. This chapter examines their view and its evidence and offers a way of synthesizing that view with the present theory.

MASOCHISM, PATHOLOGY, AND ASSESSMENT

There is a long tradition of viewing masochism as evidence of mental illness. In that view, masochism was a form of psychopathology, and people who engaged in it were mentally ill. It was considered abnormal to derive pleasure from masochism.

We have seen, however, that masochism can be understood on the basis of what is known about normal human behavior. Moreover, we have seen that many people who engage in masochism are apparently quite healthy, capable, and typical in other respects and show no signs of abnormality or mental illness.

The implication is that masochism itself should not be considered a form or a sign of mental illness. The fact that someone engages in masochism and enjoys it is not a reason to classify that person as mentally ill. Masochism is an unusual form of sexual pleasure and one that runs contrary to the norms and morals that govern prevailing attitudes about sex in our society. Accordingly, masochism can be regarded by some perspectives as weird, as deviant, and even as immoral. But it should not be regarded as pathological or sick.

Does this mean that all masochists are healthy? Certainly not; one would expect a group of masochists to contain their share of mentally ill, just like any other group. Masochism itself, however, is not a sign of mental illness.

It is also quite conceivable that one's involvement in masochism could become so extreme that it would be taken as a sign of illness or perversion. Perhaps the best rough guideline would be Freud's remarks on the nature of perversion. Freud said that no form of sexual pleasure is itself perverse, unless it comes to replace all other forms. That is, if some activity (apart from intercourse or orgasm) becomes indispensable to sexual enjoyment, then one may call it a perversion.

Freud's suggestion is probably quite applicable to masochism. If someone enjoys masochistic sex on occasion, there is no reason to regard that person as mentally ill, perverted, or sick. But if the person becomes unable to enjoy sex without masochistic submission, then masochism has apparently taken over that person's entire sexuality, and that would be an indication of illness and perversion.

There is a further important implication of applying Freud's insight to masochism. It concerns what the problem is. The individual who is only able to enjoy sex in connection with masochism may indeed be regarded as pathological. This person's problem is not the presence of masochistic sexuality, however. Rather, it is the *absence* of nonmasochistic sexuality. The fact that the individual enjoys masochism is not the problem. The problem is that the individual does not enjoy other forms of sex.

The approach to treating the perverse masochist thus shifts. The therapeutic goal is not to remove the enjoyment of masochism, but rather to restore the enjoyment of other sexual activities. The first step should be to explore the reasons for the lack of sexual response in nonmasochistic contexts.

We have seen that there is some reason to believe that masochism would enhance sexual response. Some thrill-seeking individuals may be drawn to masochism simply because it furnishes unusually intense sexual gratification. Others, however, may be drawn to masochism because they are sexually insecure, perhaps because their normal sexual responses are not strong enough in their own estimation. They may become masochists because submission reliably produces strong sexual responses in them. They may adopt an exclusively masochistic approach to sex, insisting that they do not desire sex without masochism, because they are afraid of an inadequate response. Their problem, then, is that their overall level of sexuality is weak, perhaps because of insecurities or other inhibiting factors, or perhaps because of a low endowment of libidinal energy. Somehow they discovered that masochism produced a strong enough response in them, quite possibly simply by virtue of the way masochism strengthens sexual responses.

With such individuals, again, the problem is not the presence of the masochistic pleasure, but the absence or weakness of other forms of sexual pleasure. The therapeutic approach to them should begin not by trying to analyze or eliminate their interest in masochism. Rather, it should explore the reasons for the weakness of their sexual responses outside the context of masochism.

The general point, once again, is that masochism should not be considered a sign or form of mental illness. One may make the analogy to homosexuality. For a long time, homosexuality was considered a form of mental illness, and treatment focused on trying to prevent patients from responding sexually to homosexual erotic materials. For example, some forms of therapy sought to pair homosexual stimuli with unpleasant sensations (aversive counterconditioning). Sometimes these treatments helped damage the person's enjoyment of homosexual sex, but they were not very effective at getting the person to start enjoying heterosexual sex.

Now, however, homosexuality has begun to be accepted as a normal form of sexual preference. The fact that the person experiences homosexual desires and pleasures is not taken as a sign of mental illness. Sexual masochism may be similar.

MASOCHISTS IN THERAPY

The preceding section has already made some indications of how therapy with masochists should be approached. The most extreme masochists in sex therapy, and perhaps the ones most in need of therapy, are the ones who are unable to enjoy sex apart from masochistic submission. As we have seen, the clinical focus should not be on the masochism but on the absence of sexual response apart from masochism. The goal of therapy is to teach or help the individual learn to enjoy other, more conventional forms of sex—not to discourage or prevent the masochistic sexual responses.

Treatment of such individuals would thus resemble treatment of people whose general level of sexual desire is weak. Again, causes may be inhibitions and insecurities, or general lack of libidinal energy. People who can only enjoy sex through masochistic response can probably be considered similar to people who are sexually unresponsive. Masochists show the same lack of sexual response and pleasure in many contexts. The only difference is that masochists have adapted, in a sense, to their own low level of sexual response by finding one context (masochism) in which they do respond strongly enough. In many cases, again, the reason may simply be that masochism does strengthen and enhance sexual response, for several techniques of masochism parallel those used in sex therapy with sexually unresponsive individuals (see chapter 6).

Problems of this sort may apply only to a small minority of masochists. It seems quite plausible that many masochists enjoy conventional sexual activities on other occasions. Certainly the majority of letters to *Variations* expressed that attitude, and Scott's observations likewise suggest that most masochists enjoy conventional sex, too.

Perhaps a more common presenting problem that brings masochists into clinical therapy is the negative reaction to discovering one's own masochistic sexual desires. One therapist who specializes in treating masochists described them as often normal, healthy, even admirable individuals, who are consumed with fear and doubt about their masochistic fantasies and desires (Cowan, 1982). They come to therapy fearing that they are sick and wanting to be restored to having only "normal" (i.e., nonmasochistic) sexual desires.

One can well understand the distress faced by such individuals. (Indeed, several masochists mentioned to me that they suffered similar doubts and dilemmas.) They notice that thoughts or fantasies of masochistic submission are exciting to them, and they feel aroused and drawn to explore these matters further. At the same time, they are well aware that masochism carries a stigma of perversion and mental illness. They fear that their desires and fantasies may be a sign of some very serious underlying problem. In other words, they are not sure what their own sexual desires and responses mean, and they fear that their masochistic inclinations prove that they are mentally ill or perverted.

When individuals feel insecure about themselves, they tend to engage in some form of information seeking to ascertain whether their problems are real or not. To be sure, some people deal with these insecurities by trying to avoid and suppress them; but these are unlikely to be the ones who show up in psychotherapy. Besides, recent experimental evidence suggests that thought suppression is not very effective (Wegner, in press; Wegner, Schneider, Carter, & White, 1987). Trying not to think about something is more likely to produce an obsession than the comfortable absence of the forbidden thought.

One's efforts to obtain information about masochism may well intensify one's fears and worries. Budding masochists find it difficult to talk about their desires and worries with others, for they may well encounter a negative, stigmatizing reaction—and one that may have disastrous practical consequences. If instead of talking with friends, the masochist goes to the library to look up information about masochism, he or she finds very disturbing portrayals of masochism as deviant, sick, and perverted. Past works on masochism have often treated masochists as severely disturbed individuals, engaging in shocking activities (clinical case histories tend to favor the most vivid and flamboyant examples), ridden with guilt, filled with unconscious homicidal tendencies, and so forth.

Thus, by the time that a masochist shows up in therapy, he or she may be pretty well convinced that having masochistic fantasies is a sign of some catastrophic pathology that is about to explode and ruin his or her life.

The first step in treating these individuals should be to promote self-acceptance. In essence, they have a pattern of sexual desire that is somewhat widespread and normal, but they mistakenly regard it as extremely unusual and sick. They probably have no idea that a significant minority of the population, perhaps as much as 20%, reports some sexual arousal in response to masochistic stories or thoughts, and probably there are even more who experience the response but do not admit this to interviewers. And, of course, in the past there was little basis for understanding the psychology of masochism without invoking mental illness, so many such patients probably suffer unduly from fears that their desires prove them to be mentally ill.

Merely telling the patient that masochistic desires are normal is probably not going to be sufficient, of course. Promoting self-acceptance may take more strenuous therapeutic efforts. Still, the goal of therapy with such cases is to teach the person to be comfortable with the fact of having masochistic desires and inclinations, alongside his or her desires for more conventional sexual activities.

As the individual begins to accept his or her masochistic desires, there is likely to develop a brief pattern that may seem alarming at the time. Several experimental studies have examined what occurs when people try not to think about something in particular. In some of these experiments, the stimulus was a white bear. So people spent some time trying to prevent themselves from thinking about a white bear, usually without great success. In the next phase of the experiment, however, the person was told to go ahead and think about whatever he or she wanted, even a white bear. These people often found themselves thinking constantly about white bears. Thus, removing the mental restriction produced a huge "rebound effect," in which the forbidden thought flooded the mind (Wegner et al., 1987).

One might well anticipate a similar occurrence in therapy with patients of the sort we have been discussing. These people are worried about their masochistic desires and probably have been devoting some effort to suppressing these desires. They come to therapy simply because they have not managed to suppress these desires effectively enough, and they want the therapist to make the masochistic thoughts go away. Suppose the therapist uses the approach advocated here and encourages the patient to accept his or her masochistic feelings; and suppose the patient goes along with this, perhaps after some initial resistance. At this point, then, the patient removes the mental restriction and stops trying to suppress masochistic thoughts. The result is likely to be a flooding of the mind with masochistic thoughts.

This onslaught of masochistic thoughts would probably be temporary, but of course the patient would not know this at the time. All the patient knows is that therapy is seemingly making the original problem worse rather than better, for the patient's mind is now constantly filled with masochistic thoughts.

The effect on the person's sex life may be equally worrisome. The individual has been struggling to enjoy normal sex and suppress masochistic inclinations. Now, however, the patient begins to accept masochistic sexual desires; these desires, freed from their recent suppression, may temporarily seem to engulf all the person's sexual imagination, crowding out nonmasochistic sexuality. This could convince patient and therapist alike that the individual is a much more extreme masochist than was previously thought, perhaps qualifying as a masochistic pervert as earlier described (i.e., someone who cannot enjoy sex apart from masochism).

The therapist should anticipate this problem and help the patient to realize that it is a common, temporary, and normal reaction to removing a mental restriction. After a time, the flood of masochistic desires should diminish, and the patient's sexuality will return to a normal state of having both masochistic and nonmasochistic desires.

The final stage of therapy with such individuals is in a way the most difficult, for it requires finding a way of integrating these masochistic desires into one's life. If the first stage is successful, the person comes to accept his or her masochistic desires and experience them regularly along with more conventional desires. But someone who regularly experiences desires that cannot be fulfilled is hardly the optimal outcome of psychotherapy.

Clinical Implications

Integrating one's masochistic desires into one's life is not going to be an easy task. In the first place, society stigmatizes masochism, and it will probably be quite some time before masochism is accepted as a normal and acceptable expression of human sexuality. One might make the analogy to homosexuality. Although it has now been decades since the experts began considering homosexuality as a normal and acceptable form of sexual behavior, society at large is still far from tolerance. Masochism is quite a bit farther from social tolerance than homosexuality, for there is not even much evidence of progress toward tolerance, and there is no organized movement comparable to Gay Liberation.

Society's intolerance cannot be dismissed. It is difficult to live out a lifestyle regarded by many mainstream citizens as deviant and objectionable. In short, therapists may teach masochists to accept themselves, but they should not expect society at large to accept them in the near future.

A more pressing and practical problem is finding a partner. Nearly all research studies on masochism cite the difficulties in finding sex partners, and this is not likely to change. People who wish to participate in sadomasochistic sex are a distinct minority of the population and they tend to be secretive; for both reasons, it will continue to be hard to locate them.

A further problem is the shortage of people interested in playing the dominant role, as we have already seen. Even if a masochist does manage to find someone else interested in S&M sex, that other person is more likely to be a masochist, too, rather than a sadist or dominant. This problem is often apparently resolved by having pairs of masochists exchange roles; that is, they take turns at playing the dominant role. Such individuals should probably consider themselves lucky to have found a partner for these games at all. Indeed, the frequent exchange of roles may be best for the relationship (cf. Greene & Greene, 1974). And, as we saw in the chapter on sadism, a true sadist may not be the ideal partner for a masochist; a sympathetic fellow masochist may be preferable.

An alternate solution to the shortage of partners is to try to convince one's spouse or lover to engage in these activities. Scott (1983) described the difficulties and obstacles that various masochistic men encountered in trying to convince their sexually conventional wives to dominate them. Probably the odds on persuading a sexually conventional partner to help act out one's masochistic fantasies are mediocre at best. The partner, after all, is likely to share the social stereotypes of masochism as perversion and mental illness. Even if these initial obstacles can be overcome, the partner probably simply does not have sexual desires for such activities, and so he or she may be reluctant to engage in them.

The problem is further compounded by the fact that the partner is presumably being pressured to take the dominant role, which is more difficult and uncertain. As we have seen, the typical S&M career begins with masochistic submission and then (sometimes) proceeds to taking the dominant role; by that time, the individual has probably developed some understanding of how to play the dominant role. But the masochist's spouse may be asked to leap right in to taking the dominant role, making all decisions, knowing how much pain to inflict, and so forth.

A partial solution that apparently worked for some of Scott's (1983) subjects was to start the partner off in the submissive role. Thus, she said some masochistic men were successful at getting their wives to dominate them by starting the wife off as submissive. They would tie up the wife, perhaps spank her lightly, and so forth. Once the woman began to accept these activities and perhaps enjoy them, the man would initiate an exchange of roles, so that she would dominate him.

Yet another approach is to seek new partners actively, either through going to prostitutes, joining S&M clubs, or advertising in sexually oriented publications. All of these are risky and probably unsatisfying in most cases. Moreover, in this era of dangerous diseases transmitted through sexual contact, such methods should probably not be encouraged. Still, some people will try them, and some of those will have good experiences.

Live sexual activity is of course not the only form of dealing with sexual desires. Fantasy, pornography, and masturbation have long been the solace of individuals unable to enact their desires with real partners. Scott (1983) suggested that masochists are especially interested in pornographic or erotic literature (especially pertaining to S&M), as well as fantasy. This may be a very reasonable way of adapting to the difficulty of finding real partners.

In general, then, one's chances of living a life full of masochistic sex do not seem very large. Encouraging self-acceptance may be an important step toward freeing the masochist of anxiety, guilt, fear, and doubt, but the masochist should not be led to believe that these desires will be easy to satisfy. It may be best to encourage such an individual to accept his or her masochistic fantasies as such, without expecting to act them out. The person should concentrate on developing a normal, more conventional sex life with activities that are mutually satisfying to both partners. Perhaps the individual can convince the partner to experiment with S&M games on an occasional basis, but expectations should be kept low regarding the quality and quantity of such experiences. For the most part, the masochistic desires will have to remain at the level of fantasy, perhaps buttressed by pornographic or erotic literature.

These practical obstacles to masochistic sexual pleasure underscore the importance of nonmasochistic sexual pleasure discussed earlier. The individual who has both masochistic and nonmasochistic desires is in a fairly good position to have a satisfying sex life based on conventional sexual activities, with masochism as an occasional change of pace or a recurrent fantasy. In contrast, the individual whose sexuality is exclusively masochistic has very poor prospects of achieving a satisfactory sex life.

NARCISSISM THEORY OF MASOCHISM

Recently, some theorists have put together a new view of masochism based on psychoanalytic views of narcissism. They suggest that masochists are individuals with a damaged or deficient sense of self, and that masochism is a way of building up, repairing, or restoring this sense of self (Stolorow & Lachmann, 1980).

On the surface, the view of masochism as a means of building up a sense of self is completely opposed to the view of masochism as a means of escaping from self-awareness, as this book has argued. As general theories of masochism, the two views are quite incompatible. On the other hand, there may be some way of reconciling them, in view of their quite different basis. This book has emphasized the behavior of normal individuals and proposed a theory about masochism that applies to people who are mentally well and healthy. Stolorow and Lachmann are careful to restrict their discussion to people who are mentally ill, or *structurally deficient,* in their preferred term. It is conceivable that the promoting of a low-level sense of self as a body, experiencing sensations in the immediate present moment, is both a way of escaping the elaborate self-concept of a healthy person and a way of building a foundation for a sense of self among sick, deficient individuals.

Thus, the two views can perhaps be reconciled, especially if each is restricted to a separate sphere. Let us first take a closer look at the theory and evidence put forward by Stolorow and Lachmann.

They begin with the observation that masochistic phenomena occur among mentally ill individuals who have narcissistic disturbances. That is, the person's representation of self (the self-concept) is somehow damaged early in life, and this damage propels the person toward masochism. Stolorow and Lachmann conclude from this that masochism is a means of restoring or repairing an impaired representation of self. Of course, this is hardly the only possible conclusion. Perhaps, instead, the damage to the self-concept makes the individual want to escape from awareness of self, for such awareness might bring a troubling or anxiety-filled recognition of the self-deficiencies. In short, the alleged correlation between narcissistic factors and masochism does not support either the self-negating or the self-restoring view of masochism over the other. (It does, however, underscore the relevance of the self to masochism, and so it favors either of these theories over other possible theories that do not emphasize the self.)

Pain is explained by Stolorow and Lachmann as a way of affirming one's sense of being real and alive. In their words, "The masochistic quest for pain in the structurally deficient individual may, then, represent a desperate exaggeration of experiences in which a temporarily disorientated person expresses the wish to be pinched or slapped to affirm the reality of the self" (1980, p. 32; polysyllabificationizing in original). Such requests among normal people are of course quite rare, but the argument does seem to rest on the assumption that pain promotes awareness of self as a body existing in the immediate present. This is compatible with both theories of masochism.

Stolorow and Lachmann also cite evidence that "skin contact with a beloved person relieved anxiety in the masochist" (p. 33). Although this would fit their view, there are difficulties with generalizations of this sort. In particular, there may be a base-rate fallacy: Bodily contact with a beloved person may reduce anxiety in nearly everybody, not just "structurally deficient" masochists. Indeed, being held seems capable of calming an infant, long before it has had much chance to develop a concept of self. The skin contact argument is therefore probably useless.

Next, they cite the "exhibitionistic" aspect of masochism, and this is perhaps their best evidence. They observe that masochists want to be the center of attention, which they see as a "primitive means" of strengthening the sense of self. In other words, if someone pays attention to you and reacts to you, then you exist. "The common theme . . . is that he is not being ignored" (p. 34). Masochistic desires for an audience or mirror likewise support an interpretation based on drawing attention to self.

I have treated the exhibitionistic aspect of masochism as a way of strengthening or underscoring the removal of the typical identity. That is, the Congressman or executive who watches his submission, humiliation, and chastisement in a mirror is being reminded not of his (or her) normal, powerful identity, but of his loss of that identity. The mirror says "See what you have become," rather than "Remember who you really are." There is no way of telling which interpretation is correct at present. Still, both Stolorow and Lachmann's theory and the present theory emphasize that the mirror draws attention to the self that exists only in the immediate present moment. This is compatible with both functions. For the competent, healthy, normal individual, the mirror or audience may draw attention to the transformed self during the masochistic episode, thus facilitating the escape from the normal identity. For the structurally deficient individual, the attention to self may produce a rudimentary awareness of self that is an improvement over a totally lacking or unfocused sense of self.

Stolorow and Lachmann simply ignore the masochistic desire to relinquish control through bondage and other practices. These features of masochism are the hardest to reconcile with their view, so it is not surprising that they were reluctant to mention them. The self is strongly oriented toward gaining and maintaining control; it is hard to see the wish to *relinquish* control as a means of building up the self. Being tied up is simply a loss of control, and the wish to be tied up is a wish to restrict and impair the self's capacity to function.

One way to salvage the Stolorow and Lachmann theory would be to suggest that mentally ill masochists are less interested in bondage than in other aspects of masochism (i.e., pain and humiliation). One could investigate this empirically. Perhaps the masochistic episodes of "structurally deficient" individuals will tend to downplay the loss of control and emphasize pain and being the center of attention. This would be consistent with the view that their theory is correct, at least as applied to the mentally ill (which is all they claim for it).

The issue of control raises another, more broadly troubling aspect of Stolorow and Lachmann's theory, however: It has great difficulty distinguishing between the appeal of masochism and that of sadism. All their arguments about the possible appeal of masochism seem to apply much better to sadism, and one is left wondering why anyone would prefer masochism. Thus, Stolorow and Lachmann acknowledge that the sadist can obtain the feeling of being alive and real by inflicting pain on someone else. If the masochist derives a sense of self from being the object of the sadist's attentions, how much more must the sadist derive a sense of self from being the object of the masochist's attention. The sadist controls the scene, evokes responses from the masochist, makes the commands and decisions, receives pleasant skin contact (e.g., oral sex), and receives many tributes and boosts to his or her self-worth. In the S&M scene, the submissive obeys and worships the dominant, so the dominant's self is the one that is strengthened and glorified. Sadism seems an almost ideal means of strengthening one's sense of self through playing fantasy games. In contrast, masochism is a relatively weak, inconsistent, and dubious means of accomplishing the same ends.

Perhaps Stolorow and Lachmann's view could be salvaged by reviving Freud's suggestion that, among the mentally ill, sadism is the primary attraction and masochism is a secondary, derivative, or converted form of sadism. The "structurally deficient" individual seeking to build up a sense of self might be best served by taking a dominant, sadistic role, but some inability or guilt causes that individual to take the masochistic role as a substitute. This book has argued extensively that that is not the case among normal, mentally healthy individuals; but perhaps it is true for the mentally ill who are drawn to sadomasochism.

A last consideration is the role of sexual pleasure and satisfaction. Stolorow and Lachmann claim that the orgasm has some function for building a sense of self. This is a tenuous claim, especially in view of the fact that lower animals without elaborate selves apparently have orgasms, and the prevailing view of orgasms probably views them as an ecstatic loss of self-awareness rather than a source of self-awareness. Stolorow and Lachmann acknowledge that orgasms dissolve the self, which is the opposite of their view, but they do not try to resolve this paradox; rather, they simply say that orgasms are "Janus-faced."

If we accept that orgasms involve a temporary loss of self-awareness, however, there may be room to salvage Stolorow and Lachmann's view anyway. They recognize that sexual intimacy involves a merging of self with another and say that this merging is threatening to people with deficient senses of self. Masochists, in their view, need to have their sense of self bolstered (through pain and so forth) before they are willing to undergo the loss of self required for sexual intimacy. This argument, although hardly compelling, is plausible. To be sure, sex therapists tend to find that a loss of self-awareness is more conducive to sexual satisfaction than is an increase in self-awareness (as we saw in chapter 5), but perhaps mentally ill masochists are highly unusual in this regard.

Stolorow and Lachmann give only the outline of a theoretical treatment of masochism, and they do not attempt to explain several of the important aspects of it that have been covered in this book. Their theory does appear to be able to handle several of these facts better than other psychoanalytically based theories, however. For example, they could probably give a better explanation for the cultural and historical relativity of masochism than some other views, for they at least have recognized the central importance of the self. Likewise, the distinction between pain and injury does not conflict with their account, unlike views of masochism as self-destructiveness.

To conclude, then, let us examine once more the possibility of reconciling Stolorow and Lachmann's theory with the present theory of escape from self. In the escape theory, masochism is a means of denying the broadly meaningful aspects of the self in favor of focusing awareness on the self as a physical body and locus of sensations, existing in the immediate present. For normal people, this must represent a drastic reduction in the scope and breadth of the self. The self is reduced from a complex, symbolically constructed entity, sustaining involvements and commitments that persist across time, and so forth, to a mere here-and-now physical thing. For normal individuals, masochism thus involves a substantial loss of self, and its appeal probably resides in precisely that loss.

The matter may be quite different, however, for people who do not have such a solid sense of self. The "structurally deficient" individuals on which Stolorow and Lachmann focus may well lack the high-level sense of self with its complex identity and ongoing commitments. For them, the masochistic focus on the body and its movements and sensations may be an improvement in sense of self.

In short, both views see masochism as focusing self-awareness at an extremely low level: body movements and sensations, a target of embarrassment and sexual desire, and so on. The masochistic self is the bare minimum, the merest foundation or most primitive form of self-awareness. For normal individuals, this is a drastic loss of self. But for some mentally ill individuals, this may be a positive step. One may make the analogy to having only the foundation of a house. If one previously had a complete house, a mere foundation is an extreme loss; but if one started with nothing, a foundation is a good way to begin.

Chapter Ten
Conclusion

This book has covered much ground, in the attempt to shed light on one of psychology's oldest and most challenging paradoxes. We have examined evidence from many quite different sources, including statistical analyses of anonymous letters in sex magazines to cross-cultural comparisons of sexual practices, from participant observation studies of S&M clubs to historical surveys of documents, from laboratory research to clinical impressions. This last source, clinical observation, has been deliberately downplayed in the effort to compensate for its overemphasis in past psychologies of masochism. Clinical observations have great value, but they are not the only or even necessarily the best source of evidence about many phenomena. And when dealing with something as complex and misleading as masochism, it is important to approach it from as many different angles as possible.

The outcome of this book's approach has been to suggest a new way of looking at masochism. It is a way that does not characterize the masochist as mentally ill or disturbed, although as we saw it can be made compatible with some past clinical portraits of mentally ill masochists. Rather, it furnishes a view of masochism that uses what is known about the psychology and behavior of normal, mentally healthy individuals, and it evaluates this view in the context of a wide range of empirical evidence.

In this final chapter, we take a look back at the book's major points, then a brief look forward at some issues remaining to be studied, and finally a look at some important implications of what we have found.

SUMMARY OF MAIN IDEAS

A first major point was the primacy of masochism. Despite past theories that portrayed masochism as derived from sadism, the weight of the evidence shows masochism to be more widespread and common, more fundamental, and often more strongly motivated than sadism. Masochism deserves to be emphasized in psychological theory about sadomasochistic behavior.

A second point is that masochism appears to be culturally and historically relative. Masochism should not be explained as arising mainly from the instincts and intrapsychic dynamics of the individual. Rather, masochism appears to be a product of social and cultural factors—indeed, fairly unusual ones, for sexual masochism has apparently been unknown in most cultures and in most historical periods. Social conditions create certain appetites or needs that masochism is able to satisfy.

We found much support for the view that masochism may appeal to psychologically normal people as a way of escaping from the self. That is, masochism divests the person of awareness of self in high-level, symbolic, meaningful terms, extending into the past and future. In its place, masochism focuses awareness on the self at extremely low levels; as a physical entity existing in the immediate present, passively experiencing sensations and simple movements. Masochism deconstructs the self, providing escape from identity into body.

The majority of masochists appear to be psychologically normal and healthy people, and the escape from the pressures, demands, and anxieties of self-awareness may explain a large part of the appeal of masochism. The appeal of masochism to the occasional mentally ill person may be related but different in one important way. The emphasis on the absolutely minimal self is a loss of self for a normal person, but for certain psychologically impaired individuals it may be an improvement. A minimal self is less than a normal self, but it is more than no self at all. The capacity of masochism to create a here-and-now sense of self may thus appeal to different people for different reasons, and one must be hesitant about generalizing between clinical and nonclinical groups of people.

Another important feature of masochism is that it can supply certain meanings that may help remedy certain feelings of emptiness or meaninglessness that some people may have. This aspect of masochism may be especially important among people who fantasize or desire an ongoing, stable arrangement in which they become full-time slaves to a beloved dominant partner. Such relationships are an important fantasy for many masochists, but the evidence indicates that they are often impractical and problematic when people attempt to make them come true. Still, the desire for such an arrangement may involve more than a desire for permanent escape from one's identity. Masochism offers the hope (even if it is unrealistic) of intense, prolonged fulfillment, which is something that our culture has had difficulty with during the last couple centuries. Masochism offers fulfillments of sexual pleasure and emotional intimacy. Indeed, by merging one's own will and personality with the dominant partner, masochism may offer an unusually intense form of emotional satisfaction, akin to love. We return to the relationship between masochism and love later in this chapter.

Masochism also seems to hold the promise of absolute certainty about what is right and wrong, about what is good and correct to do. As our culture has come to struggle more and more with questions of ultimate values, people have increasing difficulty finding sure guidelines to moral issues. As a result, more and more people may be drawn to masochism, which seemingly offers a solid, reliable way of ending those uncertainties. Follow the commands of the dominant partner, satisfy his or her needs, and you will be freed from responsibility, uncertainty, and anxiety. And if one misbehaves, punishment is quick (and sexually exciting), and there is no need for lingering worries or feelings of guilt.

Last, we examined the sexual aspect of masochism in some detail. Perhaps surprisingly, the evidence seems to support the claim that masochism may enhance sexual arousal and response. A number of masochistic practices resemble techniques used to enhance sexual pleasure and performance. The case is not closed, but for now it seems quite plausible that masochism does indeed intensify sex. It seems unlikely that very many people will try masochism simply for the sake of intense sexual pleasure, but it could well be that that intense pleasure helps keep some masochists coming back for more. Further, the link to sexual pleasure probably is a vital aspect of masochistic motivation, for it links the escape to a powerful and recurrent source of motivations and it provides a very positive, pleasurable ending to each episode. Beatings and humiliation without sexual pleasure would probably be much less appealing.

UNANSWERED QUESTIONS

It is hard to get solid, convincing data about masochism, and indeed this difficulty has probably been an important reason for psychology's failure to solve the problem of masochism decades ago. Throughout this book, we have repeatedly noted that the evidence is frustratingly incomplete, such as regarding the effects of masochistic practices on sexual arousal.

The history of research on masochism has had two different threads. One thread runs through the clinical work on masochism. This work has emphasized psychoanalytic theories about masochism and has worked from clinical observations, often involving severely disturbed individuals, small samples, and no control or comparison groups. The other thread has involved empirical studies, generally operating with nonclinical populations. These studies have typically not used psychoanalytic theory, but they have often had nothing to replace the Freudian approach they rejected, and so these studies have taken the form of atheoretical collections of participant impressions and of statistical analyses.

This book has offered a theoretical framework that future empirical studies might use. It is aimed specifically at studies dealing with nonclinical populations, for it is not a clinical theory of masochism. The hypotheses of escape from self and elaboration of meaning can serve to orient further research. Let us quickly review several main predictions or issues to be tested.

A first issue concerns situational causes of masochism. What events or circumstances contribute to masochistic desires or tendencies? If masochism is escape from self, then people should feel masochistically inclined when events make the self especially burdensome. In particular, when external demands or expectations place a great deal of pressure on the self, and when the individual privately finds it difficult or threatening to live up to these demands, masochism should increase. When individuals are required to make many choices or decisions, to take substantial responsibility, or to act in ways that make them uncomfortable, they may desire masochistic escape. Feedback that portrays the self in a negative light (incompetent, undesirable, guilty) may likewise enhance the appeal of masochistic escape.

A good approach would be to get masochists to keep diaries of the events in their daily lives and in their sex lives. These diaries could be examined to see what events are correlated with masochistic desires and activities.

A second issue is the relation of masochism to other escapes. Drugs and alcohol can cause escape from self-awareness similar to the effects of masochism. Is masochism correlated with these other forms of escape? To be sure, alcohol and masochism may be a poor mixture for other reasons: Masochism seeks intensified sensations whereas alcohol dulls them (although other drugs such as marijuana seem designed to intensify sensations and experiences and therefore might be similar to masochism), and the impairment of judgment caused by alcohol might increase safety risks in S&M. Still, there are important theoretical parallels between masochism and chemical escapes, and these deserve to be explored.

Personality factors in masochism deserve a fresh look. Reliable statistical data on the personality traits of masochists would reveal a great deal about what causes masochism. Levels of self-awareness, self-esteem, and locus of control might well predict masochistic tendencies. Chronic traits versus fluctuating states may be a further important issue. Vulnerability to anxiety may predict some desires for escape. Discrepancies between one's private self-concept and one's public self or reputation may be especially important. For example, many masochists may be people who are externally powerful, important, and capable, but who privately feel insecure and uncertain. Such a discrepancy might produce a strong desire to escape periodically from the everyday self with its burdensome public image.

To study the personality predictors of masochism, it is probably necessary to distinguish two types of masochists. Scott (1983) suggested that the majority of masochists are only passive and submissive during their episodes of sexual escape, but that there is a minority who are passive and submissive in all phases of their lives. These two forms may have quite different personalities. Additionally, the discrepancies between masculine and feminine forms of masochism may indicate different personality factors.

One last possible set of predisposing factors that deserve study involves arousal thresholds and desire for intense sensations. Masochism seems designed to provide unusually intense experiences, so it may appeal to people who need greater than normal levels of sexual stimulation, or to those who desire unusually strong and powerful experiences.

There are theoretical implications beyond masochism that deserve research. Do people tire of exerting control—that is, if someone makes a large number of decisions, might the person then reach a state of fatigue in which he or she desires to be passive and free of responsibility? We have argued that pain brings awareness to low levels of awareness, and although the evidence is substantial, there does not seem to be any direct laboratory proof yet. The direct effects of bondage and restraint on self-awareness need to be verified. Likewise, the effectiveness of pain and bondage for helping the person repress unwanted thoughts deserves direct experimental study.

MASOCHISM AS SELF-DESTRUCTION

Many past theories of masochism have equated it with self-destructive tendencies or desires. Indeed, current debates about clinical diagnoses continue to equate the two, focusing on whether *masochism* is a proper term for a "self-defeating personality disorder" (Franklin, 1987). But this book has argued against seeing masochism as self-destructive behavior. Because of the importance of this issue, it is useful to review the arguments once more.

Past observers saw that masochists desired to suffer, and so they regarded masochism as the desire for harm to the self. We have seen, however, that masochists typically maintain a rather strict distinction between pain and injury. They desire pain but carefully avoid injury. Masochism may be the desire to feel pain, but it is not a desire for harm to the self. Rather, pain is sought as a narcotic, as a means of focusing one's mind on immediate sensations and experiences, away from the concerns, responsibilities, and other factors that make up the typical contents of self-awareness. Masochists use pain to forget the self; they do not desire harm or injury.

Outside of masochism, pain and injury are usually linked, so it is easy to understand how past theorists could have been misled. But there is now ample evidence that the masochistic desire for pain is not accompanied by any desire for injury.

A partial exception (which may also have helped throw some researchers off the track) may be an occasional masochistic fantasy about harm to self. Some masochists may occasionally enjoy fantasies about suffering harm that would help remove the self from awareness. The most obvious forms would probably be fantasies of death or castration (cf. Friday, 1980), both of which are symbolically potent means of denying selfhood. There is nothing to suggest that normal masochists would want to act out such fantasies—indeed, they probably would immediately reject any thought of doing so. Moreover, there is no evidence to suggest that such fantasies are common among masochists, even as purely imaginary episodes. But they would be plausible and might occur in extreme cases. Their meaning, however, is not a desire to harm the self, but an extreme form of denying and forgetting the self.

Another approach to the issue of self-destructive behavior is to look at the research on such actions by normal individuals. Recently, a colleague and I compiled a thorough review of laboratory studies dealing with self-defeating behavior patterns among normal (nonclinical) people (Baumeister & Scher, 1988). Over a dozen such patterns have been demonstrated and replicated. People do self-destructive things in tradeoff circumstances, often seeking short-term relief or pleasure and incurring long-term costs or risks in exchange (e.g., smoking cigarettes, consuming alcohol, neglecting to take their prescribed medicines, procrastinating). Other self-destructive behaviors include selecting strategies that fail or backfire (e.g., staying too long with bad investments or bad relationships; adopting ineffective negotiation strategies). In none of these, however, does the person both desire and foresee the harm to self. Rather, the harm to self is either accepted as a cost that accompanies some perceived benefit, or it is an unintended consequence of some poorly designed strategy.

Two implications follow for the psychology of masochism. First, this evidence suggests that normal people are rarely, if ever, guided by self-destructive motives in their actions. The view of masochism as self-destructiveness thus does not fit well with the psychology of normal people, although it is plausible that mentally ill people sometimes do desire to harm themselves. Second, some of the self-destructive tradeoffs were apparently motivated by the desire to escape from aversive states, especially involving high self-awareness. This may be the place where masochism most closely resembles self-destructive behavior, for masochism too may often be a way of escaping from an unpleasant awareness of self. But the resemblance does not mean that masochism is self-destructive. Instead, if there is a resemblance, it means that what looks like self-destructiveness may often result from a desire to escape.

Thus, at present there is no justification for regarding masochism as a form of self-destructive behavior. Masochists are not self-destructive in what they do. Moreover, normal and mentally healthy individuals (including most masochists) do not appear to act from self-destructive motives. There are some resemblances between masochism and some forms of self-destructive behavior, but some of these resemblances are simply superficial and misleading, and in others the resemblance appears to tell us more about self-destructive actions than about masochism. Sometimes self-destructive actions arise from desires to escape, such as when a person begins to drink heavily in order to forget some failure or trauma. Masochism can be fully understood as escape, without reference to any desire to harm or defeat the self. Masochists want to forget the self, not to cause it permanent harm.

NONSEXUAL MASOCHISM

Early in this book I mentioned that many psychologists have used the term masochism to refer to nonsexual behavior, even though sexual masochism is the original and fundamental form of masochism. Usually they use the term to refer to self-destructive behaviors. But we have just seen that this is a false analogy. Masochism is not self-destructiveness, and self-destructive behavior, if it occurs at all among mentally healthy individuals, does not arise out of masochistic motivations. It is fair to ask, then, what nonsexual behaviors do resemble masochism?

If masochism is a means of escaping the self, then other forms of escape are its closest relatives. We have already noted that alcohol and drugs are powerful, popular means of escaping self-awareness. Research by Hull and his colleagues (e.g., Hull, 1981) have shown repeatedly that people are less aware of themselves after drinking alcohol, that people drink more alcohol when they want to escape from self-awareness, and so forth. The sophisticated research by Hull's group far surpasses anything available about masochism, partly because it is much more practical and viable to study alcohol consumption than sexual masochism under controlled laboratory conditions. The resemblance is fundamental, and it is important. Getting drunk, or consuming mind-altering drugs, may be one of the closest analogs to masochism among nonsexual behaviors.

Another comparable form of escape involves physical exercise. Indeed, several masochists I spoke with specifically drew analogies between exercise and masochism. Jogging and similar activities take one's mind off one's affairs and bring it to low levels by absorbing it in the immediate present, emphasizing direct sensations and movements, setting off opponent processes, and so forth. Indeed, some have noted that exercise may use pain in ways similar to masochism. The pain of fatigue and muscular exertion is sought systematically, even for its own sake; injury is carefully avoided; the pain has an element of pleasure associated with it, perhaps especially afterward; and so forth. The analogy should not be overworked, but there certainly are some important parallels between exercise and masochism.

We saw that some masochists may well be motivated by the desire for unusually intense, novel experiences. That view of masochism certainly has its analogs in nonsexual behavior. Skydiving, racing cars, mountain climbing, hang-gliding, and similar practices may provide intense sensations, and they probably also function to provide an escape from the normal self of everyday affairs. Indeed, people who enjoy such pastimes frequently comment on how the office or other concerns seem remote and trivial (or disappear entirely) when they are engaged in these activities. Although it seems odd to call skydiving "masochistic," there are important similarities.

Another aspect of masochism is the gain in meaning through linking oneself to an important authority figure. The person derives self-worth, satisfaction, and meaningfulness from the dominant one. A wide range of nonsexual behaviors fit this pattern. The groupies who draw their worth and esteem from sleeping with famous rock musicians could well be described as masochistic. Indeed, many of them accept degrading and even abusive treatment from their rock stars but still seek these attachments. A very different example would involve religious feelings. The noted scholar Peter Berger (1967) has described Protestant Christianity as an extreme form of religious masochism, for the individual humbles him or herself before God and derives all his or her value and worth from his or her relationship to God.

A last feature of masochism is the strengthening of sexual desire or response by focusing on sensations, screening out the everyday world, using artificial rules to restrict sexual activities, and so forth. We have already noted how these masochistic practices resemble techniques of sex therapy. It seems misleading to call sex therapy masochistic; rather, perhaps one should regard masochism as sexually therapeutic. Again, however, the resemblance is probably genuine and theoretically meaningful. There may well be other sexual practices that have similar effects.

Thus, there are several varieties of nonsexual behavior that resemble masochism in important ways. Masochism is not a totally isolated or unique phenomenon, unrelated to other forms of behavior. It is one form, possibly an extreme form, of behavior that produces effects resembling those that guide many other actions.

Should these other forms of behavior be called masochistic? If the resemblance to masochism is genuine, then that would be reasonable and appropriate. One could call joggers, skydivers, alcoholics, Protestants, groupies, and so forth masochistic. But what value is served by labeling them as masochists? The term masochism has already been used in too many misleading ways, because of misunderstandings, false analogies, and the like. It has gained several unsavory and inflammatory connotations.

Probably the best approach, therefore, is to confine the term masochism to its original, fundamental meaning, namely sexual masochism. The similarities and resemblances to nonsexual behavior patterns need to be noted and recognized, especially where these help to furnish a broader picture of human behavior. But it seems advisable to limit the use of the term to the purest forms of masochism.

MASOCHISM AND LOVE

How do masochism and love go together? This is not an easy question, for several reasons. Some people clearly do masochism with their loved ones, and others clearly do not. Masochists seem to desire a strong relationship as context for their sexual actions, but obviously most people experience love without engaging in sexual masochism.

A review of all the theories about love would take us far afield. For present purposes, what matters is that love is an intense form of emotional and often sexual intimacy, frequently described as the merging of two selves.

Masochism likewise involves the merging of selves, but it is a one-sided merging. The two may become one, but that one is the dominant partner. The masochist escapes self by becoming immersed in someone else.

Love is neither necessary nor sufficient to produce masochism. There is ample evidence of masochism without love, and of love without masochism. In short, masochism and love are not the same thing, nor are they necessarily linked.

Combining these observations, we can draw the tentative conclusion that masochism accomplishes something of the same ends as love, namely the ecstatic merging with another human being. Masochism can thus be regarded as an alternative to love—an alternative form of intimacy. They are different routes to the same destination.

This does not mean, however, that love is irrelevant to masochism, for (again) masochists apparently prefer submitting to partners they love. If masochism and love are separate paths to the same end, then taking them both may double the experience of merging with another person. When both masochism and love are present, the bond may be twice as intense, and the ecstatic merging twice as fulfilling. Masochists' comments suggest as much. They describe masochism as removing the entire world, of eliminating everything from awareness except self and partner in the immediate present. As one told me, the combination of masochistic submission and love makes "you feel like you're blending in to each other."

Thus, it may be most correct to describe masochism as an "alternative intimacy," that is, an alternative to love. It can occur without love, or it can combine with love. The experience of intimate merger with another person is an intense feature of masochism, as of love. Masochism may augment love, or it may substitute for it.

CONCLUSION

A complex set of puzzling behaviors has long been grouped together under the heading of sadomasochism. This book has sought to shed some light on some of those behaviors. Masochism, not sadism, appears to be the more prevalent and important phenomenon in that set. Even masochism is far from homogeneous, for men and women show somewhat different patterns of masochistic activity. In particular, masculine masochism seems to focus on deconstructing the normal stereotypes of male identity, whereas feminine masochism seems to elaborate and exaggerate some features of typical stereotypes of female identity.

Moreover, masochism has both constructive and deconstructive aspects. It provides a powerful escape from self, in the sense of removing the person's typical awareness of his or her normal identity. Once this is cleared away, however, masochism sometimes elaborates a new, fantasy identity in its place. The escape from self is thus completed by becoming someone else. Identity is not merely removed from awareness but is transformed.

Masochists derive important benefits from their participation. The escape from the normal identity probably brings valuable relief from the pressures, responsibilities, and anxieties that are associated with maintaining identity in the modern world. The achievement of a set of meanings, justifications, and intense fulfillments through creating and realizing a fantasy world probably appeals to many individuals whose lives seem uncertain and unfulfilling. Masochism may plausibly claim to provide unusually intense forms of sexual pleasure. And although it has no essential link to love, it provides an alternative form of intimacy that may provide some of the same satisfactions people experience from love. Indeed, potentially it would augment the intimacy in a normal loving relationship.

Past views have portrayed masochism as a mixture of femininity, guilt, and self-destructiveness. These views are conceptually flawed and they are not consistent with the available facts. Instead, masochism can be understood as a somewhat unusual and extreme form of many of the behavior patterns exhibited by normal adult individuals. In the final analysis, sexual masochism is neither harmful nor beneficial, except that it offers brief and intense doses of escapist pleasure. That perspective, I think, makes it possible finally to begin to solve the puzzle of masochism.

Appendix

The purpose of this Appendix is to supply information about the original research behind this book. It begins by discussing methods and procedures, and then presents the statistical data regarding the letter descriptions of masochistic fantasies and experiences.

One main source of evidence for this book is based on letters to the magazine, *Variations*, a sexually oriented magazine aimed at a wide audience. It may be described as a spinoff from *Penthouse,* a popular magazine that has regularly published letters from readers reporting alleged sexual experiences. Whereas *Penthouse* features letters reporting typical, mainstream sexual practices, *Variations* features letters describing unusual sexual practices, including masochism. It is organized by sections. In its typical format, each section begins with a fictional article by someone who is presumably a professional writer. This article is then followed by several letters relating sexual incidents that fall in the same broad category as the article. At the end of the magazine, there is a collection of miscellaneous letters.

For present purposes, the relevant sections dealt with S&M. This sample of letters was based on three years' worth of issues (1984–1986). Nearly every issue included a section dealing with S&M, and most issues also had additional S&M letters in the miscellaneous section at the magazine's end.

The sample was restricted to the letters themselves. The fictional articles were not included. Likewise, letters from the advice column at the beginning of the magazine were not included.

Some judgment was required as to whether S&M was involved, especially in selecting letters from the miscellaneous section. An effort was made to include as many letters as possible so as to avoid restricting the sample in artificial, possibly biasing ways. Still, some letters were omitted if they lacked any S&M practices beyond using the label of *sex slave*. As long as any form of pain, or symbolic domination, or humiliation, or bondage was used, the letter was included in the sample.

The authenticity of the letters has been questioned, especially by casual readers who find it hard to imagine that people really do such things. Indeed, some of the letters reported incidents that seemed implausible. The authenticity question must be divided into two questions: Are these letters actually written by anonymous readers (as opposed to being written by staff members working for the magazine, for example)? And do they report actual experiences?

Regarding the first question, the answer is apparently yes. *Penthouse* has vouched for the authenticity of the letters' origins in print elsewhere (Springer, 1976), and my own inquiry yielded an assurance that every letter they published came from the mail bag (McCarty, personal communication, 1987). Indeed, the editor informed me that they regularly receive more letters on masochism than they can publish.

My own impressions support the view that the letters originate from actual, anonymous readers from around the United States. First, there was a noticeable difference in literary quality between the fictional articles, which are quite clearly written by the magazine's staff and freelance writers, and the letters. Thus, the letters do not seem like the products of professional writers. Second, given the longstanding rivalry between the *Penthouse* magazines and their competitors (e.g., *Playboy*), it strikes me as quite implausible that the *Penthouse* staff could have been writing their own letters. Surely at some point in the past two decades they would have been exposed, and *Playboy* could have scored a major competitive victory by discrediting their competitors' letters.

Regarding the second question (did the events actually take place as described), the most likely answer is "sometimes." Some letters are quite clearly labeled as fantasies. Others claim to report actual experiences, but one doubts that the events actually occurred as reported. Of course, it is difficult to judge the plausibility of such unusual activities and experiences, and it is possible that they all report actual events exactly as they occurred. More likely, however, many of the allegedly real experiences are actually fantasies, and others report real events but embellish them with fantasy.

For present purposes, fortunately, the distinction between actual occurrence and fantasy embellishment is unimportant. The goal was to learn about the scripts and schemas that give structure to masochistic desires. The object of study was what masochists want; their imagination and fantasy life is as good a source as their actual behavior. Indeed, actual behavior is often constrained by mundane and irrelevant considerations, including fear of detection, equipment failure, misunderstanding or poor communication with partner, the vagaries and vicissitudes of opportunities to act out one's desires, and so forth. It seems reasonable to assume that when writers of these letters embellished their experiences, they did so in order to achieve what they regarded as a more perfect masochistic experience (e.g., omitting the interruptions to answer the telephone, exaggerating their degree of helplessness and excitement).

All behavioral self-report measures are suspect and problematic, and sexual self-report measures may be especially so—at least as a means of learning about actual behavior. But as a means of learning about fantasy and desire, the presumed embellishments of these letters are not an obstacle. It is only necessary to keep in mind that the letters should not be taken for reliable, accurate self-reports of behavior. Indeed, even if they were precise and thorough accounts, they could not be taken as an accurate picture of the behavior of masochists. It is doubtful that people choose a random or representative experience to write about; rather, they probably choose their favorite or prototypical experience.

In short, these letter describe what masochists would like to happen, not necessarily what actually happens.

The possibility of editorial bias must be considered. The editor of *Variations* (V. McCarty) informed me that some editing is done. In particular, unsafe and illegal practices are deleted. Additionally, there is some effort to make the letters intelligible and to correct descriptions that are blatantly erroneous or implausible.

Coding the letters presented certain difficulties, although less than with many psychological codings. The standard procedure was to code the incident described in the letter for the presence or absence of various features. Because of ambiguities, not all letters could be coded on all dimensions, and so not all analyses reported below have the same n. For example, "Later, we made love" is ambiguous as to whether oral, anal, or genital intercourse is involved. Some letters reported more than one incident. Making multiple data entries for such a letter would have artificially inflated the sample n and would have also raised statistical problems of independence of observations. So such letters were handled by treating them as if they reported a single incident. For example, if a letter described two incidents, and only one of them involved anal sex, the letter was coded as "yes" with respect to anal sex. This problem applied to relatively few letters and is therefore a minor consideration.

To ascertain the reliability of the coding, a subsample of five issues was selected at random. These issues yielded 33 letters, and a separate judge (blind to the original codings and findings) coded them. Interrater agreement was .933, that is, the two sets of ratings agreed 93% of the time. Discrepancies were found to be produced by simple oversights, differential interpretation of scoring rules, and the ambiguities of some letters. All such differences were easily resolved by brief discussion, yielding a final agreement of 100%. In short, the coding must be regarded as highly reliable, although not perfect.

Another source of information was a series of interviews with masochists. Five individuals were interviewed. They were not systematically recruited but rather volunteered to talk about their experiences after hearing about my research. The first interview lasted only 10 minutes, partly because of subject shyness and lack of opportunity to talk privately. After this, I sensed the potential value of such contacts, and whenever a subsequent opportunity to talk with a masochist arose I arranged for a longer interview in a private office. Two masochists were interviewed at length, including multiple sessions each lasting over an hour.

In view of the nonsystematic nature of these interviews (both in recruitment and structure), I have used them as confirmatory and illustrative rather than as primary sources of data.

RELIABILITY OF CODING

Thirty-three letters were coded by a second coder who was blind to the research hypotheses. Across all categories, the raters agreed on 693 codings and disagreed on 50, for 93.3% agreement. Disagreements arose from letters reporting more than one incident (with different properties), from ambiguity of coding verbal humiliation, and other minor differences or ambiguities. Brief discussion raised agreement to 100%.

TABLES AND STATISTICS

What follows is a presentation of the data from the *Variations* letters.

TABLE 1
Sex Acts

	Submissive	Dominant
Give oral sex	147	47
Receive oral sex	51	139
Neither	61	68
Anal sex—Receive	73	3
Penetrate partner	31	91
Vaginal penetration	67	35
No anal or vaginal sex	85	95

TABLE 2
Anal Sex Received by Submissive Partner

	Author	
	Dominant	Submissive
Male Author		
Anal sex	12 (39%)	29 (34%)
No anal sex	19	57
Female Author		
Anal sex	9 (30%)	26 (38%)
No anal sex	21	43

No comparisons are significant.

TABLE 3
Oral Sex Performed by Submissive Partner

	Author	
	Dominant	Submissive
Male Author		
Oral Sex	22 (73%)	58 (69%)
No oral sex	8	26
Female Author		
Oral Sex	27 (84%)	38 (57%)
No oral sex	5	29

Female dominants vs. female submissives: Chi^2 $(1, n=99)=7.35$, $p < .01$.
All dominants vs. submissives, $Chi^2(1, n=213)=5.76$, $p < .02$.

TABLE 4
Submissive Partner Engages in Genital Intercourse*

	Author	
	Dominant	Submissive
Male Author		
Genital intercourse	21 (70%)	23 (27%)
No genital intercourse	9	61
Female Author		
Genital intercourse	8 (26%)	41 (61%)
No genital intercourse	22	26

*Tabulations include penetration involving dildoes and vibrators.
Male vs. female dominated couples: $Chi^2(1, n=211)=28.68$, $p < .001$.
Male vs. female submissives: $Chi^2(1, n=151)=17.45$, $p < .001$.

TABLE 5
Performance of Oral Sex, by Role

	By Submissive	By Dominant
Performed oral sex	147 (66%)	47 (21%)
Did not perform it	76	176

$Chi^2(1, n=446)=91.23, p < .001.$

TABLE 6
Presence of Audience

	Author	
	Dominant	Submissive
Audience	11 (20%)	65 (42%)
No audience	43	90

Note: These figures delete letters in which third parties were present but unaware of the S&M activity (semipublic) and letters in which a second submissive was present.
$Chi^2(1, n=209)=8.05, p < .01.$

TABLE 7
Audience Participation in Submissives' Letter

	Male Author	Female Author
Participant audience	31 (84%)	15 (54%)
Nonparticipant audience	6	13

Note: This table excludes letters written by dominants and excludes all letters in which no audience was present.
$Chi^2(1, n=65)=7.03, p < .01.$

TABLE 8
Who Knows the Audience?

	Dominant	Submissive
Known	79 (89%)	19 (21%)
Unknown or scarcely known	10	70

$Chi^2(1, n=178)=81.73, p < .001.$

TABLE 9
Meaning of Pain Administered Within Relationship Context

	Author	
	Dominant	Submissive
Male Author		
Punishment for misbehavior	5 (19%)	12 (16%)

Not as punishment	21	65
Female Author		
Punishment for misbehavior	7 (23%)	23 (43%)
Not as punishment	23	31

Note: These data omit letters in which no ongoing relationship was described. Submissives only, male vs. female: $Chi^2(1, n=131) = 11.83$, $p < .001$. Dominants only, male vs. female: $Chi^2(1, n=56) = 0.14$, ns.

TABLE 10
Comparing Transvestite vs. Nontransvestite Male Submissives

	Transvestite	Nontransvestite
Display Humiliation		
Yes	8 (25%)	15 (29%)
No	24	36
Pain as Punishment for Misbehavior in Relationship Context		
Yes	4 (15%)	8 (19%)
No	22	35
Oral Humiliation		
Yes	13 (39%)	26 (52%)
No	20	24

Note: All three chi-square comparisons are not significant. Moreover, in the first two, the nontransvestite males are closer to the rates for female masochists than the transvestite males are. Thus, transvestite male masochists resemble other male masochists, not female masochists.

TABLE 11
Bondage: Restraint of Submissive Partner

	Author	
	Dominant	Submissive
Male Author		
Bondage	15 (50%)	58 (66%)
No bondage	15	30
Female Author		
Bondage	22 (67%)	41 (57%)
No bondage	10	31

Note: Combining by couples, $Chi^2(1, n=222) = 3.22$, $.05 < p < .10$. Other comparisons not significant.

TABLE 12
Pain Administered to Submissive Partner

	Author	
	Dominant	Submissive
Male Author		
Whipping or multiple	4	42
Spanking only	17	19
No pain	8	22
Minor/misc. pain	0	4
Female Author		
Whipping or multiple	15	19
Spanking only	13	41
No pain	5	8
Minor/misc. pain	0	3

Note: Minor/misc. pain referred to using only one slap (esp. to face) or pinching clamps, without any further mention of pain.

Presence vs. absence of pain (counting minor/misc. as no pain), male vs. female: $Chi^2(1, n=158)=4.52$, $p < .05$. Males 70%, females 85%.

Severity of pain: Comparisons of male vs. female authors, whipping & multiple vs. spanking only:
  Submissives only: $Chi^2(1, n=121)=16.73$, $p < .001$.
  Dominants only: $Chi^2(1, n=49)=6.02$, $p < .02$.

Thus, male submissives are more likely than female ones to report higher severity of pain.

TABLE 13
Relationship Context

	Past	Future
Ongoing intimate relationship including unusual sexual activities	88	185
Ongoing intimate relationship without unusual sexual activities	73	10
Mere acquaintances	30	7
Strangers, unacquainted	40	16

TABLE 14
Actual or Implied Guilt

	Author	
	Dominant	Submissive
Male Author		
Genuine guilt	8 (38%)	20 (38%)
Trumped-up	5	15

No guilt	8	18
Female Author		
Genuine guilt	6 (23%)	24 (51%)
Trumped-up	10	10
No guilt	10	13

Note: These tallies refer only to letters that reported administering pain. Letters explicitly described as fantasies are also omitted. Guilt refers to actual misbehavior or offense occurring as part of the normal, everyday relationship. Trumped-up guilt refers to some rule violation occurring in the context of the S&M scene and used as pretext for punishment.

Comparison of female dominants vs. female submissives, genuine guilt vs. other two categories combined: $Chi^2(1, n=73)=5.42$, $p < .02$.

Most other comparisons nonsignificant.

TABLE 15
Gender Role Switching by Submissive Partner

	Author	
	Dominant	Submissive
Male Author		
Gender switching	0 (0%)	35 (39%)
No gender switching	29	54
Female Author		
Gender switching	9 (29%)	0 (0%)
No gender switching	24	74

Note: No letters reported gender switching by dominant partner. Submissives only, male vs. female: $Chi^2(1, n=163)=37.06$, $p < .001$.

TABLE 16
Use of Housework as Feature of Gender Switching by Male Submissive

	Author	
	Dominant Female	Submissive Male
Housework performed by submissive	8 (89%)	18 (51%)
Submissive male is feminized but without mention of housework	1	17

$Chi^2(1, n=44)=4.16$, $p < .05$.

TABLE 17
Humiliation of Submissive Partner

	Author	
	Dominant	Submissive
Male Author		
Animal	0 (0%)	15 (17%)
Baby	0 (0%)	8 (9%)
Verbal	5 (16%)	30 (35%)
Display	10 (32%)	24 (28%)
Urination	1 (3%)	8 (9%)
Enema	2 (6%)	4 (5%)
Oral*	1 (3%)	34 (40%)
Other	2 (6%)	39 (45%)
No humiliation	15 (48%)	8 (9%)
Female Author		
Animal	5 (15%)	5 (7%)
Baby	0 (0%)	0 (0%)
Verbal	7 (21%)	19 (26%)
Display	5 (15%)	32 (44%)
Urination	4 (13%)	5 (7%)
Enema	4 (12%)	4 (6%)
Oral*	12 (36%)	5 (7%)
Other	13 (39%)	10 (14%)
No humiliation	5 (15%)	17 (24%)

*Oral humiliation includes kissing feet, kissing buttocks or anus, oral consumption of sexual juices other than through oral sex, and/or underwear held in mouth.

Some letters included multiple humiliations, so columns do not add up to total number of letters. Percentages are based on comparing letters that included vs. did not include each particular type of humiliation.

Comparisons of Male vs. Female patterns:

Oral humiliations: Submissives only: $Chi^2(1, n=158)=22.39$, $p < .001$. Dominants only: $Chi^2(1, n=64)=10.84$, $p < .001$. Combined by couples (i.e., male dominant plus female submissive authors, compared against male submissive plus female dominant authors): $Chi^2(1, n=222)=33.18$, $p < .001$.

Display humiliation: Submissives only: $Chi^2(1, n=158)=4.68$, $p < .05$. Dominants only: $Chi^2(1, n=64)=2.61$, ns. Combined by couples: $Chi^2(1, n=222)=13.86$, $p < .001$.

Animal humiliation (treating submissive as lower animal). Submissives only: $Chi^2(1, n=158)=3.91$, $p < .05$. Dominants only: $Chi^2(1, n=64)=5.10$, $p < .05$. Couples combined: $Chi^2(1, n=222)=7.89$, $p < .01$.

Baby humiliation (treating submissive as human infant): Male submissives vs. all other groups combined, $Chi^2(1, n=221)=13.03$, $p < .001$ (one letter not coded because of ambiguous implication).

Absence of all humiliations: Submissives only, $Chi^2(1, n=158)=6.02$, $p < .02$. Dominants only, $Chi^2(1, n=64)=8.22$, $p < .01$. Combined by couples, $Chi^2(1, n=222)=13.86$, $p < .001$.

Comparison of dominants vs. submissives, regardless of gender, on absence of humiliation: 20 (31%) of 64 letters by dominants reported no humiliation, whereas only 25 (16%) of 158 letters by submissives reported no humiliation, $Chi^2(1, n=222)=6.71$, $p < .01$.

TABLE 18
Absence of Humiliation, Not Counting Display

	Author	
	Dominant	Submissive
Male Author		
Humiliation	7	75
No humiliation*	28 (80%)	11 (13%)
Female Author		
Humiliation	25	29
No humiliation*	6 (19%)	42 (59%)

*These letters reported no humiliation other than displaying the masochist (usually nude).
Male submissives vs. female submissives: $Chi^2(1, n=157)=37.39$, $p < .001$.
Male dominants vs. female dominants: $Chi^2(1, n=66)=24.21$, $p < .001$.
All dominants (52%) vs. all submissives (34%): $Chi^2(1, n=223)=6.16$, $p < .02$.

TABLE 19
Sexual Intercourse With Someone Other Than Primary Partner

	Author	
	Dominant	Submissive
Male Author		
Submissive has sex*	3	28
Dominant has sex	2	10
Total number of letters coded	30	87
Female Author		
Submissive has sex	5	10
Dominant has sex	2	2
Total number of letters coded	32	69

*That is, the submissive has sex with someone other than the dominant partner.
Submissive has sex with another: Males only, dominant vs. submissive: $Chi^2(1, n=117)=5.64$, $p < .02$. Submissive authors only, male vs. female, $Chi^2(1, n=156)=6.54$, $p < .02$.
Self (author) has sex with other: Males only, dominant vs. submissive, $Chi^2(1, n=117)=7.62$, $p < .01$. Females only, dominant vs. submissive, $Chi^2(1, n=101)=1.42$, ns.
Dominant partner has sex with another: compare male vs. female submissive authors: $Chi^2(1, n=156)=4.20$, $p < .05$.

References

Alexander, M. (1982). Passion play. In Samois (Ed.), *Coming to power* (pp. 228–242). Boston, MA: Alyson.

Alloy, L. B., & Abramson, L. Y. (1979). Judgments of contingency in depressed and nondepressed students: Sadder but wiser? *Journal of Experimental Psychology: General, 108,* 441–485.

American Psychiatric Association (1980). *Diagnostic and statistical manual of mental disorders* (3rd ed.). Washington, DC: Author.

Bandura, A. (1977). Self-efficacy: Toward a unifying theory of behavioral change. *Psychological Review, 84,* 191–215.

Barker, V. (1982). Dangerous shoes, or what's a nice dyke like me doing in a get-up like this? In Samois (Ed.), *Coming to power* (pp. 101–104). Boston, MA: Alyson.

Baumeister, R. F. (1982). A self-presentational view of social phenomena. *Psychological Bulletin, 91,* 3–26.

Baumeister, R. F. (1986). *Identity: Cultural change and the struggle for self.* New York: Oxford University Press.

Baumeister, R. F. (1987). How the self became a problem: A psychological review of historical research. *Journal of Personality and Social Psychology, 52,* 163–176.

Baumeister, R. F. (1988a). Masochism as escape from self. *Journal of Sex Research, 25,* 28–59.

Baumeister, R. F. (1988b). Gender differences in masochistic scripts. *Journal of Sex Research, 25,* 478–499.

Baumeister, R. F. (in press). Anxiety and deconstruction: On escaping the self. In J. Olson (Ed.), *The Ontario symposium on self-inference.* Hillsdale, NJ: Lawrence Erlbaum Associates.

Baumeister, R. F., Hamilton, J. C., & Tice, D. M. (1985). Public versus private expectancy of success: Confidence booster or performance pressure? *Journal of Personality and Social Psychology, 48,* 1447–1457.

Baumeister, R. F., & Scher, S. J. (1988). Self-defeating behavior patterns among normal individuals: Review and analysis of common self-destructive tendencies. *Psychological Bulletin, 104,* 3–22.

Baumeister, R. F., & Steinhilber, A. (1984). Paradoxical effects of supportive audiences on performance under pressure: The home field disadvantage in sports championships. *Journal of Personality and Social Psychology, 47,* 85–93.

Beach, F. A. (Ed.). (1976). *Human sexuality in four perspectives.* Baltimore, MD: Johns Hopkins Press.

Bellwether, J. (1982). Love means never having to say oops: A lesbian's guide to s/m safety. In Samois (Ed.), *Coming to power* (pp. 69–79). Boston, MA: Alyson.

Benjamin, H., & Masters, R. E. L. (1965). *Prostitution and morality.* London: Souvenir Press.

Berger, P. L. (1967). *The sacred canopy: Elements of a sociological theory of religion.* Garden City, NY: Doubleday Anchor.

Berglas, S. C. (1986). *The success syndrome.* New York: Plenum.

Blumstein, P., & Schwartz, P. (1983). *American couples: Money, work, sex.* New York: Simon & Schuster.

Boss, M. (1949). *Meaning and content of sexual perversions.* New York: Grune & Stratton.

Brehm, J. W. (1966). *A theory of psychological reactance.* New York: Academic Press.

Brody, L. R. (1985). Gender differences in emotional development: A review of theories and research. *Journal of Personality, 53,* 102–149.

Brownmiller, S. (1975). *Against our will: Men, women and rape.* New York: Simon & Schuster.

Bullough, V. L. (1976a). *Sexual variance in society and history.* Chicago, IL: University of Chicago Press.

Bullough, V. L. (1976b). *Sex, society, and history.* New York: Science History Publications.

Bullough, V. L., & Brundage, J. (1982). *Sexual practices and the medieval church.* Buffalo, NY: Prometheus.

Bullough, V. L., & Bullough, B. L. (1964). *The history of prostitution.* New Hyde Park, NY: University Books.

Califia, P. (1982). From Jessie. In Samois (Ed.), *Coming to power* (pp. 154–180). Boston, MA: Alyson.

Califia, P. (1983). A secret side of lesbian sexuality. In T. Weinberg & G. Kamel (Eds.), *S and M: Studies in sadomasochism* (pp. 129–136). Buffalo, NY: Prometheus.

Caplan, P. (1984). The myth of women's masochism. *American Psychologist, 39,* 130–139.

Carver, C. S., & Scheier, M. F. (1981). *Attention and self-regulation: A control-theory appraoch to human behavior.* New York: Springer-Verlag.

Cleugh, J. (1951). *The Marquis and the Chevalier.* London: Melrose.

Coen, S. J. (1988). Sadomasochistic excitement: Character disorder and perversion. In R. Glick & D. Myers (Eds.), *Masochism: Current psychoanalytic perspectives* (pp. 43–60). Hillsdale, NJ: The Analytic Press.

Comer, R., & Laird, J. D. (1975). Choosing to suffer as a consequence of expecting to suffer: Why do people do it? *Journal of Personality and Social Psychology, 32,* 92–101.

Cowan, L. (1982). *Masochism: A Jungian view.* Dallas, TX: Spring Publications.

Culler, J. (1982). *On deconstruction: Theory and criticism after structuralism.* Ithaca, NY: Cornell University Press.

Curtis, R., Smith, P., & Moore, R. (1984). Suffering to improve outcomes determined by both chance and skill. *Journal of Social and Clinical Psychology, 2,* 165–173.

Davenport, W. H. (1976). Sex in cross-cultural perspective. In F. A. Beach (Ed.), *Human sexuality in four perspectives* (pp. 115–163). Baltimore, MD: Johns Hopkins University Press.

de Rougemont, D. (1956). *Love in the Western world* (M. Belgion, trans.). New York: Pantheon.

Deutsch, H. (1944). *The psychology of women.* New York: Grune & Stratton.

Diana, L. (1985). *The prostitute and her clients.* Springfield, IL: Thomas.

Diener, E., & Wallbom, M. (1976). Effects of self-awareness on antinormative behavior. *Journal of Research in Personality, 10,* 107–111.

Dutton, D. G., Aron, A. P. (1974). Some evidence for heightened sexual attraction under conditions of high anxiety. *Journal of Personality and Social Psychology, 30,* 510–517.

Duval, S., & Wicklund, R. A. (1972). *A theory of objective self-awareness.* New York: Academic Press.

Eliade, M. (1985). *A history of religious ides, vol 3: From Muhammad to the age of reforms.* Chicago, IL: University of Chicago Press.

Ellis, H. (1936). *Studies in the psychology of sex* (Vol. 1). New York: Random House. (Originally published 1905)

Falk, G., & Weinberg, T. S. (1983). Sadomasochism and popular Western culture. In T. Weinberg & G. Kamel (Eds.), *S and M: Studies in sadomasochism* (pp. 137–144). Buffalo, NY: Prometheus.

Fiedler, L. A. (1982). *Love and death in the American novel.* New York: Scarborough. (Originally published 1966)

Ford, C. S., & Beach, F. A. (1951). *Studies in psychology of sex* (Vol. 1). New York: Random House.

Franklin, D. (1987). The politics of masochism. *Psychology Today, 21* (1), 52–57.

Freedman, J. L. (1970). Transgression, compliance, and guilt. In J. Macaulay & L. Berkowitz (Eds.), *Altruism and helping behavior* (pp. 155–161). New York: Academic Press.

Freud, S. (1938). Sadism and masochism. In A. A. Brill (Ed. and Trans.), *Basic writings of Sigmund Freud.* New York: Modern Library.

Freud, S. (1961). The economic problem of masochism. In J. Strachey (Ed. and Trans.), *The standard edition of the complete works of Sigmund Freud* (Vol. 19, pp. 159–170). London, Hogarth Press. (Originally published 1924)

Friday, N. (1980). *Men in love.* New York: Dell.

Gaeddert, W. P. (1985). Sex and sex role effects on achievement strivings: Dimensions of similarity and difference. *Journal of Personality, 53,* 286–305.

Gebhard, P. H. (1969). Fetishism and sadomasochism. In J. Masserman (Ed.), *Dynamics of deviant sexuality* (pp. 71-80). New York: Grune & Stratton.

Gebhard, P. H. (1971). Human sexual behavior: A summary statement. In D. Marshall & R. Suggs (Eds.), *Human sexual behavior: Variations in the ethnographic spectrum* (pp. 206-217). New York: Basic Books.

Gebhard, P. H. (1978). Factors in marital orgasm. In J. LoPiccolo & L. LoPiccolo (Eds.), *Handbook of sex therapy* (pp. 167-174). New York: Plenum.

Gibbons, F. X., & Wicklund, R. A. (1976). Selective exposure to self. *Journal of Research in Personality, 10,* 98-106.

Gilligan, C. (1982). *In a different voice: Psychological theory and women's development.* Cambridge, MA: Harvard University Press.

Glick, R. A., & Meyers, D. I. (1988). *Masochism: Current psychoanalytic perspectives.* Hillsdale, NJ: The Analytic Press.

Greenberg, J., & Musham, C. (1981). Avoiding and seeking self-focused attention. *Journal of Research in Personality, 15,* 191-200.

Greene, G., & Greene, C. (1974). *S-M: The last taboo.* New York: Grove Press.

Greenwald, A. G. (1980). The totalitarian ego: Fabrication and revision of personal history. *American Psychologist, 35,* 603-618.

Harris, M. B., Benson, S. M., & Hall, C. (1975). The effects of confession on altruism. *Journal of Social Psychology, 96,* 187-192.

Heidegger, M. (1927). *Sein und Zeit [Being and time].* Tuebingen, West Germany: Niemayer.

Higgins, E. T. (1986). Self-discrepancy: A theory relating self and affect. *Psychological Review, 94,* 319-340.

Hoffman, M. L. (1975). Sex differences in moral internalization and values. *Journal of Personality and Social Psychology, 32,* 720-729.

Horner, M. (1972). Toward an understanding of achievement-related conflicts in women. *Journal of Social Issues, 28,* 157-176.

Houghton, W. E. (1957). *The Victorian frame of mind, 1830-1870.* New Haven, CT: Yale University Press.

Howe, D. W. (1976). Victorian culture in America. In D. Howe (Ed.), *Victorian America* (pp. 3-28). Philadelphia, PA: University of Pennsylvania Press.

Hull, J. G. (1981). A self-awareness model of the causes and efects of alcohol consumption. *Journal of Abnormal Psychology, 90,* 586-600.

Hull, J. G., & Young, R. D. (1983). Self-consciousness, self-esteem, and success-failure as determinants of alcohol consumption in male social drinkers. *Journal of Personality and Social Psychology, 44,* 1097-1109.

Hull, J. G., Young, R. D. & Jouriles, E. (1986). Applications of the self-awareness model of alcohol consumption: Predicting patterns of use and abuse. *Journal of Personality and Social Psychology, 51,* 790-796.

J. (1982). Proper orgy behavior. In Samois (Eds.), *Coming to power* (pp. 41-43). Boston, MA: Alyson.

Janus, S., Bess, B., & Saltus, C. (1977). *A sexual profile of men in power.* Englewood Cliffs, NJ: Prentice-Hall.

Juliette (1983). Autobiography of a dominatrix. In T. Weinberg & G. Kamel (Eds.), *S and M: Studies in sadomasochism* (pp. 87-93). Buffalo, NY: Prometheus.

Kamel, G. W. L. (1983). The leather career: On becoming a sadomasochist. In

T. Weinberg & G. Kamel (Eds.), *S and M: Studies in sadomasochism* (pp. 73–79). Buffalo, NY: Prometheus.

Kant, I. (1968). [Critique of the faculty of Judgment]. Hamburg, FRG: Felix Meiner. (Originally published 1790)

Kinsey, A. C., Pomeroy, W. B., Martin, C. E., & Gebhard, P. H. (1953). *Sexual behavior in the human female.* Philadelphia, PA: Saunders.

Krafft-Ebing, R. V. (1983). Psychopathia sexualis (F. S. Klaff, trans.). In T. Weinberg & G. Kamel (Eds.), *S and M: Studies in sadomasochism* (pp. 25–29). Buffalo, NY: Prometheus.

Langer, E. (1975). The illusion of control. *Journal of Personality and Social Psychology, 29,* 253–264.

Lasch, C. (1978). *The culture of narcissism: American life in an age of diminishing expectations.* New York: Norton.

Lee, J. A. (1983). The social organization of sexual risk. In T. Weinberg & G. Kamel (Eds.), *S and M: Studies in sadomasochism* (pp. 175–193). Buffalo, NY: Prometheus.

Lepanto, R., Moroney, W., & Zenhausern, R. (1965). The contribution of anxiety to the laboratory investigation of pain. *Psychonomic Science, 3,* 475.

Lewis, H. B. (1985). Depression vs. paranoia: Why are there sex differences in mental illness? *Journal of Personality, 53,* 150–178.

Licht, H. (1934). *Sexual life in ancient Greece.* New York: Dutton.

Liebling, B. A., Seiler, M., & Shaver, P. (1974). Self-awareness and cigarette smoking behavior. *Journal of Experimental Social Psychology, 10,* 325–332.

Lifton, R. J. (1986). *The Nazi doctors: Medical killing and the psychology of genocide.* New York: Basic Books.

Linden, L. L. (1982). *Against sadomasochism: A radical feminist analysis.* East Palo Alto, CA: Frog in Well Press.

LoPiccolo, J. (1978). Direct treatment of sexual dysfunction. In J. LoPiccolo & L. LoPiccolo (Eds.), *Handbook of sex therapy* (pp. 1–18). New York: Plenum.

LoPiccolo, J., & LoPiccolo, L. (Eds.). (1978). *Handbook of sex therapy.* New York: Plenum.

Lord, C. G., & Saenz, D. S. (1985). Memory deficits and memory surfeits: Differential cognitive consequences of tokenism for tokens and observers. *Journal of Personality and Social Psychology, 49,* 918–926.

Lucy, J. (1982). If I ask you to tie me up, will you still want to love me? In Samois (Ed.), *Coming to power* (pp. 29–40). Boston, MA: Alyson.

MacIntyre, A. (1981). *After virtue: A study in moral theory.* Notre Dame, IN: University of Notre Dame Press.

Markus, J., & Wurf, E. (1987). The dynamic self-concept: A social psychological perspective. *Annual Review of Psychology, 38,* 299–337.

Marshall, D. S. (1971). Sexual behavior on Mangaia. In D. Marshall & R. Suggs (Eds.), *Human sexual behavior: Variations in the ethnographic spectrum (pp. 103–163).* New York: Basic Books.

Mass, L. (1983). Coming to grips with sadomasochism. In T. Weinberg & G. Kamel (Eds.), *S and M: Studies in sadomasochism* (pp. 45–56). Buffalo, NY: Prometheus.

Masters, W. H., & Johnson, V. E. (1970). *Human sexual inadequacy.* Boston, MA: Little, Brown.

Meyer, D. H. (1976). American intellectuals and the Victorian crisis of faith. In D. Howe (Ed.), *Victorian America* (pp. 59–80). Philadelphia, PA: University of Pennsylvania Press.
Money, J. (1987). Masochism: On the childhood origin of paraphilia, opponent-process theory, and antiandrogen therapy. *Journal of Sex Research, 23,* 173–175.
Otis, L. L. (1985). *Prostitution in medieval society.* Chicago, IL: University of Chicago Press.
Panken, S. (1983). *The joy of suffering: Psychoanalytic theory and therapy of masochism.* New York: Aronson.
Patterson, O. (1982). *Slavery and social death.* Cambridge, MA: Harvard University Press.
Pennebaker, J. W. (1985). Traumatic experience and psychomatic disease: Exploring the roles of behavioral inhibition, obsession, and confiding. *Canadian Psychology, 26,* 82–95.
Pennebaker, J. W. (in press). Stream of consciousness and stress: Levels of thinking. In J. S. Uleman & J. A. Bargh (Eds.), *The direction of thought: Limits of awareness, intention, and control.* New York: Guilford.
Pennebaker, J. W., Hughes, C., & O'Heeron, R. C. (1987). The psychophysiology of confession: Linking inhibitory and psychomatic processes. *Journal of Personality and Social Psychology, 52,* 781–793.
Reage, P. (1966). *Story of O.* New York: Grove Press. (Originally published 1954)
Regan, J. W. (1971). Guilt, perceived injustice, and altruistic behavior. *Journal of Personality and Social Psychology, 18,* 124–132.
Reik, T. (1957). *Masochism in modern man.* (M. H. Beigel & G. M. Kurth, trans.). New York: Grove Press. (Originally published 1941)
Rhodewalt, F., & Davison, J. (1983). Reactance and the coronary-prone behavior pattern: The role of self-attribution in responses to reduced behavioral freedom. *Journal of Personality and Social Psychology, 44,* 220–228.
Rodgers, D. T. (1978). *The work ethic in industrial America: 1850–1920.* Chicago, IL: University of Chicago Press.
Rosenhan, D. L., Salovey, P., Karylowski, J., & Hargis, K. (1981). Emotion and altruism. In J. P. Rushton & R. M. Sorrentino (Eds.), *Altruism and helping behavior* (pp. 233–248). Hillsdale, NJ: Lawrence Erlbaum Associates.
Rothbaum, F., Weisz, J. R., & Snyder, S. (1982). Changing the world and changing the self: A two process model of perceived control. *Journal of Personality and Social Psychology, 42,* 5–37.
Samois (Ed.). (1982). *Coming to power.* Boston, MA: Alyson.
Santini, R. (1976). *The secret fire: How women live their sexual fantasies.* New York: Grove Press.
Scarry, E. (1985). *The body in pain: The making and unmaking of the world.* New York: Oxford University Press.
Schachter, S. (1971). *Emotion, obesity, and crime.* New York: Academic Press.
Schachter, S., & Singer, J. (1962). Cognitive, social, and physiological determinants of emotional state. *Psychological Review, 69,* 378–399.
Schlenker, B. R. (1985). *The self and social life.* New York: McGraw-Hill.
Scott, G. G. (1983). *Erotic power: An exploration of dominance and submission.* Secaucus, NJ: Citadel Press.

Seta, J. J., & Hassan, R. K. (1980). Awareness of prior success or failure: A critical factor in task performance. *Journal of Personality and Social Psychology, 39,* 70–76.

Shainess, N. (1984). *Sweet suffering: Woman as victim.* New York: Simon & Schuster.

Solomon, R. L., & Corbit, J. D. (1974). An opponent-process theory of motivation: I. Temporal dynamics of affect. *Psychological Review, 81,* 119–145.

Smith, H., & Cox, C. (1983). Dialogue with a dominatrix. In T. Weinberg & G. Kamel (Eds.), *S and M: Studies in sadomasochism* (pp. 80–86). Buffalo, NY: Prometheus.

Spence, J. T., & Sawin, L. L. (1984). Images of masculinity and femininity: A reconceptualization. In V. O'Leary, R. Unger, & B. Wallston (Eds.), *Sex, gender, and social psychology* (pp. 35–66). Hillsdale, NJ: Lawrence Erlbaum Associates.

Spengler, A. (1977). Manifest sadomasochism of males: Results of an empirical study. *Archives of sexual behavior, 6,* 441–456.

Springer, E. (1976). *The Penthouse letters: The sexual state of the union.* New York: Warner.

Stekel, W. (1953). *Sadism and masochism: The psychology of hatred and cruelty* (E. Gutheil, trans.). (Vol. 1). New York: Liveright. (Originally published 1929).

Steenbarger, B. N., & Aderman, D. (1979). Objective self-awareness as a nonaversive state: Effect of anticipating discrepancy reduction. *Journal of Personality, 47,* 330–339.

Stolorow, R. D., & Lachmann, F. M. (1980). *Psychoanalysis of dvelopmental arrests.* New York: International Universities Press.

Stone, L. (1977). *The family, sex, and marriage in England 1500–1800.* New York: Harper & Row.

Suggs, R. C., & Marshall, D. S. (1971). Anthropological perspectives on human sexual behavior. In D. Marshall & R. Suggs (Eds.), *Human sexual behavior: Variations in the ethnographic spectrum* (pp. 218–243). New York: Basic Books.

Swann, W. B. (1985). The self as architect of social reality. In B. R. Schlenker (Ed.), *The self and social life* (pp. 100–125). New York: McGraw-Hill.

Swann, W. B. (1987). Identity negotiation: Where two roads meet. *Journal of Personality and Social Psychology, 53,* 1038–1051.

Symanski, R. (1981). *The immoral landscape: Female prostitution in Western societies.* Toronto, Canada: Butterworth.

Tannahill, R. (1980). *Sex in history.* New York: Stein & Day.

Taylor, G. R. (1970). *Sex in history.* New York: Harper & Row. (Originally published 1954)

Trilling, L. (1971). *Sincerity and authenticity.* Cambridge, MA: Harvard University Press.

Vallacher, R. R., & Wegner, D. M. (1985). *A theory of action identification.* Hillsdale, NJ: Lawrence Erlbaum Associates.

Vallacher, R. R., & Wegner, D. M. (1987). What do people think they're doing: Action identification and human behavior. *Psychological Review, 94,* 3–15.

Walker, L. E. A., & Browne, A. (1985). Gender and victimization by intimates. *Journal of Personality, 53,* 179–195.

Weeks, J. (1985). *Sexuality and its discontents: Meanings, myths, and modern sexualities.* London: Routledge & Kegan Paul.

Wegner, D. M. (in press). *Unwanted thoughts*. New York: Vintage.
Wegner, D. M., Schneider, D. J., Carter, S. R., & White, T. L. (1987). Paradoxical effects of thought suppression. *Journal of Personality and Social Psychology, 53,* 5–13.
Wegner, D. M., & Vallacher, R. R. (1986). Action identification. In R. M. Sorrentino & E. T. Higgins (Eds.), *Handbook of cognition and motivation* (pp. 550–582). New York: Guilford Press.
Weinberg, M. S., Williams, C. J., & Moser, C. (1984). The social constituents of sadomasochism. *Social Problems, 31,* 379–389.
Weinberg, T., & Kamel, W. L. (Eds.). (1983). *S and M: Studies in sadomasochism.* Buffalo, NY: Prometheus
Weinberg, T. S. (1987). Sadomasochism in the United States: A review of recent sociological literature. *Journal of Sex Research, 23,* 50–69.
Weinberg, T. S., & Falk, G. (1980). The social organization of sadism and masochism. *Deviant Behavior, 1,* 379–393.
Weinberger, D. A., Schwartz, G. E., & Davidson, R. J. (1979). Low-anxious, high-anxious, and repressive coping styles: Psychometric patterns and behavioral and physiological responses to stress. *Journal of Abnormal Psychology, 88,* 369–380.
Weintraub, K. J. (1978). *The value of the individual: Self and circumstance in autobiography.* Chicago, IL: University of Chicago Press.
Weiss, J. M. (1971a). Effects of coping behavior in different warning signal conditions on stress pathology in rats. *Journal of Comparative and Physiological Psychology, 77,* 1–13.
Weiss, J. M. (1971b). Effects of coping behavior with and without a feedback signal on stress pathology in rats. *Journal of Comparative and Physiological Psychology, 77,* 22–30.
Wicklund, R. A. (1975a). Objective self-awareness. In L. Berkowitz (Ed.), *Advances in experimental social psychology* (Vol. 8, pp. 233–275). New York: Academic Press.
Wicklund, R. A. (1975b). Discrepancy reduction or attempted distraction? A reply to Liebling, Seiler & Shaver. *Journal of Experimental Social Psychology, 11,* 78–81.
Yardley, K., & Honess, T. (Eds.). (1987). *Self and identity: Psychosocial perspectives.* Chichester, England: Wiley.
Zoftig, S. (1982). Coming out. In Samois (Ed.), *Coming to power* (pp. 86–96). Boston, MA: Alyson.

Author Index

A

Abramson, L., 6
Aderman, D., 90
Alexander, M., 149
Alloy, L., 6
Aron, A., 138

B

Bandura, A., 6
Barker, V., 149
Baumeister, R., 5, 17, 29, 34, 39, 40, 88, 92, 112, 134, 152, 205
Beach, F., 54, 139
Bellwether, J., 14, 76
Benjamin, H., 52
Benson, S., 95
Berger, P., 207
Berglas, S., 92
Bess, see Janus
Blumstein, P., 149f, 157, 165, 167, 169, 171, 173
Boss, M., 9
Brehm, J., 6, 7
Brody, L., 145, 169
Browne, A., 146
Brownmiller, S., 163
Brundage, J., 49
Bullough, B., 52
Bullough, V., 45, 46, 47, 48, 49, 50, 51, 52, 135, 163

C

Califia, P., 12, 15, 23, 62, 73, 102, 103
Caplan, P., 7, 61, 145, 146
Carter, S., 191–192
Carver, C., 5, 28, 29, 89
Cleugh, J., 3, 12, 83, 162
Coen, S., 117
Comer, R., 134
Corbit, J., 104
Cowan, L., 4, 9, 10, 61, 66, 101–104, 135, 173, 190
Cox, C., 78, 93, 97, 113, 119, 150, 160, 178
Culler, J., 29
Curtis, R., 96, 134

D

Davenport, W., 55, 64
Davidson, R., 94
Davison, J., 79
de Rougemont, D., 66
Deutsch, H., 7, 144, 163
Diana, L., 78
Diener, E., 131

Dutton, D., 138
Duval, S., 89

E

Eliade, M., 50, 96, 134
Ellis, H., 45, 46, 50, 51, 139

F

Falk, G., 16, 51
Fiedler, L., 66
Ford, C., 54, 139
Franklin, D., 9, 14, 204
Freedman, J., 70, 95, 135
Freud, S., 3, 7, 11, 20, 21, 38, 47, 57, 144, 145, 147, 152, 188, 197
Friday, N., 22, 123, 205

G

Gaeddert, W., 172
Gebhard, P., 4, 39, 55, 56, 57, 140, 146
Gibbons, F., 90
Gilligan, C., 66, 169, 171
Glick, R., 3, 38
Greenberg, J., 90
Greene, C., 4, 9, 13, 15, 16, 19, 22, 65, 93, 193
Greene, G., 4, 9, 13, 15, 16, 19, 22, 65, 93, 193
Greenwald, A., 5

H

Hall, C., 95
Hamilton, J., 92
Hargis, see Rosenhan
Harris, M., 95
Hassan, R., 92
Heidegger, M., 94
Higgins, E., 5
Hoffman, M., 156, 169
Houghton, W., 43
Honess, T., 5
Horner, M., 8
Howe, D., 43
Hughes, C., 92

Hull, J., 91, 206

J

"J", 13, 65, 73
Janus, S., 22, 62, 78, 84, 86, 92, 93, 108, 113, 155
Johnson, V., 124–129
Jouriles, E., 91
Juliette, 78, 81, 178, 180, 181

K

Kamel, G., 21, 23, 25, 93, 103, 178, 182
Kant, I., 43, 101
Karylowski, see Rosenhan
Kinsey, A., 4, 146
Krafft-Ebing, R., 2, 3

L

Lachmann, F., 195–199
Laird, J., 134
Lasch, C., 88
Lee, J., 14, 19, 23, 24, 76, 103, 140, 178, 181
Lepanto, R., 63
Lewis, H., 156, 170
Licht, H., 46
Liebling, B., 91
Lifton, R., 28
Linden, R., 11, 62, 104
LoPiccolo, J., 124, 131
LoPiccolo, L., 124
Lord, C., 85
Lucy, 62, 102

M

MacIntyre, A., 43
Markus, H., 5
Marshall, D., 55, 56
Martin, C., 4, 146
Mass, L., 104
Masters, R., 52
Masters, W., 124–129
McCarty, V., 17, 18, 212, 213
Meyer, D., 43

Meyers, D., 3, 38
Money, J., 105
Moore, R., 96
Moroney, W., 63
Moser, C., 13, 65, 160
Musham, C., 90

O

O'Heeron, R., 92
Otis, L., 52
Otway, T., 50

P

Panken, S., 3
Patterson, O., 85
Pennebaker, J., 28, 92, 136
Petronius, 46
Pomeroy, W., 4, 146

R

Reage, P., 111, 184
Regan, J., 95
Reich, A., 144
Reik, T., 3, 9, 14, 15, 21, 60, 63, 65, 82, 84, 86, 118, 138, 146, 149, 152, 158, 183, 185
Rhodewalt, F., 79
Rodgers, D., 44
Rosenhan, D., 70, 95
Rothbaum, F., 6, 79
Rousseau, J.-J., 43, 51

S

Sacher-Masoch, L. von, 2, 12, 83, 162
Saenz, D., 85
Salovey, see Rosenhan
Saltus, see Janus
Samois, 22, 65, 148f, 180
Santini, R., 79, 185
Sawin, L., 92
Scarry, E., 29, 71–74
Schachter, S., 136, 138
Scheier, M., 5, 28, 29, 89
Scher, S., 134, 205

Schlenker, B., 5
Schneider, D., 191–192
Schwartz, G., 94
Schwartz, P., 149f, 157, 165, 167, 169, 171, 173
Scott, G., 4, 5, 9, 12, 14, 17, 18, 19, 23, 24, 31, 62, 65, 66, 67, 78, 83, 86, 88, 93, 97, 103, 106, 107, 109, 110, 111, 113, 119, 120, 122, 123, 140, 150, 155, 160, 163, 178, 183, 184, 190, 193, 194, 204
Seiler, B., 91
Seta, J., 92
Shainess, N., 8, 82, 118, 128, 133, 146, 162, 173
Shaver, P., 91
Singer, J., 138
Smith, H., 78, 93, 97, 113, 119, 150, 160, 178
Smith, P., 96
Snyder, S., 6, 79
Solomon, R., 104
Spence, J., 92
Spengler, A., 4, 9, 16, 17, 19, 23, 24, 62, 103, 107, 119
Springer, E., 17, 212
Steenbarger, B., 90
Stekel, W., 9, 10, 24, 38, 57, 93, 118, 128, 135, 138, 185
Steinhilber, A., 92
Stolorow, R., 195–199
Stone, L., 40, 44
Suggs, R., 55, 56
Swann, W., 5, 180
Symanski, R., 78

T

Tannahill, R., 45, 48, 49, 51, 56, 66, 135
Taylor, G. R., 45, 46
Tice, D., 92
Trilling, L., 40

V

Vallacher, R., 27, 28, 29, 74, 96

W

Walker, L., 146

Wallbom, M., 131
Weeks, J., 102
Wegner, D., 27, 28, 29, 74, 96, 191–192
Weinberg, M., 13, 65, 160
Weinberg, T. 16, 21, 25, 51, 93, 182
Weinberger, D., 94
Weintraub, K., 40
Weiss, J., 79, 91, 92
Weisz, J., 6, 79
White, T., 191–192
Wicklund, R., 89, 90, 91
Williams, C., 13, 65, 160

Wurf, E., 5

Y

Yardley, K., 5
Young, R., 91

Z

Zenhausern, R., 63
Zoftig, S., 67, 77

Subject Index

A

Abortion, 48, 49
Abused women, 7–8, 11, 61, 144–146, 157
Action identification theory [see also Deconstruction], 27–30, 74, 80, 96
Addiction, 104, 106
Adhesive tape, 76
Adolescence, 55
Adult baby, see Baby humiliations
Adultery, 48, 49, 52, 161
Advance punishment [see also Punishment], 95, 96, 133–138
Advertising, 194
Advice columnists, 9
Aesthetic pleasure, 101
Aging, 32
Agnostics, 43
Alcohol, 83, 91, 99, 105, 203, 205–208
Altruism, 95, 98–99
Anal sex, 47–48, 49, 83, 121–122, 132, 149f, 164; also Appendix, Tables 1, 2
Abstraction [see also Deconstruction], 27, 28, 31, 85, 86
Anesthesia, 64
Ancient world, 39, 45–48, 51–52, 53, 59
Animal humiliations, see Humiliation
Anticipation, see Pain
Anxiety, 32, 36, 100, 102, 107, 110, 111, 114, 115, 116, 129, 132, 174, 194, 195, 196, 201, 202, 204, 209
Apologizing, 67
Appeal of masochism, 1, 2, 15, 28, 68, 88–116, 201
  Differential appeal, 15, 203–204
Aquinas, 49
Arousal, 54, 55, 64, 127, 136, 138–142, 202, 204
Assyria, 45
Atheism, 43
Atonement, see Guilt, Punishment, 98–100, 115, 133
A Treatise on the Use of Flogging, (1718), 51
Attention [see also Deconstruction, Self-awareness, Audience], 71–75, 85, 91, 166, 197
Audience [see also Display humiliation], 11, 77, 82, 85, 165–166, 167, 168, 169, 196; also Appendix, Tables 6–8
Authority, 3, 8, 39, 55, 76, 117, 134, 207
Autobiography, 40, 51, 53

B

Baby humiliations, see Humiliation
Bath, 77
Beauty, 101
Bed, 76, 93

Begging, 31, 82, 84, 173
Bestiality, 48, 49, 52
Biography, 40
Biological causes and factors, see Instinct
Biting during sexual intercourse, see Pain
Blindfold, 1, 12, 76, 79–80, 111
Blood, 62
Body, 26, 30, 31, 74, 85, 86, 87, 104–105, 196, 198–199, 201
Bondage, 3, 6, 12, 14, 26, 31, 45, 54, 76–81, 86, 105–106, 111, 128, 136–137, 139, 154–157, 166, 167, 174, 178, 197; also Appendix, Table 11
Boredom, 184
Brassieres, see Underwear, Lingerie, Transvestism, Humiliation
Bruises, see Injury
Brutality, 11
Burden of selfhood, 30, 31–32, 39–42, 57, 58, 59, 88–93, 100, 114–115, 116, 172, 203

C

Candles, 46, 62
Cannibalism, 9
Castration, 123, 205
Catharsis, 102–103, 106, 111, 116
Catholics [see also Christianity, Religion, God], 95, 133–136, 137
Cattle, 48
Chains, 76, 77
Chairs, 76
Cheating [see Sexual infidelity]; on exams, 131–132
Childbirth, 64
Children, 9, 18, 48, 145
China, 45–46
Church ritual and ceremony, 43, 46, 55, 95, 133–134
Christianity, 34, 41, 42–44, 48–50, 58, 59, 95, 112, 133–136, 207
Cigarettes, see Smoking
Cleaning, see Housework
"Cleaning up," see Oral Humiliations
Clinical observation, 2, 9–10, 14, 187–199, 200, 203
Clothespins, 61

Clubs (for S&M), 9, 22–23, 51, 119, 122, 194
Cocaine, see Drug use
Cognitions, 18–19
"Coital connection," 126
Collar, as badge of servitude, 77, 79–80, 159
Commands, 76, 80, 86, 109, 110, 111, 126–127, 137, 174, 197
Communication between partners, 19, 78, 102
Confession, 95, 133
Concubinage, 52
Congressmen, see Politicians
Consenting adults, 11
Contraception, 48, 49
Control, and loss of [see also Bondage], 6, 12–13, 23, 24, 33–36, 56, 63, 76–81, 86–87, 92, 93, 105–106, 107, 111, 112–114, 127–128, 129, 155, 168, 174, 179, 185, 197
Conventional sex [see also Perversion], 190, 194–195
Cooking, see Housework
Coprophilia, 49
Couples, entry into masochism, [see also Reluctance of partners] 12, 23
 conflicts, 113
Creativity, 89, 112
Criminality, 9, 28, 97
Cross-cultural evidence, 16, 38, 53–59, 64, 200
Cross-dressing, see Transvestism
Cruelty, 11, 20, 177
Crusades, 134
Cuckolding, see Humiliation, Sexual fidelity, Sexual infidelity, Adultery
Cult movements, 49, 50
Culture, effects of, 11, 16, 34–35, 38–59, 147, 150, 173, 177, 198, 201
Cunnilingus, see Oral sex

D

Danger, 10, 18, 76, 108, 160, 181, 203
Death, 34, 43, 90, 205
Decisions, 12, 30, 31, 78, 79, 87, 91–92, 106, 114, 184, 197, 203, 204
Deconstruction, 26, 29, 36, 71–75, 80, 81, 85, 87, 92, 131, 175–176, 201, 209
 Appeal of deconstructed state, 28, 72–73

Deconstruction (continued)
  Defined, 29
Defecation, see Excrement
Definitions of masochism, 2–4, 47, 54, 55
Degradation, see Humiliation
Demands made by masochists, 12, 181
Dentistry, 13, 65
Depression, 105, 170
Desire for masochistic activities, 1, 18–19, 24, 81, 120, 188–195
Diagnostic and Statistical Manual (DSM-III), 9
Dieting, 69, 97
Dignity [see also Self-esteem, Pride, Humiliation], 84
Dildoes, 49, 121, 164, 165
Dishes (washing of), see Housework
Display, see Humiliation
Dominant partners [see also Reluctance of partners; Sadism]
  Role, 12, 111, 113, 120–122, 164, 180
  Distinguished from sadism, 24, 178, 180, 186
  Shortage of, 24–25, 178
Dominatrices see Prostitutes, Dominant partners, Sadism
Driving, 95
Drug use, 11, 18, 104–105, 203

E

Early Modern Period, 40–41, 45, 53, 58
Ecstasy, 100–101, 115, 198, 209
Education, 9, 34
Efficacy, see Control
Egotism, see Self-esteem
Egypt, 47–48
Ejaculation, see Orgasm, Semen
Electric shock, 96
Embarrassment, see Humiliation
Emotion, 28, 32, 99, 110, 111, 138, 168, 170–171, 202
Enema, see Humiliation
Enlightenment, historical period of, 43
Epidemiology, see Prevalence
Epilepsy, 9
Escalating involvement, 103–104
Escape from self theory, overview 26–32
  Applied to guilt, 98–99
  and sex differences, 171–173
  Contrasted with narcissism theory, 195–199
Evaluation, 89, 112
Evidence, Difficulties in obtaining, 15–17, 202
  Quality/flaws of empirical, 4, 14–19, 20, 59, 202–203
  Statistical interpretation, 18, 81, 143, 152–153, 211–221
  Types, 14–19
Exchange of roles, 78, 193, 194
Excitation transfer theory, 138–139, 141
Excrement, 18, 83, 159–160
Exercise, 105, 139, 207–208
Exhibitionism [see also Display humiliation], 196
Expiation, 98, 99, 115
Exploitation, 11

F

Face, 83
Faith, 43
Fantasies, 4, 5, 18, 19, 22, 31, 63, 64–65, 106, 108–109, 119, 124, 184, 194–195, 197, 205, 210
Fear, 5, 60, 63, 139, 141, 145, 194
Feces, see Excrement
Feet, 1, 31, 83, 84, 87, 160, 168
Fellatio, see Oral sex
Feminine masochism, hypothesis that women are masochistic, 5, 7–8, 144–147, 150–151, 210
Feminism, 7–8, 11, 144–146
Fetishism, 11
First-person accounts of masochism, 15–16, 103–104
Flagellants (religious sect), 49–50, 96
Flagellation [see also Whipping], 46, 49, 50, 52, 53
Flogging, see Whipping, Flagellation
Foreplay, 129, 140, 142
Fornication, 49
Frigidity, see Sexual dysfunction
Fulfillment, 32–37, 39, 42–44, 53–54, 56, 58–59, 102, 106, 107–115, 169, 173, 174, 202, 210

G

Gags, 76

Games, as analogy to masochistic activities, 26
Genocide, 11
Gladiators, 177
God, 33, 42, 49–50, 96, 101, 109, 207
Golden showers, see Excrement
Greek civilization, ancient, 39, 46, 52
Groupies, 207
Group sex, 122
Guilt, 21, 28, 36, 56, 60, 68–71, 73, 75, 77–78, 87, 93–100, 103, 111, 115, 116, 133–138, 156–157, 170–171, 191, 194, 197, 202, 210; also Appendix, Tables 7 and 14
  Effects of, 94–98
  Ontological, 94
  Relief from, 94, 111, 115
  Sexual, 94, 123, 133–138, 141, 156

H

Handcuffs [see also bondage], 76, 84
Hang-gliding, 207
Happiness and unhappiness, 43–44, 170
Harm, see Injury, Self-destructiveness
Headaches, 64, 65
Heaven, 43
Helping, see Altruism
Homeostasis, see Opponent process
Heroin, see Drug use
Historical evidence about masochism, 16, 38–53, 57–59, 198
Homeostasis, see Opponent process
Homicide, see Murder
Homosexual activities and homosexuality, 3, 15, 47–48, 49, 52, 77–78, 122, 132, 136–137, 149, 161, 165, 173, 189, 193
  Tolerance of homosexuality, 10, 15
Hooks in ceiling, 76
Horus, 47–48
Housework, 35, 69–70, 77, 80, 87, 97, 113, 148, 149, 150, 179; also Appendix, Table 16
Humiliation, 3, 6, 26, 31, 45, 54, 56, 81–87, 105–106, 127, 139, 157–162, 165, 166, 169, 171, 174, 178; also Appendix, Tables 15–19
  Animal humiliations, 1, 82, 159, 167, 168, 169, 172
  Baby humiliations, 82, 159, 168, 169, 172
  Cuckolding, see also Sexual infidelity, 83, 160, 161–162, 166; also Appendix, Table 19
  Degradation, 82, 84, 158–159, 160, 167, 168, 174
  Display, 81, 82, 84, 85, 109, 154, 157–158, 162, 167, 169, 171, 172
  Embarrassment 3, 26, 69, 81, 105, 141, 158, 171, see Humiliation
  Enema, 82–83
  Lingerie [see also Underwear], 82, 84, 160
  Oral humiliations, 83, 84, 154, 160–161, 168
  Oral consumption of sexual fluids, 47–48
  Techniques, 82–83
  Transvestism as [see also Transvestism], 82, 172
  Verbal insults, 1, 12, 81, 82, 90
  Verbal humiliations, 77, 82, 159
Humor, 55
Hyperemia, reactive, 139

I

Identity change, 31, 85, 196
Identity crisis, 39
Illusion in masochism, 12–14, 63
Illusion of control, 6, 12, 79
Imagination, 18–19, 65, 81, 120, 182–183, 192
Impotence, [see also sexual dysfunction], 46, 118, 185
Imprisonment, see Prison, Legal issues
Incarceration, see Prison, Legal issues
Incense, 46
Incest, 48, 49
Income, 9
Individuality, 40–42, 53, 57, 58, 59
Indulgences, 134
Industrial Revolution, 43, 58
Infantilism, see Baby humiliations
Information seeking, 191
Inhibitions, 131–133, 136–137
Initiation rites [see also Church ceremonies and rituals], 54–55
Initiative, 12, 79, 80, 86
Injury, 3, 13–14, 46–47, 62, 71, 144, 198, 205–206, 207
Insanity, see Mental illness

Instinct, 38–39, 42, 53, 57, 144, 147, 201
Intelligence, 89
Intentionality, 66–67
Internal spectator [see also Self-awareness], 129
Interviews, as research technique, 19, 178
Intimacy, 36, 37, 73, 102, 110–111, 114, 169–171, 173, 198, 202, 208–209, 210
    and sadism, 183–184
Isolation, see social isolation

J

Jail, see Prison, Legal issues
Jock straps, see Underwear
Jogging, 105
Jokes, 55
Justification, as need for meaning, 32–36, 39, 42–44, 58–59, 107–115, 174, 210
Justify masochism, need to, 15, 102, 106

K

Kant, philosophical work, 43
Kitchen, see Housework
Kneeling, 46, 77
Knives, 62

L

Labels 1, 8, 147, 208
Latin, 46
Laundry, see Housework
Learning, 27, 61, 102–104
Legal issues, 11, 18, 53, 70
Legitimation gap, 35
Leprosy, 13
Lesbianism, see Homosexuality
Letters to sex-oriented magazines, as research methodology, 17–19, 152–154, 211–214
    Editing, 17
    Interrater agreement, 17, 214
Lettuce, 47
Libidinal energy, level of, 189, 190, 204
Library, as source of information about masochism, 191
Life-scheme, 110–112
Limits [see also Safe words], 62–64, 72–73, 139
Lingerie, see Underwear, Humiliation, Panties
Literature 2, 46, 50–51, 53
Loss of control, see Control
Low level awareness or thinking, see Deconstruction
Love, 29, 34, 40, 44, 54, 66, 67, 68, 75, 87, 101, 108, 112, 144, 202, 208–209

M

Magic, 46
Masking tape, 76
Masochistic attitude, 45, 46, 54
Masochistic tests, 86
Mass media, 9, 23, 51, 82, 177
Masturbation, 47–48, 49, 62, 77, 80, 82, 88, 119, 174, 194
Mechanical devices, 49
Meaning in life [see also Deconstruction, Justification, Fulfillment], 32–36
Menstrual cramps, 8, 146
Mental illness, 1, 2, 8–11, 15, 20, 101–104, 179, 180, 181, 187–199, 203, 205–206
Mesopotamia, 48
Middle Ages, 40, 48–50, 51, 53, 59, 96
Migraine headaches, 64
Mirrors, use in experiments 89–91; in masochism, 196
Misunderstandings, 12–14, 19
Modest speech, 55
Monasteries, 50
Money, 34, 35, 53, 145, 167, 178
Morality, 10–12, 33–35, 36, 41, 42, 43, 44, 74, 99, 132
"Moral masochism," 93
Motels, 124
Mountain climbing, 207
Mouth [see also oral], 80, 83, 87, 159, 168
Movie, 23, 51, 177
Murder, 9, 70, 191
Muscle movement, 27, 30, 80
Mythology, 47–48

Subject Index   239

N

Nakedness, see Nudity, Display humiliation
Names, 149
Narcissism, theoretical perspective on masochism, 195–199
Narcotics, Analogy to masochistic pain, 72–76, 103–104
"Natural submissives," 113
Nazis, 11
Neckties, 76, 148
Necrophilia, 9
Needles, 62
Newlyweds, 29
Negative connotation of masochism, 8, 9, 15, 25, 102, 147, 190–191, 193–194
New York, 78
Nipple clamps, 61, 155
Nonsexual masochism 3, 9, 45, 46–47, 49–50, 54–55, 117
Normality [see also Mental illness], 1, 2, 9–11, 15, 20, 195, 197, 200, 205, 206–208
Nudity, see also Display, 76, 82, 84

O

Ontological guilt, see Guilt
Opponent process effects, 104–107, 115, 116, 207
Opportunities for masochistic sex, lack of, 19
Oppression, 11, 44
Oral Humiliation, see Humiliation
Oral sex, 48, 49, 52, 76–77, 80, 83, 87, 109, 120–121, 140, 156, 163, 164–165, 166, 167, 185–186, 197; also Appendix, Tables 1, 3
Orgasmic dysfunction, see Sexual dysfunction
Orgasms [see also Sexual pleasure, Sexual dysfunction, various sexual activities], 24, 77, 78, 82, 83, 110, 118, 119, 123, 125, 126, 127, 129, 174, 185, 198
  Multiple, 123, 174
Orgies, see group sex

P

Pain, 1, 2, 3, 6, 13, 26, 31, 45, 50, 54, 55, 60–76, 86, 105, 106, 109, 124, 139, 154–157, 166, 167, 171, 172, 177, 178, 196, 198, 205–206, 207; also Appendix, Tables 9, 12
Anticipation, 60, 63, 65, 72–73, 139, 171
Becomes pleasure, 8, 13, 64–65
Biting and scratching, 54, 55, 56, 62, 64, 65f, 139
Context for, 13, 66–71, 156–157, 167, 176; also Appendix, Table 9
Desire for, 1, 8, 60, 68, 196
as Narcotic, 72–76, 205
Pride over endurance of, 62, 155, 172
Regulation of severity, 12, 13
Relation to sexual arousal, 1, 50, 54
Sensitivity to, 13–14, 155,
Severity, 13, 65, 155, 168
Spanking, 1, 8, 24, 31, 61, 82, 124, 127, 136, 154–157; Humiliating, 83, 84
Techniques for administering, 61–63
Thresholds and Tolerance levels, 54, 61, 62–64, 72–73, 155
Panties [see also Humiliation, Underwear], 77, 84, 109, 160
Pantyhose, 76
Participant observation, as research technique, 16
Passivity, 7, 77, 80, 141, 151
Passion, 44, 54, 112
Pederasty, 9, 48, 52
Permission, 31, 78, 125–127, 141
Perrier, 83
Personality differences, 9–10, 27, 44, 113, 146, 203–204
Perversion, 8–11, 144, 188, 190, 192
Pigs, 48
Pleasure, 1, 2
Poetry, 44, 46, 51
Political realities, 12, 44
Politicians, 9, 78, 84, 92–93, 196
Pornography, 50–51, 183, 194
Practical problems of masochistic activity 5, 12, 19, 108–109, 181, 192–195, 201
Pressures, 91–93, 124, 141, 201, 203, 209
Prevalence of masochism, 4–5, 49, 51, 53, 55–57, 59, 193, 201
  Co-occurrence with sadism, 20–26, 182–183
  of sadism, 178, 193
Pride, 62, 86

Primacy of masochism, 20–26, 36, 201
Prison, 97, 98, 134
Procrastination, 205
Professional dominatrices, see Prostitutes
Prostitutes and Prostitution, 5, 7–8, 12, 22, 48, 49, 51–53, 62, 67, 78, 81, 88, 92, 106, 107–108, 119, 178
Psychotherapy, 28, 187–195
Pubic hair, 77, 109
Punishment [see also Pain, Guilt], 68–71, 82, 87, 90, 94–100, 117, 133–138, 141, 154, 156–157, 167, 170, 173, 174, 176, 202; also Appendix, Table 9
  Advance, 95, 96, 133–138
  Desire for, 97, 99, 135

R

Racing cars, 207
Rape, 49, 52, 134
Razors, 62
Reage, see *Story of O*
Rebound effect, 192
Recitation of speeches, 77
Rejection, 90, 100
Relationship, 66–68, 75, 77, 102, 104, 107–112, 125, 141, 154–156, 167, 168, 169–171, 172, 173, 174, 184, 185, 201–202; also Appendix, Tables 9, 13
  as source of meaning, 32–36
Religion, 33, 40, 42–44, 46–47, 48–50, 53, 55, 58, 101, 109–110, 112, 135–136, 207
Reluctance, of partners, 12, 19, 23, 66, 83, 180, 193–194
Renaissance, 40, 51, 53, 59
Responsibility, 74, 77–81, 86, 87, 91–93, 94, 106, 126–127, 136–137, 141, 173, 202, 203, 209
  masochists' sense of, 10
Retaliation, 95–96
Rock musicians, 207
Role switching, 24–25
Roman civilization and empire, 39, 46, 48, 52
Romantic era, 40, 44, 58, 112
Ropes, 76
Rousseau, philosophical views, 43–44
  autobiography, 51
  masochism, 51

Rules 1, 3, 77, 78, 86, 109, 126–127, 141, 174, 207

S

Sacher-Masoch, Leopold von, 2–3, 12, 83, 162
Sadism, 15, 20–26, 48, 63, 177–186, 193
  Relation to masochism, 15, 20–26, 179–183, 185, 186, 197, 201
"Safe words," 13, 113
Safety, 108, 160, 181, 203
Salvation, 43
Sampling biases, 15, 16, 17–18
Satyricon, literary work, 46
Scarves, 76
Scat, see Excrement
Scratching the skin during intercourse, see Pain
Scripts, 12, 19, 23, 69–70, 183
Secrecy, desire for, 16, 19, 25, 125, 191, 193
Seduction, 49
Self [see also narcissism], 5–7, 15, 26–32, 71, 79, 102–104, 168, 180, 187, 195–199, 201, 203–204
  Burden of selfhood, 30, 31–32, 39–42, 57, 58, 59, 88–93, 100, 114–115, 116, 172, 203
  Escape from self theory, overview 26–32; applied to guilt, 98–99; and sex differences, 171–173; contrasted with narcissism theory, 195–199
Self-acceptance, 191–194
Self-actualization, 34, 112
Self-awareness, 26, 29–32, 71–75, 79–80, 85, 86, 93, 100, 101, 107, 128–133, 141, 179, 195, 198, 201, 203, 205–206; Causes of unpleasantness, 89–91, 195; and sadism, 179–180
  Structurally deficient, 195–199
Self-control, 172–173
Self-destructive behavior, 3, 8, 14, 15, 45, 46, 198, 204–206, 210
  Self-mutilation, 46–47
Self-esteem, 6–7, 26, 33, 35, 62, 84, 85, 87, 89–90, 92, 107, 112–114, 130–131, 141, 179–180, 197, 203
Self-knowledge, 61, 101–104
Self-worth, see Self-esteem
Semen, 47–48, 83

Senators, see Politicians
Sensate focus, 124–125, 141, 207
Sensation-seeking [see also Thrill-seeking], 3
Sensations, physical, 30
Sensuous Woman, 8
Servants, 46, 51
Seth, 47–48
Sex (gender) differences, 3, 7–8, 121, 122, 135, 143–176, 204
Sex guilt, see Guilt
Sex manuals, 8, 45–46, 53, 76
Sex roles, 92, 147–151, 166–176, 204
Sexual abuse, see Abused women
Sexual dysfunction and inadequacy, 15, 46, 118, 122–130, 163, 185
Sexual fidelity [see also Sexual infidelity], 49, 161, 169; also Appendix, Table 19
Sexual guilt, see Guilt
Sexual infidelity [see also Sexual fidelity, Adultery], 3, 122, 161–2
Sexual intercourse, 121, 163–164, 169, 170–171, 174
  Frequency of, 118–119, 121, 163–164, 167
  Types of, 119–122
Sexual permissiveness, 56
Sexual pleasure, 1, 55, 88, 117–142, 173–174, 185, 186, 190, 198, 202
Shaving, 77, 109
Sheep, 48
Shyness, 8
Sin, 49, 50
  Hierarchy of sexual sins, 49
Skin contact, 196, 197
Skydiving, 207
Slaps, 61, 196
Slave, as prototype of masochistic role, 31, 35, 85, 86, 87, 147–148, 201
  Full-time sex slave, 31, 201–202
  "good slave," 35, 86, 87, 112, 120
  Meaning of slavery, 85
Smoking, 69, 91, 205
Social injustice, 7, 97
Social isolation, 124, 185
Socioeconomic class, 9–10, 17, 35, 78, 180
Spanking, 1, 8, 24, 31, 61, 82, 124, 127, 136, 154–157, see also Pain
  Humiliating, 83, 84
Spanish Inquisition, 11
Spectators, see Audience

Speeches, 77
Speeding ticket, 95
Spouse abuse, see Abused women
Stigma, see Negative connotation
Stockings, 76
Story of O, 111, 184
Strangers, 108
Stress, 31, 92, 100, 103, 105–106
Subculture (S&M), 16, 23
Survey data, 4, 16, 64, 103
Suspension bridge (experiment), 138–139
Symbolism, 27–32, 72, 86, 168
  in masochism, 12, 66–68, 75, 83, 85, 149, 163–164, 171, 172, 176

T

Technology, 34
Telephone, 18
Television set, 82
Ten Commandments, 42, 134
Tennis, 27
Texas, 29
Theological writings, 48–50, 52, 53
Therapeutic effects of masochism, 101–104, 106, 116, 122–128, 129–133, 202, 207–208
Thought suppression, 190–192, 204
Thrill-seeking, 128, 189, 204, 207–208
Time, 30, 86, 140, 142, 196, 198
Tobacco, see Smoking
Tokenism, 85
Tolerance [see also Stigma, Negative connotation], 11, 18, 51, 52, 56, 191, 193
Tongue, see Oral sex, Humiliation
Torture, 64, 71–72
Transsexualism, 48
Transvestism, 48, 49, 77, 148–151, 153–154, 158, 166; also Appendix, Tables 10, 15, 16
"Trumped-up" guilt [see also Guilt, Punishment], 69, 70, 98, 156; also Appendix, Table 14
Trust, 108

U

Ulcers, 33, 79, 91–92
Unconscious motivations, 69–71, 97, 144

Underwear, 11, 83, 84, 148–150
Undressing, see Nudity, Display humiliation
Urination, see Excrement

V

Value base [see also Justification], 33, 39, 44, 58–59, 109–112
Venereal disease, 48, 194
Venice Preserv'd, 50
Verbal humiliations, see Humiliation
Vibrator, see Dildo
Vicarious pleasure, 182–183, 186
Victorian era, 11, 43, 56, 59
Violence, 11, 44
Virginity, 7

Voyeurism, 48

W

Washington, 78
Watching, see Audience
Welts, 62
"Whatever-you-say-mistress syndrome" 184
Whipping, 1, 3, 31, 46, 50, 51, 61, 62, 65, 96, 109, 154–157, 167
Wife abuse, see Abused women
Wife-beating, see Abused women
Wife-swapping, 118
Wine, 83
Work, 43, 44, 78, 79, 86, 92, 93, 94, 99
Work ethic, 44, 112